W9-AQS-212

PERMANENT ADDRESSES

PERMANENT ADDRESSES

A Guide to the Resting Places of Famous Americans

Jean Arbeiter

Linda D. Cirino

M. Evans and Company, Inc.   New York

Library of Congress Cataloging in Publication Data

Arbeiter, Jean S.
  Permanent addresses.

  Includes index.
  1. United States—Biography.   2. Cemeteries—United
States—Guide-books.   3. United States—Description and
travel—1981-   —Guide-books.   I. Cirino, Linda D.
II. Title
CT215.A73   1983   917.3'04927   83-1618

ISBN   0-87131-402-9

Copyright © 1983 by Jean Arbeiter and Linda D. Cirino
Illustrations © 1983 by M. Evans and Company, Inc.

All rights reserved. No part of this book may be reproduced or trans-
mitted in any form or by any means without the written permission of
the publisher.

M. Evans and Company, Inc.
216 East 49 Street
New York, New York 10017

DESIGN BY RONALD F. SHEY

Manufactured in the United States of America

9 8 7 6 5 4 3 2 1

CONTENTS

PREFACE

This book focuses on the famous American dead and where they can be found. Our interest in the celebrated does not end with their deaths, nor does our affection and admiration for them. A few years ago we read about a woman in Hollywood who decided to sell maps of movie stars' graves instead of movie stars' homes. Her first edition sold out rapidly, and she found it hard to keep up with the demand. People wanted to know where and how to visit the permanent addresses of their favorites. That's what made us decide to write this book. It is a "star trek" to the resting places of the celebrated throughout the United States.

When you picked up *Permanent Addresses*, you were probably moved by genuine interest, not morbidity. The presence of celebrated entertainers, writers, artists, musicians, military figures, scientists, and government leaders imparts glamour to a cemetery or churchyard. We all have historical figures we admire, as well as contemporaries. By visiting a grave site, our desire to become close to the famous can be vicariously fulfilled. A gravestone is a reaffirmation of a presence that once moved the world. It offers the chance to remember the dead person's struggles and accomplishments and to experience them once again.

Many cemeteries that house the rich and famous are worthwhile tourist sites because they were designed to be enjoyed by visitors as well as bestow dignity upon the departed. Such "cemetery parks" are noted for their meandering paths, sentimental and charming Victorian cemetery sculpture, and beautiful landscaping, besides the sense of timelessness and serenity they offer. Among them are Green-Wood and Woodlawn in New York City, Graceland in Chicago, Crown Hill in Indianapolis, Mount Auburn in Cambridge, Massachusetts, Albany Rural Cemetery in Albany, New York, Lake View in Cincinnati, Laurel Hill in Philadelphia, Allegheny in Pittsburgh, and Forest Home in Milwaukee. A number offer walking tours and maps to the grave sites of their celebrity residents. Many go back to the days before public parks—they were the first green spaces set aside in the great cities and were widely visited by the public.

Other resting places are well visited because they have become sites of pilgrimage for fans, as the thousands of visitors to Elvis Presley's grave on his Memphis estate indicate. For decades, admirers of the silent screen's Latin lover, Rudolph Valentino, visited his crypt in Hollywood Memorial Park on the anniversary of his death. One of them, an unknown "lady in black" bearing flowers, managed to create such an aura of mystery that she inspired imitators. The James Dean cult still draws devotees to his grave in Park Cemetery in his home town of Fairmount, Indiana. Harry Houdini, the great escape artist and student of spiritualism, died on Halloween leaving a promise to send a message back to the living, if possible. His grave site in New York City's Machpelah Cemetery appeared to be the perfect place to test out his progress, and séances have been held there by the faithful on Halloween eve.

Many grave sites of the famous have a story to tell in themselves. During the Civil War, the body of Confederate statesman John C. Calhoun was removed from its grave in St. Philip's Churchyard, Charleston, and reburied beneath the church to avoid possible Yankee desecration. The grave of Bessie Smith, the great blues singer, went unmarked for thirty-three years until an admirer, Janis Joplin, backed a campaign to raise funds for that purpose.

Permanent addresses aren't always permanent, we learned. Naval hero John Paul Jones died abroad in obscurity and rested in a small Parisian cemetery for a century. President Theodore Roosevelt, bent on strengthening America's image as a naval power, brought Jones home, and today his body is enshrined in a magnificent tomb at the U.S. Naval Academy in Annapolis. Al Capone's family had his body moved from one Chicago cemetery to another, leaving the original headstone to fool visitors.

Some people have a hard time getting buried at all. The Catholic Church is loath to allow the interment of gangsters like

Capone in consecrated ground, although he finally obtained rest therein. Lawsuits sometimes follow death; the body of feisty showman Billy Rose remained in a vault for over a year while his sister and executors haggled over the purchase of a plot and mausoleum. The assassins of presidents have the most difficulty in obtaining a permanent address. The federal government kept the body of John Wilkes Booth for four years before his family received permission to bury him in Baltimore; even then, President Andrew Johnson insisted that the grave remain unmarked. The cemetery where Lee Harvey Oswald lies in Fort Worth, Texas, tried to forestall his burial there, and the corpse of Leon Czolgosz, the murderer of President McKinley, was disintegrated by prison officials who poured acid on the coffin.

Some are removed from their permanent addresses, never to be found again. The body of revolutionary spokesman Tom Paine was snatched from its grave in New Rochelle, New York, and surfaced briefly in England before disappearing from history. No trace can be found of the original coffin of another Revolutionary War hero, Ethan Allen. Did it go to medical students or the devil, as some of the detractors of the free-thinking Allen claimed? And where—if anywhere—are the ashes of the defenders of the Alamo, Davy Crockett and Jim Bowie among them, whose bodies were burned by the Mexicans after the fall of that beseiged outpost?

For some, a future change of address was part of the original burial plan. Polish patriot Jan Paderewski, one of the few foreigners honored with burial in Arlington National Cemetery, is said to lie there only until Poland is free once more.

Hope, awe, nostalgia, hero worship, a sense of history or mystery—all of these feelings can be nurtured by following some of the paths suggested in *Permanent Addresses*. We hope that our readers will enjoy wandering through underground history as much as we did. We wish them good reading and good visiting.

ACKNOWLEDGMENTS

As we worked on this book, many individuals responded to our queries. They were cemetery employees who provided us with directions and other details, town or municipal officials who helped track down obscure cemeteries, and relatives of the celebrated who were most gracious in steering us to the right places. All of these people were generous with their time and information. This book would not have been possible without their assistance and enthusiasm. To us it was proof of how much Americans value the final resting places of the celebrated.

Many institutions helped us with photographs and other research. We are indebted to them all, but particularly to Rita Heffler of the Hackensack Library in New Jersey for her cheerful help. We owe a special and personal debt to our families for their constant support and encouragement.

HOW TO USE THIS BOOK

Permanent Addresses is divided into two parts: a biographical section and a geographical one. The biographical portion is divided into categories of celebrated people, such as Entertainers, Social Reformers, and Writers. If you are interested in a specific person, simply look in the subject area where you would expect to find him or her, or consult the index at the back of the book. Within each category, celebrities are listed in alphabetical order, along with brief information about them and the town and name of the cemetery where they are buried. Some biographical entries contain more anecdotal information than others; these concern people about whom we found unusual and interesting stories relating to death and/or burial. More detailed information about the cemeteries and how to find them is included in the Geographical Guide to Cemeteries, which follows the biographical data.

Not all permanent addresses are known. In the biographical section you'll also find information about those whose ashes are scattered over land or sea and those who are simply permanently missing. We've also included brief data about famous Americans and others who spent a large part of their careers in the United States but found a permanent address abroad.

PERMANENT ADDRESSES

ENTERTAINERS

MAUDE ADAMS (1872–July 17, 1953) **Cenacle Convent, Lake Ronkonkoma, Long Island, New York**   The first actress to play Peter Pan is buried on the grounds of her former estate, which she gave to the sisters of St. Regis in gratitude for their care after she suffered a nervous breakdown. Other religious orders had refused to treat her because she was an actress.

JACOB ADLER (1855–April 1, 1926) **Mount Carmel Cemetery, Glendale, Queens, New York**   When the great actor of the Yiddish stage died, fifty thousand people took to the streets in demonstration and hucksters sold buttons with his portrait, reading "We mourn our loss."

FRED ALLEN (1894–March 17, 1956) **Gate of Heaven Cemetery, Hawthorne, New York**   The caustic radio comedian, whose weekly show in the 1930s and '40s equaled that of Jack Benny in popularity, had this word on actors' funerals: "By the time an

17

actor gets ready to die he hasn't enough friends left out there to act as pallbearers. At most funerals the six men you see motivating the casket are from Central Casting." The widely respected Allen had no such problem at his funeral, where the mourning was genuine.

GRACIE ALLEN (1906–August 27, 1964) **Forest Lawn Memorial Park, Glendale, California** Gracie and her husband, George Burns, were a perennial comedy favorite. Burns was determined that death would not separate the team. He had Gracie buried with Protestant Episcopal rites in a nonsectarian cemetery even though she was a Roman Catholic, so that he, a Jew, could be buried near her later on.

RICHARD ARLEN (1900–March 28, 1976) **Holy Cross Cemetery, Los Angeles, California** Silent movie star; he appeared in *Wings* (1927), the first motion picture to win an Academy Award.

TALLULAH BANKHEAD (1903–December 12, 1968) **Saint Paul's Churchyard, Chestertown, Maryland** Throaty-voiced Tallulah was noted for her performances both on and off stage, the offstage being the more outrageous. When she was near death and on a breathing machine she could utter only two words close to her heart—"codeine" and "bourbon." At a friend's suggestion, the casket chosen for her was her favorite color, baby blue. Bankhead was buried wearing one of her silk wrappers, cigarette burns showing, and a rabbit's foot was placed in the coffin.

P. T. BARNUM (1810–April 7, 1891) **Mountain Grove Cemetery, Bridgeport, Connecticut** As he lingered near death, the great showman wondered what the newspapers would say about him after he was gone. He asked the New York *Evening Sun* to publish his obituary in advance so that he could enjoy it. On March 24, 1891, the newspaper ballyhooed, "Great and Only Barnum. He Wanted to Read His Obituary; Here it Is." The inventor of hokum must have gone to his grave satisfied with this pre-event publicity. The crowd at his funeral was so large that a pickpocket was arrested.

ETHEL BARRYMORE (1879–June 8, 1959) Calvary Cemetery, Los Angeles, California   Member of famous acting family, called "First Lady of the American Theater."

JOHN BARRYMORE (1882–May 29, 1942) Calvary Cemetery, Los Angeles, California   Noted for his Shakespearean performances and such films as *Dr. Jekyll and Mr. Hyde* (1920) and *Grand Hotel* (1932).

LIONEL BARRYMORE (1878–November 16, 1954) Calvary Cemetery, Los Angeles, California   In a wheelchair after 1938, he is best remembered as Dr. Gillespie in the *Dr. Kildare* movies.

NORA BAYES (1880–March 19, 1928) Woodlawn Cemetery, Bronx, New York   Popular singing comedian of vaudeville.

WARNER BAXTER (1891–May 7, 1951) Forest Lawn Memorial Park, Glendale, California   Silent star, usually featured in he-man roles.

WALLACE BEERY (1886–April 15, 1949) Forest Lawn Memorial Park, Glendale, California   Character actor renowned for his tough-guy performances in such films as *Tugboat Annie* (1933) and *Viva Villa* (1934).

DAVID BELASCO (1853–May 14, 1931) Linden Hills Cemetery, Maspeth, Queens, New York   Known as "the wizard of

the American theater," he discovered a long line of stars and produced more than two hundred sensational dramas, among them *Zaza* (1898), *The Return of Peter Grimm* (1911), and *Laugh, Clown, Laugh* (1923).

JOHN BELUSHI (1949–January 24, 1982) **Abel's Hill Cemetery, Chilmark, Massachusetts** Comedian; star of TV's *Saturday Night Live* (1975–79). Died of drug overdose in Hollywood.

WILLIAM BENDIX (1906–December 14, 1964) **San Fernando Mission Cemetery, Mission Hills, California** TV's Riley in *The Life of Riley* series (1953–58).

CONSTANCE BENNETT (1905–July 24, 1965) **Arlington National Cemetery, Arlington, Virginia** Star of the popular *Topper* (1933), and the fashionably haughty blonde beauty in other films.

JACK BENNY (1894–December 26, 1974) **Hillside Memorial Park, Los Angeles, California** In his will the beloved comedian arranged for the delivery of one red rose to his wife, Mary Livingstone, each day for the rest of her life.

GERTRUDE BERG (1900–September 14, 1966) **Clovesville Cemetery, Fleischmanns, New York** Radio and TV's "Molly Goldberg," she wrote, produced, and starred in the popular series about a Jewish family in the Bronx.

EDGAR BERGEN (1903–October 1, 1978) **Inglewood Park Cemetery, Inglewood, California** Ventriloquist and creator of Charlie McCarthy.

DAN BLOCKER (1928–May 13, 1972) **DeKalb Cemetery, DeKalb, Texas** Hoss Cartwright on the hit TV series *Bonanza* (1959–63).

BEN BLUE (1901–March 7, 1975) **Hillside Memorial Park, Los Angeles, California** Sad-faced and limber-limbed vaudeville comedian who made successful transition to films.

HUMPHREY BOGART (1899–January 14, 1957) Forest Lawn Memorial Park, Glendale, California   Top box-office star of the 1940s and '50s, often appeared as the cynic turned hero; his ever-popular films include *The Maltese Falcon* (1940), *Casablanca* (1943), and *To Have and Have Not* (1943); died after a long bout with cancer.

EDWIN BOOTH (1833–June 7, 1893) Mount Auburn Cemetery, Cambridge, Massachusetts   A great tragic actor, Booth helped found the Players Club in Manhattan's Gramercy Park and spent his final years there. As his daughter hovered by the dying Booth's bedside, all of the lights in the building and on the street failed. "Don't let Father die in the dark!" she cried, but he died just as the light was restored a few minutes later. At the very moment his coffin was being carried from a New York church, three stories of Ford's Theater in Washington collapsed with a violent roar and killed twenty people. It was at that building that the actor's brother, John Wilkes Booth (see Criminals), had shot and killed Abraham Lincoln.

CLARA BOW (1905–September 26, 1965) Forest Lawn Memorial Park, Glendale, California   The "it" girl of silent movies; she planned her own funeral, which featured quiz-show host Ralph Edwards reading passages from Kahlil Gibran's *The Prophet.*

MAJOR EDWARD BOWES (1874–June 13, 1946) Sleepy Hollow Cemetery, North Tarrytown, New York   Host of the 1930s–'40s radio show *Major Bowes and His Original Amateur Hour.*

CHARLES BOYER (1899–August 26, 1978) Holy Cross Cemetery, Los Angeles, California   His film career as the irresistibly romantic lover spanned more than forty years and was highlighted by his performance as Pépé-Le-Moko in *Algiers* (1938); other films include *Gaslight* (1944) and *Cluny Brown* (1948). Boyer was devoted to his wife of many years, Patricia, and killed himself two days after her death.

FANNY BRICE (1891–May 29, 1951) **Home of Peace Cemetery, Los Angeles, California**   Popular comedian, got her start in the *Ziegfeld Follies*, played "Baby Snooks" on radio.

JOE E. BROWN (1892–July 6, 1973) **Forest Lawn Memorial Park, Glendale, California**   Wide-mouthed movie comedian.

LENNY BRUCE (1926–August 3, 1966) **Eden Memorial Park, Mission Hills, California**   Stand-up comedian, known for his bitter satire and off-color material. Died of drug overdose.

FRANCIS X. BUSHMAN (1883–August 23, 1966) **Forest Lawn Memorial Park, Glendale, California**   Major male screen idol of Hollywood's early days; died forty years to the day after the death of Rudolph Valentino.

SEBASTIAN CABOT (1918–August 23, 1977) **Westwood Memorial Park, Los Angeles, California**   Character actor, appeared as the dauntless butler "Mr. French" in the TV series *Family Affair* (1966–71).

LOUIS CALHERN (1895–May 12, 1956) **Hollywood Memorial Park, Los Angeles, California**   Character actor of the 1940s and '50s, remembered for his portrayals of stately figures. Among his films: *Duck Soup* (1933), *The Asphalt Jungle* (1950), and the title role in *Julius Caesar* (1953).

GODFREY CAMBRIDGE (1933–November 29, 1976) **Forest Lawn Memorial Park, Glendale, California**   Black comedian of the 1960s and a satirical commentator on racial issues. In *The Watermelon Man* (1970) he played a white bigot whose skin turns black.

EDDIE CANTOR (1892–October 10, 1964) **Hillside Memorial Park, Los Angeles, California**   Zippy singing comedian of vaudeville and later radio.

JACK CARSON (1910–January 2, 1963) **Forest Lawn Memorial Park, Glendale, California**   Supporting actor and comedian in such films as *Stage Door* (1937) and *A Star Is Born* (1954). Died on the same day as Dick Powell.

IRENE CASTLE (1893–January 25, 1969) **VERNON CASTLE** (1887–February 15, 1918) **Woodlawn Cemetery, Bronx, New York** Popular brother/sister dance team of the early 1900s.

JEFF CHANDLER (1919–June 17, 1961) **Hillside Memorial Park, Los Angeles, California** "He-man" of the movies in the 1950s, starred in *The Broken Arrow* (1950) and *The Sign of the Pagan* (1954). Died of blood poisoning following an operation.

LON CHANEY (1883–August 26, 1930) **Forest Lawn Memorial Park, Glendale, California** The silent screen's "Man of a Thousand Faces," he terrified audiences in *The Phantom of the Opera* (1925).

MONTGOMERY CLIFT (1920–July 22, 1966) **Friends Cemetery, Brooklyn, New York** By the time the screen idol of the 1950s died his body was aged way behind its years by drug and alcohol abuse. His funeral service was Episcopal, although Clift had wanted a Quaker one. He *is* buried in a Quaker cemetery, however. Actress Nancy Walker, a close friend, planted two hundred crocuses at the grave site, which also features a granite marker created by John Benson, the man who designed John F. Kennedy's gravestone at Arlington.

RONALD COLMAN (1891–May 19, 1958) **Santa Barbara Cemetery, Santa Barbara, California** British actor, romantic lead of the films of the 1930s and '40s. His wife had Shakespeare's words engraved on his gravestone: "We are such stuff as dreams are made of, and our little life is rounded with a sleep."

RICHARD CONTE (1914–April 15, 1975) **Westwood Memorial Park, Los Angeles, California** Movie gangster of the 1940s and '50s. He is interred near Marilyn Monroe, who made her first screen test with him.

GARY COOPER (1901–May 12, 1961) **Sacred Heart Cemetery, Southampton, Long Island, New York** "Papa, I bet I beat you back to the barn," the popular movie star told Ernest Hemingway when he knew he was dying of cancer. Originally buried in Los Angeles, he was moved thirteen years later to Long Island to be near his wife, who had married a Southampton physician.

Katharine Cornell's grave site is on Martha's Vineyard where she spent many summers. (Dennis Hirschfelder)

KATHARINE CORNELL (1893–June 8, 1974) **Village Cemetery, Tisbury, Massachusetts**   For more than thirty years, Cornell, one of the most celebrated leading ladies of the American stage, never missed a summer on Martha's Vineyard, Massachusetts. Cornell was so devoted to the island that she financed the renovation of the Tisbury Town Hall. When she died, Tisbury honored her wish to be buried in the old cemetery behind the town hall, even though there was no room left in it. Space was found by moving an air tank. "It's what she wanted, so she will have it," said one selectman.

LOU COSTELLO (1906–March 3, 1959) **Calvary Cemetery, Los Angeles, California**   The small, bouncy comedian died in a Beverly Hills hospital after sending his manager out to get an ice cream soda. "That was the best ice cream soda I ever tasted," he said, and expired. Bud Abbott, Costello's partner, led the pallbearers at his funeral but had soothed his grief with so much whiskey that he leaned on the casket instead of carrying it. Costello is interred in a crypt a short distance away from his two-year-old son "Butch," who drowned in the family pool.

LOTTA CRABTREE (1847–September 25, 1924) **Woodlawn Cemetery, Bronx, New York** The Golden West's favorite actress spent the last fifteen years of her life planning how to dispose of her four-million-dollar fortune. Her charities included drinking fountains for animals and funds for needy war veterans. In the months following her death more than a hundred people came forward arguing some kind of relationship with the performer. The "daughter's" case lost credibility in the face of medical testimony that Lotta was probably still a virgin in her old age. Eventually most of the fortune went to the causes she favored, though not every city remembered by her wanted the animal drinking fountains.

JOAN CRAWFORD (1908–May 10, 1977) **Ferncliff Cemetery, Hartsdale, New York** Leading star of "women's pictures" of the 1930s and '40s: *A Woman's Face* (1941), *Mildred Pierce* (1946).

BING CROSBY (1904—October 14, 1977) **Holy Cross Cemetery, Los Angeles, California** Only a few entertainers were present at Crosby's funeral, and Kathryn Crosby told reporters, "He hated funerals. I'm sure he didn't plan to come to this one." The singer was buried next to his first wife, Dixie.

CHARLOTTE CUSHMAN (1816–February 18, 1876) **Mount Auburn Cemetery, Cambridge, Massachusetts** America's first great stage actress, affectionately known as "Our Charlotte"; she triumphed in such Shakespearean roles as Lady Macbeth and Hamlet, and once played Romeo to her sister's Juliet.

DOROTHY DANDRIDGE (1923–September 8, 1965) **Forest Lawn Memorial Park, Glendale, California** The beautiful black singer and actress, whose life was marked by unhappiness, died in Hollywood of what was inaccurately termed a drug overdose. A few days before her death she had broken a tiny bone in her right foot and neglected to have it set. Marrow from the broken bone got into her bloodstream, where the fatlike particles clotted and cut off the flow of blood to the lungs and brain, causing her death.

LINDA DARNELL (1921–April 10, 1965) **Union Hill Cemetery, Kennett Square, Pennsylvania**   Brunette leading lady of the 1940s, starred in *Forever Amber* (1947); died of burns suffered in a fire.

MARION DAVIES (1900–September 22, 1961) **Hollywood Memorial Park Cemetery, Los Angeles, California**   Longtime mistress of newspaper magnate William Randolph Hearst (see Journalists), who spent seven million dollars trying to make her a star.

JAMES DEAN (1931–September 30, 1955) **Park Cemetery, Fairmount, Indiana**   To the generation of the 1950s Dean symbolized restless, rebellious youth. His death in a car accident, minutes after he had been given a speeding ticket, was followed by mass hysteria. *Rebel Without a Cause*, the movie that secured his position as a cult figure, was released after the troubled young actor's demise, and it intensified interest in Dean. Articles appeared claiming that Dean was still alive, and the souvenir market produced James Dean busts, "wallet pix," rings (some purporting to contain a chip from his gravestone), bits of paint and aluminum that supposedly came from the death car, and a record called "Jimmy Dean's First Christmas in Heaven."

In the ten years following Dean's death, Warner Brothers received as many as seven thousand letters a month addressed to the actor from fans who refused to accept the fact that he was dead. Dean's pinkish granite headstone has lost part of its letters and numbers to zealous souvenir hunters. The stone is nearly obscured by two tall trees (Arborvitae, tree of life) planted by a member of the Dean family because they would be difficult to uproot.

CECIL B. DE MILLE (1881–January 21, 1959) **Hollywood Memorial Park Cemetery, Los Angeles, California**   Pioneer motion picture director, famed for such biblical spectacles as *The*

Ten Commandments (1923; remade thirty years later) and *Samson and Delilah* (1949).

WALT DISNEY (1901–December 15, 1966) **Forest Lawn Memorial Park, Glendale, California**   Cinematic genius, creator of the animated feature film.

MARIE DRESSLER (1869–July 28, 1934) **Forest Lawn Memorial Park, Glendale, California**   Gravel-voiced actress, appeared in *Anna Christie* (1930) and *Min and Bill* (1930), becoming a star at age sixty-one.

JIMMY DURANTE (1893–January 29, 1980) **Holy Cross Cemetery, Los Angeles, California**   Teased about the amount of money he gave to panhandlers, the popular comedian once responded, "Maybe we ain't born equal, but it's a cinch we all die equal."

DOUGLAS FAIRBANKS, SR. (1883–December 21, 1939) **Hollywood Memorial Park Cemetery, Los Angeles, California** Hero of the silent screen, first of the great swashbucklers.

WILLIAM FARNUM (1876–June 5, 1953) **Forest Lawn Memorial Park, Glendale, California**   Silent movie star, appeared in *The Man Who Fights Alone* (1924), *Ben Hur* (1927), *Ten Nights in a Bar Room* (1931), and *Cleopatra* (1934).

LOUISE FAZENDA (1889–April 17, 1962) **Inglewood Park Cemetery, Inglewood, California**   Sparkling comedian of the silents and wife of producer Hal Wallis, made screen appearances in *Tillie's Punctured Romance* (1928), *No, No, Nanette* (1930), and *Ready, Willing and Able* (1937).

W. C. FIELDS (1880–December 25, 1946) **Forest Lawn Memorial Park, Glendale, California**   Being an undertaker in Philadelphia was the most difficult business in the world, Fields once said, because "a mortician can hardly tell if he's burying a dead person or a live one." The comedian did not get a chance to test this theory about his home town, for he died, after many years of hard drinking, in a sanitarium in Pasadena, California. "Just cremate me," he instructed his mistress, Carlotta Monte, "I had enough of the cold ground in my youth." The request was not carried out, because his widow argued it was contrary to the laws of the Catholic Church. But Fields was laid to rest aboveground in a crypt.

PETER FINCH (1916–January 14, 1977) **Hollywood Memorial Park Cemetery, Los Angeles, California** English actor, won Oscar posthumously for *Network* (1976).

ERROL FLYNN (1909—October 14, 1959) **Forest Lawn Memorial Park, Glendale, California** The swashbuckling actor told Ida Lupino that when he died he wanted his ashes scattered at sea, but added, "I can tell you I know my wishes will not be carried out." One of his recurring dreams was that he stood staring at his own unmarked grave in Forest Lawn, a burial place he could not abide. The dream turned out to be one of Flynn's many instances of prescience. After his death, his third wife, Patrice Wymore, refused to have the body cremated or buried in a Jamaican churchyard, as he had requested, but shipped it to Forest Lawn instead. Twenty years later, Flynn's children supplied a marker for his grave.

MICHEL FOKINE (1880–August 22, 1942) **Ferncliff Cemetery, Hartsdale, New York** Choreographer of the Russian ballet, creator of the Ballet Russe, and one of the founders of modern dance.

JOHN FORD (1895–August 31, 1973) **Holy Cross Cemetery, Los Angeles, California** Director; only person to win the Academy Award for four feature films.

EDWIN FORREST (1806–December 16, 1872) **St. Paul's Episcopal Churchyard, Philadelphia, Pennsylvania** Considered by many to be America's greatest actor of the nineteenth century. Forrest's will created the Edwin Forrest Home "for decayed actors," which continues in operation in Philadelphia. In its heyday the Home housed about twelve "guests," with an even larger retinue of servants. Scrupulously observed were Forrest's last wishes: each July 4 the Declaration of Independence was recited "as written by Thomas Jefferson, without expurgation," and on Shakespeare's birthday residents performed scenes from his plays.

EDDIE FOY (1857–February 16, 1928) **Holy Sepulchre Cemetery, New Rochelle, New York**   Vaudeville trouper; he and his family performed as "The Seven Little Foys."

WILLIAM FRAWLEY (1893–March 3, 1966) **San Fernando Mission Cemetery, Mission Hills, California**   Comedian, played "Fred Mertz" in the *I Love Lucy* TV series (1951–60).

CLARK GABLE (1901–November 16, 1960) **Forest Lawn Memorial Park, Glendale, California**   The funeral of "The King," perhaps Hollywood's greatest idol ever, was held with closed casket because he had said, "I don't want a lot of strangers looking down at my wrinkles and my big fat belly when I'm dead." He is interred next to his third wife, Carole Lombard.

JOHN GARFIELD (1913–May 21, 1952) **Westchester Hills Cemetery, Hastings-on-Hudson, New York**   Powerful dramatic star, gained prominence in the stage production of *Golden Boy* (1937).

JUDY GARLAND (1922–June 22, 1969) **Ferncliff Cemetery, Hartsdale, New York**   One of the great superstars of all time. Her vitality and poignancy touched millions, from her first starring role in *The Wizard of Oz* (1939) to *Judgment at Nuremberg* (1961). "Your wife will be the star of Ferncliff," the cemetery representative told Garland's fifth and final husband, Mickey Deans, when he selected her mausoleum.

HOOT GIBSON (1892–August 23, 1962) **Inglewood Park Cemetery, Inglewood, California**   Cowboy star of the silents.

WILLIAM GILLETTE (1853–April 29, 1937) **Riverside Cemetery, Farmington, Connecticut**   Leading stage actor and author of the turn of the century; best known for his role as Sherlock Holmes, which he first played in 1899 and revived up until his retirement in 1932; authored successful Civil War spy dramas like *Held by the Enemy* (1886) and *Secret Service* (1895).

SAMUEL GOLDWYN (1884–March 31, 1974) **Forest Lawn Memorial Park, Glendale, California** For thirty years one of Hollywood's top producers; his films, noted for their technical excellence, include *Wuthering Heights* (1939), *The Little Foxes* (1941), and Academy Award winner *The Best Years of Our Lives* (1946). Also remembered for such "Goldwynisms" as "An oral agreement isn't worth the paper it's written on."

BETTY GRABLE (1916–July 3, 1973) **Inglewood Park Cemetery, Inglewood, California** Musical comedy star and pinup favorite of the 1940s.

SYDNEY GREENSTREET (1879–January 19, 1954) **Forest Lawn Memorial Park, Glendale, California** In "fat man" roles, a leading film villain of the 1940s.

JACK HALEY (1899–June 6, 1979) **Holy Cross Cemetery, Los Angeles, California** Stage and screen comedian, appeared as the "Tin Man" in *The Wizard of Oz* (1939).

OLIVER HARDY (1892–August 7, 1957) **Valhalla Memorial Park, North Hollywood, California** With Stan Laurel, starred in over two hundred comedy features and short subjects.

JEAN HARLOW (1911–June 7, 1937) **Forest Lawn Memorial Park, Glendale, California** The platinum-haired star's films include *Red Dust* (1932) and *China Seas* (1935).

WILLIAM S. HART (1870–June 23, 1946) **Green-Wood Cemetery, Brooklyn, New York** The original motion picture cowboy.

GABBY HAYES (1885–February 9, 1969) **Forest Lawn Memorial Park, Glendale, California** Best known for his portrayal of Hopalong Cassidy's sidekick.

SUSAN HAYWARD (1919–March 14, 1975) **Our Lady's Memory Garden, Cemetery of Our Lady of Perpetual Help Church, Carrollton, Georgia** Red-haired leading lady of such dramatic films as *I'll Cry Tomorrow* (1955) and *With a Song in My Heart* (1952).

ANNA HELD (1873–August 12, 1918) **Gate of Heaven Cemetery, Hawthorne, New York**   Turn-of-the-century musical comedy star.

JUDY HOLLIDAY (1923–June 7, 1965) **Westchester Hills Cemetery, Hastings-on-Hudson, New York**   Stage and movie comic actress of the 1950s, won Academy Award for *Born Yesterday* (1950).

HARRY HOUDINI (1874–October 31, 1926) **Machpelah Cemetery, Glendale, Queens, New York**   Setting out on his last tour, the great magician and escape artist had a premonition that he was marked for death. He had made a pact years earlier with his wife: whoever died first would send back a coded message consisting of ten words to prove whether or not spirits could communicate. Only Mrs. Houdini knew the code, and for years following his death she consulted spiritualists and held a séance on the anniversary of his passing—Halloween. The actual message was never received, and after a decade of trying Mrs. Houdini gave up the vigil. Houdini is buried beside his beloved mother, whose grave he visited every day and also every night. A black bag containing his mother's letters was placed in his coffin before it was closed, and the president of the Society of American Magicians broke a magic wand over it.

SOL HUROK (1888–March 5, 1974) **Temple Israel Cemetery, Hastings-on-Hudson, New York**   Best-known impresario of the century; at his funeral Isaac Stern played, Jan Peerce sang, and Marian Anderson delivered the eulogy.

GEORGE JESSEL (1898–May 20, 1981) **Hillside Memorial Park, Los Angeles, California**   Jessel, who gained fame as a vaudeville comedian, became celebrated as a Hollywood toastmaster and deliverer of eulogies at funerals. Beginning with Fanny Brice and Al Jolson, he delivered several hundred of the latter. Jessel claimed he had already planned the inscription for his own tombstone: "I tell you here from the shade it is all worthwhile." The big question was: who would deliver the eulogy at Jessel's funeral? The honor fell to Milton Berle.

The Al Jolson memorial in Hillside Memorial Park in Los Angeles is visible from the freeway. (Daniel and Claire Feins)

AL JOLSON (1886–October 23, 1950) Hillside Memorial Park, Los Angeles, California Vaudeville's great entertainer experienced a new surge of popularity when his film biography, *The Jolson Story* (1946), appeared a few years before his death. In the cemetery there is a statue of the jazz singer, resting on bended knee, arms stretched out, singing his famous rendition of "Mammy."

BUSTER KEATON (1895–January 31, 1966) Forest Lawn Memorial Park, Glendale, California A leading comedian of silent films, usually wore a porkpie hat and deadpan expression.

EMMETT KELLY (1898–March 28, 1979) Rest Haven Memorial Park Cemetery, Lafayette, Indiana The sad clown, "Weary Willy," of the Ringling Brothers and Barnum and Bailey Circus.

ERNIE KOVACS (1919–January 12, 1962) Forest Lawn Memorial Park, Glendale, California First important comedy star of the "Golden Age" of television.

ALAN LADD (1913–January 29, 1964) Forest Lawn Memorial Park, Glendale, California Popular actor, starred in *This Gun for Hire* (1942) and *Shane* (1953); died from a self-inflicted gunshot wound.

BERT LAHR (1895–December 3, 1967) Union Field Cemetery, Ridgewood, Queens, New York Vaudeville and radio performer, the endearing "Cowardly Lion" in *The Wizard of Oz* (1939).

CAROLE LANDIS (1919–July 5, 1948) Forest Lawn Memorial Park, Glendale, California Blonde film actress, the first "sweater girl." A suicide; her body was discovered by Rex Harrison.

CHARLES LAUGHTON (1899–December 15, 1962) Forest Lawn Memorial Park, Glendale, California British stage and film actor remembered for his performances as Captain Bligh in *Mutiny on the Bounty* (1935) and Quasimodo in *The Hunchback of Notre Dame* (1939).

STAN LAUREL (1890–February 23, 1965) Forest Lawn Memorial Park, Glendale, California Oliver Hardy's partner in comedy classics.

GYPSY ROSE LEE (1914–April 26, 1970) Inglewood Park Cemetery, Inglewood, California Leading striptease artist of 1940s burlesque, appeared on Broadway in *Star and Garter* (1942); also a successful mystery novelist. The musical *Gypsy* (1959) was based on her early life.

JOE E. LEWIS (1902–June 4, 1971) Cedar Park Cemetery, Paramus, New Jersey Noted nightclub stand-up comic.

HAROLD LLOYD (1893–March 8, 1971) Forest Lawn Memorial Park, Glendale, California Film comedian whose daredevil stunts belied his persona as the self-effacing all-American boy. Highest-paid film star of the 1920s, he died one of the wealthiest men in Hollywood.

CAROLE LOMBARD (1908–January 16, 1942) **Forest Lawn Memorial Park, Glendale, California**   The blonde comedian was anxious to get home from a wartime bond tour to her husband, Clark Gable. Lombard's mother and an M-G-M publicity man tossed a coin for her. "Tails we go by plane, heads by train." Tails came up, and the party took off aboard a TWA transport. Gable had a practical joke ready for his bride, who loved them. He had placed a wax dummy of a blonde woman in her bed, and was about to leave for the airport when he got the message that the plane was down near Las Vegas. Lombard's charred remains were identifiable only by the long black gloves and strapless evening gown she had been wearing when she rushed to the plane.

PETER LORRE (1904–March 23, 1964) **Hollywood Memorial Park Cemetery, Los Angeles, California**   Character actor, appeared as the wispy-voiced weirdo in *The Maltese Falcon* (1941) and *Casablanca* (1942).

FRANK LOVEJOY (1914–October 2, 1962) **Holy Cross Cemetery, Los Angeles, California**   Character actor and tough guy in *Beachhead* (1954) and *Strategic Air Command* (1955).

BELA LUGOSI (1882–August 16, 1956) **Holy Cross Cemetery, Los Angeles, California**   As a portrayer of supernatural villains Lugosi "died" in over a hundred screen and stage appearances, by every means possible. His favorite was in *The Son of Frankenstein* (1939), in which he lingered pathetically after receiving a gunshot wound. "It's a living," he would remark with a shrug. No wonder Lugosi's real funeral gave friends and fans a sense of *déjà vu*. "I have seen Bela lying in his coffin so often that it was a familiar sight," someone remarked. According to one witness, after most of the guests had left a woman, with a screaming small boy in tow, charged toward the coffin to show her terrified son that Dracula was dead and could frighten him no more. Lugosi was laid out and buried in his Dracula cape.

WILLIAM LUNDIGAN (1914–December 20, 1975) **Holy Cross Cemetery, Los Angeles, California** Screen, radio, and television star; films include *House on Telegraph Hill* (1951), *Salute to the Marines* (1943), *The Way West* (1967).

ALFRED LUNT (1892–August 3, 1977) **Forest Home Cemetery, Milwaukee, Wisconsin** For forty years he and his wife, Lynn Fontanne, were the leading couple of the American stage.

JACKIE "MOMS" MABLEY (1897–May 23, 1975) **Ferncliff Cemetery, Hartsdale, New York** Black stage, screen, and vaudeville comedian.

MARJORIE MAIN (1890–April 10, 1975) **Forest Lawn Memorial Park, Glendale, California** The indomitable "Ma Kettle" of films, Main is buried next to her husband, who died in 1935, forty years before she did. In 1953 she had his body moved to Forest Lawn, saying, "I've been lonely so much of my life, I'd like to be with him in death."

JAYNE MANSFIELD (1932–June 29, 1967) **Fairview Cemetery, Pen Argyl, Pennsylvania** Sex-symbol blonde actress, killed in a car-truck crash. Her grave is marked by a heart-shaped tombstone, the same shape as the swimming pool she had in her Hollywood mansion.

RICHARD MANSFIELD (1854–August 29, 1907) **Gardner Cemetery, New London, Connecticut** Renowned nineteenth-century actor, acclaimed as "Beau Brummel" and "Cyrano de Bergerac."

CHICO MARX (Leonard) (1887–October 11, 1961) **Forest Lawn Memorial Park, Glendale, California**   To the Marx Brothers comedy team he brought a fractured Italian accent and piano-playing interludes.

GROUCHO MARX (Julius) (1890–August 20, 1977) **Eden Memorial Park, Mission Hills, California**   Contributed irreverent rapier wit to the Marx Brothers films and later to the hit TV quiz show *You Bet Your Life* (1947–62).

HARPO MARX (Arthur) (1888–September 28, 1964) **Forest Lawn Memorial Park, Glendale, California**   Girl-chasing, non-talking, impish scoundrel in such Marx Brothers hits as *Coconuts* (1929), *Monkey Business* (1931), and *Duck Soup* (1935).

LOUIS B. MAYER (1885–October 29, 1957) **Home of Peace Memorial Park, Los Angeles, California**   Movie mogul, founder of M-G-M.

VICTOR McLAGLEN (1883–November 7, 1959) **Forest Lawn Memorial Park, Glendale, California**   Character actor, won 1935 Academy Award for *The Informer*.

ADOLPHE MENJOU (1890–October 29, 1963) **Hollywood Memorial Park Cemetery, Los Angeles, California**   Suave, debonair actor; films include *The Front Page* (1931) and *State of the Union* (1948).

MARILYN MILLER (1898–April 7, 1936) **Woodlawn Cemetery, Bronx, New York**   Musical comedy star of such Broadway hits as *Sally* (1920) and *Rosalie* (1928).

FLORENCE MILLS (1895–November 1, 1927) **Woodlawn Cemetery, Bronx, New York**   Singer and comedian, one of the most popular black Broadway stars of the 1920s. Among her many successes: *Blackbirds* (1926).

SAL MINEO (1939–February 12, 1976) **Gate of Heaven Cemetery, Hawthorne, New York**   Played teenage roles in *Rebel Without a Cause* (1955), *Giant* (1956), and *Exodus* (1960); stabbed to death.

TOM MIX (1880–October 12, 1940) **Forest Lawn Memorial Park, Glendale, California** "Empty Saddles" was the cowboy star's favorite song, and Rudy Vallee sang it at his funeral. The actor's body had been retrieved from an auto accident in Arizona, his cream-colored western dress suit virtually unwrinkled. Mix was found attired in boots, a diamond-studded belt buckle, and a white ten-gallon hat; his pockets were stuffed with $6,000 in cash and $1,500 in traveler's checks. At the crash site a seven-foot-high statue of a riderless pony was erected in Mix's memory.

MARILYN MONROE (1926–August 5, 1962) **Westwood Memorial Park, Los Angeles, California** Monroe's life was lived on the front pages, but after her death from a drug overdose her devoted ex-husband, Joe DiMaggio, determined that she would have a dignified funeral. In making arrangements he barred crowds and restricted guests to a few close friends, insulting not a small number of Hollywood celebrities who thought they belonged in that category. Marilyn was buried in a flowing sea-green Pucci dress. According to biographer Eunice Murray, DiMaggio "bent down and kissed her on the forehead murmuring 'I love you, I love you, I love you.'"

LOLA MONTEZ (1818–January 17, 1861) **Green-Wood Cemetery, Brooklyn, New York** World-famous dancer, actress and courtesan, she died impoverished and alone.

PAUL MUNI (1895–August 25, 1967) **Hollywood Memorial Park Cemetery, Los Angeles, California** Major star of the Yiddish theater, then a highly respected film actor in such 1930s hits as *Scarface* (1932), *I Am a Fugitive from a Chain Gang* (1932), *The Good Earth* (1937), *The Life of Emile Zola* (1937).

MAE MURRAY (1890–March 23, 1965) **Valhalla Memorial Park, North Hollywood, California** In her heyday as a silent star, Murray managed to go through a fortune of more than three million dollars; a year before her death she was found wandering the streets of St. Louis, Missouri, penniless.

NITA NALDI (1899–February 17, 1961) **Calvary Cemetery, Woodside, Queens, New York**   A leading vamp of the silents.

ALLA NAZIMOVA (1879–July 13, 1945) **Forest Lawn Memorial Park, Glendale, California**   One of the most successful silent stars; among her films, *The Madonna of the Streets* (1924).

RAMON NOVARRO (1899–October 31, 1968) **Calvary Cemetery, Los Angeles, California**   The first of Hollywood's Latin lovers, he was bludgeoned to death in his Hollywood Hills home.

JACK OAKIE (1903–January 23, 1978) **Forest Lawn Memorial Park, Glendale, California**   Comedian, appeared in over a hundred films, including *The Great Dictator* (1940).

ANNIE OAKLEY (1860–November 3, 1926) **Brock Cemetery, Greenville, Ohio**   The famous sharpshooter requested that her funeral be totally secret, and it was.

MARY PICKFORD (1893–May 29, 1979) **Forest Lawn Memorial Park, Glendale, California**   "America's sweetheart," and its first movie star, earned at least a million dollars a year in her heyday. In 1965 she took to her bed, announcing that she had worked hard since the age of five and intended to rest. By and large she remained there for the rest of her life.

DICK POWELL (1904–January 2, 1963) **Forest Lawn Memorial Park, Glendale, California**   Titles of a few of his films reflect his versatility as both a song-and-dance man and a dramatic actor: *Flirtation Walk* (1934), *Gold Diggers of 1935*, *Mrs. Mike* (1949), and *The Bad and the Beautiful* (1952); he died of cancer with wife June Allyson holding his hand.

TYRONE POWER (1914–November 15, 1958) **Hollywood Memorial Park Cemetery, Los Angeles, California**   Sex symbol and dashing swashbuckler, star of such films as *The Mark of Zorro* (1940), *Blood and Sand* (1940), and *The Razor's Edge* (1946); at the funeral his young third wife sat by the casket, holding the actor's hand throughout the half-hour ceremony.

FREDDIE PRINZE (1954–January 22, 1977) **Forest Lawn Memorial Park, Glendale, California** Popular star of hit TV series *Chico and the Man* (1974–77), he shot himself in the head.

GEORGE RAFT (1896–November 24, 1980) **Forest Lawn Memorial Park, Glendale, California** Movie tough guy in over sixty motion pictures.

CLAUDE RAINS (1889–May 30, 1967) **Red Hill Cemetery, Moultonborough, New Hampshire** British-born character actor; his best-known films include *Casablanca* (1942) and *Lawrence of Arabia* (1962).

BASIL RATHBONE (1892–July 21, 1967) **Ferncliff Cemetery, Hartsdale, New York** Remembered for his portrayal of Sherlock Holmes in the 1930–'40s film series.

WALLACE REID (1891–January 18, 1923) **Forest Lawn Memorial Park, Glendale, California** Reid died in a Hollywood sanitarium after a long battle with drugs. Because he was one of the silent screen's most admired leading men, his wife, Dorothy, publicized the cause of his breakdown, hoping to alert the public to the drug menace. Later, as a tribute to his memory, she directed a movie on the same subject, *Human Wreckage*. Reid was one of the first Hollywood celebrities to be buried in Forest Lawn.

MAX REINHARDT (1873–October 31, 1943) **Westchester Hills Cemetery, Hastings-on-Hudson, New York** Producer and director, introduced expressionism to the German stage in the 1920s and '30s. With the rise of the Nazis, he fled to the U.S. and made a Hollywood version of *A Midsummer Night's Dream* (1934).

BILL "BOJANGLES" ROBINSON (1878–November 25, 1949) **Evergreen Cemetery, Brooklyn, New York** The beloved tap dancer's funeral attracted a crowd of half a million in Harlem.

EDWARD G. ROBINSON (1893–January 26, 1973) **Beth El Cemetery, Glendale, Queens, New York** Character actor, noted for gangster roles such as *Little Caesar* (1930).

Tablet marking the site of Will Rogers's fatal plane crash in Alaska.
(NBC-TV)

WILL ROGERS (1879–August 15, 1935) **Forest Lawn Memorial Park, Glendale, California**   Comedian and social commentator Rogers and his friend pilot Wiley Post (see Explorers and Settlers) took off from Barrow, Alaska, even though they had reports that the weather up ahead was poor. Their plane crashed in such an isolated area that an Eskimo witness had to run sixteen miles through rough tundra to get help. A sheet of paper found in Rogers's badly mangled typewriter contained his weekly column, which ended abruptly in mid-sentence. The last word he had typed was "death." "A smile has disappeared from the lips of America," mourned singer John McCormack, reflecting the public's adoration of the homespun Rogers. The emotional outpouring rivaled that which followed Lincoln's death. Four full pages of the New York *Times* were taken up by the event, flags flew at half-mast throughout the nation, and CBS and NBC observed a half-hour of silence. Charles Lindbergh (see Explorers and Settlers) took charge of bringing the bodies home, and fifty thousand people filed by Rogers's casket.

BILLY ROSE (1899–February 10, 1966) **Westchester Hills Cemetery, Hastings-on-Hudson, New York** The diminutive producer of hit Broadway shows was less successful in his human relationships. As a result, there was haggling over his estate when he died, some of it centering on the disposition of Rose's remains. The body remained in the vault while his sister and executors argued about how much should be spent. The sister selected a plot so huge it had gone unsold for thirty-five years, arguing that Billy had often said, "I've got to have room, I've got to have size, I've got to have space around me," and a $60,000 mausoleum was finally agreed upon. The full cost of the burial: $125,000.

LILLIAN RUSSELL (1861–June 6, 1922) **Allegheny Cemetery, Pittsburgh, Pennsylvania** Leading stage beauty of the gaslight era; buried with full military honors at President Harding's orders.

ROSALIND RUSSELL (1912–November 28, 1976) **Holy Cross Cemetery, Los Angeles, California** The fast-talking career girl in such films as *The Women* (1939) and *Auntie Mame* (1958); died of cancer after suffering for many years from rheumatoid arthritis.

IRENE RYAN (1902–April 26, 1973) **Woodlawn Memorial Park, Compton, California** "Granny" in the TV series *The Beverly Hillbillies* (1962–71).

RUTH ST. DENIS (1877–July 21, 1968) **Forest Lawn Memorial Park, Glendale, California** Dancer, a creator of the American modern dance revolution.

DIANA SANDS (1934–September 21, 1973) **Ferncliff Cemetery, Hartsdale, New York** Young black actress, remembered for the Broadway production of *A Raisin in the Sun* (1959).

MAURICE SCHWARTZ (1891–May 10, 1960) **Mount He-bron Cemetery, Flushing, Queens, New York**   Called the John Barrymore of the Yiddish theater, noted for his version of *King Lear*.

DAVID O. SELZNICK (1902–June 22, 1965) **Forest Lawn Memorial Park, Glendale, California**   Hollywood producer; among his many successes, *Gone With the Wind* (1939).

MACK SENNETT (1880–November 5, 1960) **Holy Cross Cemetery, Los Angeles, California**   Silent film producer, called the "King of Comedy."

LEE STRASBERG (1901–February 17, 1982) **Westchester Hills Cemetery, Hastings-on-Hudson, New York**   Actor and teacher, father of "method acting" in America, and mentor to such stars as Marlon Brando, James Dean, Marilyn Monroe, Al Pacino, and Robert De Niro.

MARGARET SULLAVAN (1909–January 1, 1960) **St. Mary's Whitechapel Trinity Episcopal Churchyard, Lancaster, Virginia**   Film and stage actress, *The Shop Around the Corner* (1940); died of an overdose of pills.

NORMA TALMADGE (1893–December 24, 1957) **Holly-wood Memorial Park Cemetery, Los Angeles, California**   A top star of silent films (*Smilin' Through*, 1922, *Camille*, 1927, *Du-Barry, Woman of Passion*, 1930) and one of the much-admired Talmadge sisters (with Constance and Natalie).

SHARON TATE (1943–August 9, 1969) **Holy Cross Ceme-tery, Los Angeles, California**   Actress, wife of director Roman Polanski, brutally murdered by followers of cult leader Charles Manson.

LAURETTE TAYLOR (1884–December 7, 1946) **Woodlawn Cemetery, Bronx, New York**   Stage actress, Amanda in Tennessee Williams's *The Glass Menagerie* (1944).

ROBERT TAYLOR (1911–June 9, 1969) Forest Lawn Memorial Park, Glendale, California   Leading man of such films as *Magnificent Obsession* (1935) and *The Detectives* TV series (1959–62).

IRVING THALBERG (1899–September 14, 1936) Forest Lawn Memorial Park, Glendale, California   "Boy wonder" movie executive at M-G-M, producer of many top films; movie star Wallace Berry flew his plane over the funeral procession, dropping red roses.

TOM THUMB (Charles Sherwood Stratton) (1838–December 1883) Mountain Grove Cemetery, Bridgeport, Connecticut   Circus midget, promoted by P. T. Barnum.

MIKE TODD (1907–March 23, 1958) Waldheim/Forest Home Cemetery, Forest Park, Illinois   Elizabeth Taylor and fast-talking producer Mike Todd had been married less than a year when he proposed that she join him on a trip to accept the Friars Club "Showman of the Year" award. Taylor stayed home because of a bad cold and so avoided death when the plane crashed in New Mexico.

SPENCER TRACY (1900–June 10, 1967) Forest Lawn Memorial Park, Glendale, California   Popular movie actor, died of a heart attack just after finishing *Guess Who's Coming to Dinner* with his longtime companion, Katharine Hepburn.

TRIGGER (1932–July 3, 1965) Roy Rogers–Dale Evans Museum, Victorville, California   Rogers's faithful four-legged companion in over ninety feature films; mounted in the museum.

SOPHIE TUCKER (1884–February 9, 1966) Emanuel Cemetery, Wethersfield, Connecticut   Vaudeville headliner known as "the last of the red-hot mamas."

BEN TURPIN (1869–July 1, 1940) Forest Lawn Memorial Park, Glendale, California   Comic known for his cross-eyed expressions.

Silent screen star Rudolph Valentino lying in state. His funeral attracted thousands of frenzied mourners.

RUDOLPH VALENTINO (1895–August 23, 1926) **Hollywood Memorial Park Cemetery, Los Angeles, California** Valentino died suddenly in New York City of acute appendicitis at the very height of his film popularity. At the funeral chapel hysteria set in as a crowd of twelve thousand fans of the smoldering Latin lover waited to see his remains. The funeral parlor's large plate window was broken by the crush of bodies, and three women were injured. The madness followed the two special railroad cars hired to carry the body back to Hollywood. After an equally hectic funeral, Valentino was not forgotten. In the early 1930s a mysterious woman dressed in black began to appear at his crypt for the yearly commemorative services marking his death. Others imitated the eerie "lady in black," and at one time there were as many as a dozen showing up. One turned out to be a former *Follies* girl who claimed to have been married to the star and to have borne him two children. Another was Ditra Flame, president of the Hollywood Valentino Memorial Guild, dedicated to keeping his memory alive. She continued to appear as the "lady in black" until the 1960s. "The Sheik's" crypt is marked with his legal name: Rodolfo Guglielmi Valentino.

JOHN WAYNE (1907–June 11, 1979) **Pacific View Memorial Park, Newport Beach, California** Popular star of westerns and war films from *Stagecoach* (1939) to *True Grit* (1968).

CLIFTON WEBB (1896–October 13, 1966) **Hollywood Memorial Park Cemetery, Los Angeles, California** Sophisticated character actor, portrayed the unflappable baby sitter in *Sitting Pretty* (1948).

MAE WEST (1892–November 22, 1980) **Cypress Hills Cemetery, Brooklyn, New York** Made sex both funny and tantalizing on stage and in such films as *She Done Him Wrong* (1933).

GUS WILLIAMS (1847–January 16, 1915) **Green-Wood Cemetery, Brooklyn, New York** Vaudeville performer.

ANNA MAY WONG (1907–February 2, 1961) **Rosedale Memorial Park, Los Angeles, California** First Chinese movie star.

NATALIE WOOD (1938–November 29, 1981) **Westwood Memorial Park, Los Angeles, California** The child actress who made her movie debut at age five in *Miracle on 34th Street* (1947) went on to become an adult star and was nominated for an Academy Award three times. She drowned in a boating accident near Catalina Island while her two-time husband, actor Robert Wagner, talked with her co-star Christopher Walken. Accompanied by Russian balalaika music, she was buried near Marilyn Monroe.

MONTY WOOLLEY (1888–May 6, 1963) **Greenridge Cemetery, Saratoga Springs, New York** Character actor, the egocentric critic in *The Man Who Came to Dinner* (1941).

ED WYNN (1886–June 19, 1966) **Forest Lawn Memorial Park, Glendale, California** Mild-mannered comedian known as "the perfect fool."

FLORENZ ZIEGFELD (1869–July 22, 1932) **Forest Lawn Memorial Park, Glendale, California** Producer, "glorified the American girl" in the *Ziegfeld Follies* of the 1920s and '30s.

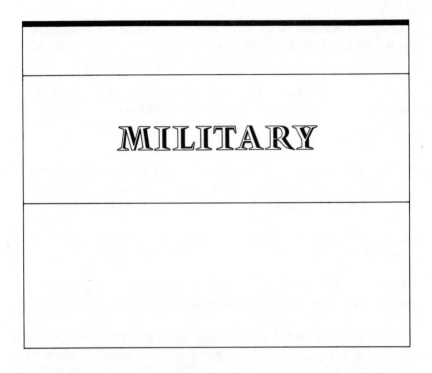

MILITARY

CREIGHTON ABRAMS (1914–September 4, 1974) **Arlington National Cemetery, Arlington, Virginia**   Army chief of staff and U.S. Commander in Vietnam, daring tank tactician.

HENRY "HAP" ARNOLD (1886–January 15, 1950) **Arlington National Cemetery, Arlington, Virginia**   Commander of the Army Air Forces during World War II.

MARY ANN "MOTHER" BICKERDYKE (1817–November 8, 1901) **Linwood Cemetery, Galesburg, Illinois**   Served as nurse, surgeon, and administrator on the battlefields of the Civil War, cut through army red tape to get supplies to the Union men, who dubbed her "Mother."

BELLE BOYD (1844–June 11, 1900) **Spring Grove Cemetery, Wisconsin Dells, Wisconsin**   Confederate spy and stage actress.

EDWARD BRADDOCK (1695–July 13, 1755) **Braddock's Grave, Farmington, Pennsylvania** General Braddock's army was ambushed on its way to Fort Duquesne during the French and Indian War, and he was fatally wounded. Braddock was carried back to Great Meadows, where he died and was buried in the road after services conducted by his aide-de-camp, George Washington. Wagons were driven over the grave to prevent the Indians from finding and desecrating it. In 1804 the body was moved to the present site.

OMAR N. BRADLEY (1893–April 8, 1981) **Arlington National Cemetery, Arlington, Virginia** General of the army, known as the "GI's general" during World War II; he commanded U.S. Second Corps in North Africa and Sicily (1943) and led U.S. ground troops in the Normandy invasion (1944).

ROGER B. CHAFFEE (1935–January 27, 1967) **Arlington National Cemetery, Arlington, Virginia** Astronaut, killed in a simulation of the Apollo I launching.

CLAIRE CHENNAULT (1890–July 27, 1958) **Arlington National Cemetery, Arlington, Virginia** Ace aviator, formed the Flying Tigers to aid the Chinese in the late 1930s.

LUCIUS D. CLAY (1897–April 16, 1978) **West Point Cemetery, U.S. Military Academy, West Point, New York** Organized the Berlin airlift during the 1948–'49 Communist blockade of the western sector.

COMANCHE (c. 1862–November 7, 1891) **Dyche Hall, University of Kansas Museum of Natural History, Lawrence, Kansas** Known as the sole survivor of Little Big Horn, Comanche was a mustang who saw action with the Seventh Cavalry and was wounded twelve times. The Custer burial party found the wounded animal and took him to Fort Lincoln, 950 miles away, where he recuperated. Honored as a symbol of the massacre, he was excused from military duties and was never again ridden in the line of duty. He died of colic at Fort Riley, Kansas, and, at the request of his officers, was mounted. Currently, he is on display in a humidity-controlled case.

MARGARET CORBIN (1751–c. 1800) **West Point Cemetery, U.S. Military Academy, West Point, New York** Took over her dead husband's cannon during a Revolutionary War battle, the first U.S. woman to earn a military pension.

GEORGE ARMSTRONG CUSTER (1839–June 25, 1876) **West Point Cemetery, U.S. Military Academy, West Point, New York** Custer had more than twenty horses shot from under him in some of the roughest fighting of the Civil War but was never seriously wounded until the massacre at Little Big Horn, Montana, in June 1876. At that lonely spot the general and his 225 men were killed by the Sioux, their bodies later stripped of clothing and all possessions by the Indian women. Custer's naked corpse was found on the highest point of the field and interred in a shallow grave. He was reburied at West Point in October 1877.

STEPHEN DECATUR (1779–March 22, 1820) **Saint Peter's Churchyard, Philadelphia, Pennsylvania** Naval hero of the War of 1812; "Our country: In her intercourse with foreign nations may she always be right, but our country right or wrong."

GEORGE DEWEY (1837–January 16, 1917) **Washington Cathedral, Washington, D.C.** Admiral; national hero, defeated the Spanish fleet at Manila Bay in 1898 during the Spanish-American War.

DAVID G. FARRAGUT (1801–August 14, 1870) **Woodlawn Cemetery, Bronx, New York** Union admiral, noted for rallying cry "Damn the torpedos—full speed ahead!"

NATHAN BEDFORD FORREST (1821–October 29, 1877) **Forrest Park, Memphis, Tennessee** Confederate general, led cavalry raids against Union supply lines.

DEBORAH SAMPSON GANNETT (1760–April 29, 1827) **Rockridge Cemetery, Sharon, Massachusetts** Served in the American Revolution disguised as a man, using the name of Robert Shurtleff, and distinguished herself as a fighter. The inscrip-

Final resting place of Deborah Sampson Gannett, "The Female Soldier," who fought in the American Revolution disguised as a man. (Patrick J. Leonard)

tion on the reverse of her stone reads: "Deborah Sampson Gannett—Robert Shurtleff/The Female Soldier/Service 1781 to 1783."

GERONIMO (1829–February 17, 1909) **Apache Cemetery, Fort Sill, Oklahoma**   Apache chief, led sensational campaign against the whites (1885–86); captured and recaptured several times, he and his tribe were finally forced to become farmers and stock raisers at Fort Sill.

NATHANAEL GREENE (1742–June 19, 1786) **Johnson Square, Savannah, Georgia**   American Revolutionary general, pursued the British into New Jersey after they evacuated Philadelphia.

VIRGIL I. GRISSOM (1926–January 27, 1967) **Arlington National Cemetery, Arlington, Virginia**   Astronaut; third man to go into space (1961); killed in a simulation of Apollo I launching.

WILLIAM F. "BULL" HALSEY (1882–August 16, 1959) **Arlington National Cemetery, Arlington, Virginia**   Admiral, commander of U.S. naval forces in South Pacific in World War II.

WADE HAMPTON (1818–April 11, 1902) **Trinity Churchyard, Columbia, South Carolina**   Confederate commander, powerful South Carolina political figure after the Civil War.

JOHN BELL HOOD (1831–August 30, 1879) **Metairie Cemetery, New Orleans, Louisiana**   The Confederate hero of Chickamauga loved military pomp and ceremony but was deprived of it in death. He died during a yellow fever epidemic in New Orleans, and without military procession and ritual went to his grave.

OLIVER OTIS HOWARD (1830–October 26, 1909) **Lakeview Cemetery, Burlington, Vermont**   Union general, head of the Freedman's Bureau, and founder of Howard University.

STONEWALL JACKSON (1824–May 10, 1863) Stonewall Jackson Memorial Cemetery, Lexington, Virginia   Confederate general and hero; at the Battle of Bull Run an officer cried, "There is Jackson standing like a stone wall," giving him his nickname.

JOHN PAUL JONES (1747–July 18, 1792) Chapel, U.S. Naval Academy, Annapolis, Maryland   America's first naval hero died in France, almost forgotten by his country, and was buried in obscurity in the Protestant Cemetery of Paris. More than a century later, Ambassador Horace Porter began what turned out to be a six-year search for Jones's remains. President Theodore Roosevelt, seeking to strengthen America's military image, sent a squadron of naval vessels to escort the Father of the Navy home. In 1913 his body was permanently enshrined in an ornamental and elaborate tomb, erected by Congress at a cost of seventy-five thousand dollars.

KIDRON (?–October 10, 1942) Smithsonian Museum of Natural History, Washington, D.C.   Loyal horse of General John H. Pershing; museum has his skin and skull, all that is left.

JAMES LAWRENCE (1781–June 4, 1813) Trinity Churchyard, New York, New York   Naval hero of the War of 1812, said "Don't give up the ship" when mortally wounded. First buried in Halifax, Nova Scotia, by the British, who admired his courage.

ROBERT E. LEE (1807–October 12, 1870) Lee Chapel Museum, Washington and Lee University, Lexington, Virginia   The Commanding General of the Confederacy spent his final years as president of Washington College, now Washington and Lee University. A few days before his death flood waters engulfed Lexington, completely cutting it off from the outside world and leaving no coffin for the great hero of the South. After a diligent search, two young men found one, but it was too small for him, and General Lee had to be buried without his shoes.

JAMES LONGSTREET (1821–January 2, 1904) Alta Vista Cemetery, Gainesville, Georgia   Lee's most distinguished lieutenant after the death of Stonewall Jackson.

DOUGLAS MacARTHUR (1880–April 5, 1964) MacArthur
Memorial, Norfolk, Virginia   The flamboyant general who commanded American forces to victory in the Pacific in World War
II was buried in a plain, gray steel government-issue casket in his
most faded suntan uniform. "It is a symbol of my life," he had
once told a subordinate. "Whatever I've done that really matters,
I've done wearing it. When the time comes, it will be in these
that I journey forth. What greater honor could come to an American and a soldier?"

FRANCIS MARION (c. 1732–February 26, 1795) Gabriel's
Plantation, Belle Isle, St. Stephen, South Carolina   American
Revolutionary hero and guerrilla leader, known as the "Swamp
Fox" because he would attack British troops and then retreat to
the Carolina swamps.

GEORGE CATLETT MARSHALL (1880–October 16,
1959) Arlington National Cemetery, Arlington, Virginia   U.S.
Army general and statesman, won Nobel Peace Prize (1953) for
creating the Marshall Plan for postwar European recovery.

GEORGE BRINTON McCLELLAN (1826–October 29,
1885) Riverview Cemetery, Trenton, New Jersey   Union general, commander of the Army of the Potomac (1861–62).

WILLIAM "BILLY" MITCHELL (1879–February 19, 1936)
Forest Home Cemetery, Milwaukee, Wisconsin   U.S. Army Air
Corps general, aviation pioneer and advocate. Court-martialed in
1926 for attacking the military for its neglect of air power.

AUDIE MURPHY (1924–May 31, 1971) Arlington National
Cemetery, Arlington, Virginia   Most decorated soldier of World
War II, he won every medal the army gives for gallantry; became
a film actor and appeared in a movie version of his own story,
To Hell and Back (1955); killed in an airplane crash.

CHESTER NIMITZ (1885–February 20, 1966) Golden Gate
National Cemetery, San Bruno, California   Admiral of the Fleet
during World War II.

MATTHEW CALBRAITH PERRY (1794–March 4, 1858)
Island Cemetery, Newport, Rhode Island Naval commodore, opened up U.S. trade with Japan (1853–54).

OLIVER HAZARD PERRY (1785–August 23, 1819) Island Cemetery, Newport, Rhode Island
Naval hero of the Battle of Lake Erie in the War of 1812; "We have met the enemy and they are ours."

JOHN J. PERSHING (1860–July 15, 1948) Arlington National Cemetery, Arlington, Virginia
During World War I, when he commanded U.S. troops overseas, "Black Jack" Pershing's was probably the best-known name in the country. Self-made funeral plans were kept in a Pentagon file marked "Top Secret"; by mid-morning after the general's death the Pentagon already had an operations center working to his strict timetable and three thousand telegraphed funeral invitations were sent out. He was buried beneath an enlisted man's marker in a plot now known as "Pershing Hill" in Arlington. Twenty years later the remains of his grandson, Richard Pershing, killed in action in Vietnam, were interred near him.

MOLLY PITCHER (Mary Ludwig Hays) (1754–January 22, 1832) Old Graveyard, Carlisle, Pennsylvania
American Revolutionary hero of the Battle of Monmouth, carried pitchers of water to thirsty troops, later took over her wounded husband's gun.

EDDIE RICKENBACKER (1890–July 23, 1973) Greenlawn Cemetery, Columbus, Ohio
By his own count Rickenbacker had cheated death 135 times before dying in bed at age eighty-two. The most-decorated flying ace of World War I was also a racing car driver, self-made business tycoon, and inveterate adventure-seeker. His funeral celebrated the skies he loved. Four jet planes shot into view; the first pulled straight up while the others went on in the missing-leader formation, the Air Force version of the Army's riderless horse.

WINFIELD SCOTT (1786–May 29, 1866) West Point Cemetery, U.S. Military Academy, West Point, New York
General, led U.S. forces in the Mexican War (1846–48).

PHILIP SHERIDAN (1831–August 5, 1888) **Arlington National Cemetery, Arlington, Virginia**   Union general, cut off Lee's line of retreat from Appomattox (1865).

WILLIAM TECUMSEH SHERMAN (1820–February 14, 1891) **Calvary Cemetery, St. Louis, Missouri**   Union general known for his comment "War is hell."

The monument to Sitting Bull, the Sioux chief who defeated Custer, dominates the landscape in Mobridge, South Dakota. (South Dakota Division of Tourism)

SITTING BULL (Tatanka Iyotake) (c. 1831–December 15, 1890) **Sitting Bull Monument, Mobridge, South Dakota**   Four months after the great Sioux chief defeated Custer at Little Big Horn, he went down to permanent defeat. After six years of exile in Canada, the Sioux were brought back to South Dakota. When he ordered his warriors to resist arrest, Sitting Bull was shot in the back of the head; the aftermath of his death was the massacre of the Sioux at Wounded Knee. In the mid-1960s the chief's remains were buried on the top of a high hill west of Mobridge close to the spot where he was killed.

FRIEDRICH WILHELM VON STEUBEN (1730–November 28, 1794) **Steuben Memorial, Remsen, New York**   At Valley Forge, Prussian officer von Steuben developed the rough Continental Army into an effective fighting force. In gratitude the victorious Americans made him a citizen and New York State gave him a 16,000-acre farm north of Utica. He died there, almost bankrupt, and was buried in an unmarked grave, wrapped in his military cloak. Years later, when a road was scheduled to go through the burial area, a devoted aide dug up the baron's body and hid it in the forest to avoid desecration. That burial site now has a tablet proclaiming that von Steuben's services were "Indispensable to the achievement of American Independence."

JAMES EWELL BROWN (JEB) STUART (1833–May 12, 1864) **Hollywood Cemetery, Richmond, Virginia**   Confederate general, outstanding cavalry leader, and regarded by Lee as the "eyes of the Army."

TRAVELLER (?–1872) **Lee Chapel Museum, Washington and Lee University, Lexington, Virginia**   Robert E. Lee's beloved horse; after some years on display, his skeleton was buried on the grounds near his master's crypt.

EMORY UPTON (1839–March 15, 1881) **Fort Hill Cemetery, Auburn, New York**   Commandant of cadets at West Point (1870–75), he wrote more on tactics and military history than any other officer of his day and developed a system of infantry tactics that bears his name; committed suicide.

JONATHAN M. WAINWRIGHT (1883–September 2, 1953) **Arlington National Cemetery, Arlington, Virginia** Commander on Corregidor, forced to surrender in 1942, and a prisoner of war until 1945.

ANTHONY WAYNE (1745–December 15, 1796) **St. David's (Radnor) Churchyard, Wayne, Pennsylvania** "Bury me at the foot of the flagstaff, boys," the Revolutionary hero requested before he expired in the military garrison at the present-day site of Erie, Pennsylvania. They obliged, and "Mad Anthony" was interred in a plain coffin. Twelve years later his son, Isaac, set out to bring his remains home to Radnor. There are conflicting versions of what happened on the return trip. One story goes that his body was boiled to remove the flesh and the bones were carried home in Isaac's saddlebags. Another tale is that the bags were stolen en route, and yet a third that nobody knows the whereabouts of the remains of Mad Anthony Wayne. Nonetheless, somebody or something was buried at St. David's. At the funeral services in 1809 the reclusive Mary Vining, an old sweetheart, emerged from her home for the first time since Wayne's death fifteen years earlier.

LEONARD WOOD (1860–August 7, 1927) **Arlington National Cemetery, Arlington, Virginia** Army general and doctor, organized the Rough Riders with Theodore Roosevelt (see Presidents); later governor of Cuba.

ALVIN YORK (1887–September 2, 1964) **Alvin York's Farm and Grist Mill, Pall Mall, Tennessee** Described by General Pershing as "the greatest soldier of the war" (World War I), Sergeant York found himself under enemy fire during the Battle of the Argonne Forest on October 8, 1918, and led seven men to wipe out the German machine gun nest, killing 25 of the enemy and capturing 132 prisoners. He was awarded the Congressional Medal of Honor and became a popular hero; Gary Cooper (see Entertainers) portrayed York in the 1941 film that won him an Academy Award.

SOCIAL REFORMERS

JANE ADDAMS (1860–May 21, 1935) **Cedarville Cemetery, Cedarville, Illinois** Founder of Chicago's Hull House, first settlement house in the U.S. (1899); her funeral was held in its courtyard.

SUSAN B. ANTHONY (1820–March 13, 1906) **Mount Hope Cemetery, Rochester, New York** American reformer and leader of the woman suffrage movement.

CLARA BARTON (1821–April 12, 1912) **North Cemetery, Oxford, Massachusetts** Founder and first president of the American Red Cross (1881–1904), noted for her service on the battlefields of the Civil War.

ELLA REEVE BLOOR (1862–August 10, 1951) **Harleigh Cemetery, Camden, New Jersey** A communist sympathizer and labor organizer known as "Mother" Bloor.

JOHN BROWN (1800–December 2, 1859) **The John Brown Farm, North Elba, New York**   John Brown's execution for his seizure of the U.S. Arsenal at Harper's Ferry, Virginia, fueled emotions on both sides of the slavery question, leading to the Civil War. Convicted of treason by the State of Virginia, the fanatical abolitionist commented, "I cannot better serve the cause I love than to die for it."

He rode to the gallows in Charlestown seated on his own coffin in the back of a truck. John Wilkes Booth (see Criminals), a member of the First Virginia Regiment from Richmond, was among the 1,500 spectators who witnessed the hanging, and it nurtured his commitment to the southern cause. Brown's body, sent north in a black walnut coffin, was placed in a new one in New York City so that he would not be buried in a southern coffin. At each stop on the long trip to Brown's upstate New York

John Brown's death is remembered each year by the John Brown Memorial Association. (New York State Office of Parks, Recreation and Historic Preservation, Bureau of Historic Sites, John Brown Farm State Historic Site)

Abolitionist John Brown requested that this self-composed inscription be placed on a stone originally intended for his grandfather's grave. (Edwin N. Cotter, Jr., Thousand Islands State Park and Recreation Commission)

farm, the carefully guarded body was greeted with tolling bells and sympathetic crowds. As the coffin was lowered into the farmyard earth, a friend, part Indian and part Negro, sang "Blow Ye the Trumpet, Blow," a hymn Brown had used as a lullaby for his children. Years earlier he had moved his grandfather's discarded gravestone to North Elba in preparation for his own use of it. His inscription, below that of his grandfather, reads: "John Brown, Born May 9, 1800, Was Executed at Charleston [*sic*], Va., Dec. 2, 1859."

CARRIE CHAPMAN CATT (1859–March 9, 1947) **Woodlawn Cemetery, Bronx, New York**   Suffragist and founder of the League of Women Voters.

59

LEVI COFFIN (1798–September 16, 1877) **Spring Grove Cemetery, Cincinnati, Ohio**   Major figure in the "underground railroad" network. Not a single fugitive given assistance by him failed to reach freedom.

EUGENE VICTOR DEBS (1855–October 20, 1926) **Highland Lawn Cemetery, Terre Haute, Indiana**   The final illness of the five-time Socialist candidate for president was attributed to campaigning and his imprisonment for wartime pacifism. Lingering near death in a sanitarium, he emerged briefly from a coma and wrote down the words of Henley's *Invictus*, which had been an inspiration to him throughout his life:

> It matters not how strait the gate,
> How charged with punishment the scroll,
> I am the master of my fate
> I am the captain of my soul.

As he scribbled the last words the pencil dropped from his fingers and he fell into a coma again. After death his body lay in state at the Labor Temple in Terre Haute and again at his home, from the front porch of which Norman Thomas conducted the funeral service. He was cremated, and his ashes were buried without religious service.

DOROTHEA DIX (1802–July 17, 1887) **Mount Auburn Cemetery, Cambridge, Massachusetts**   Crusader for improved treatment for the insane and the establishment of public hospitals and asylums.

FREDERICK DOUGLASS (c. 1817–February 20, 1895) **Mount Hope Cemetery, Rochester, New York**   Escaped slave, spokesman for abolition, and editor of an antislavery newspaper. Susan B. Anthony spoke at his funeral, and floral tributes included one from the son of his former master.

MEDGAR EVERS (1925–June 12, 1963) **Arlington National Cemetery, Arlington, Virginia**   As he walked into his home, Evers, the field secretary of the NAACP, was hit in the back by a sniper's bullet. His death touched off mass protests, during which 158 people were arrested in Mississippi. After funeral services in the Masonic Temple in Jackson, Evers's coffin was carried through the town. At his graveside civil rights colleagues sang "We Shall Overcome." His assassination fueled the voter registration drive and the campaign leading to the passage of the Civil Rights Act (1964).

WILLIAM LLOYD GARRISON (1805–May 24, 1879) **Forest Hills Cemetery, Boston, Massachusetts** Uncompromising abolitionist, publisher of the *Liberator* for thirty-five years.

HENRY GEORGE (1839–October 29, 1897) **Green-Wood Cemetery, Brooklyn, New York** Economist, exponent of a single tax on land to reduce inequalities of wealth; died while running for mayor of New York City.

EMMA GOLDMAN (1869–May 14, 1940) **Waldheim/Forest Home Cemetery, Forest Park, Illinois** Anarchist Goldman, advocate of revolution and free love, was deported from the U.S. to Russia in 1919. She went abroad after disagreements with the Bolshevik regime, eventually settling in Toronto, where she died. The exile was granted one of her deepest wishes: reentry into the U.S. She is buried near fellow radicals who were hanged for inciting violence in the Haymarket Square riot of 1886.

SAMUEL GOMPERS (1850–December 13, 1924) **Sleepy Hollow Cemetery, North Tarrytown, New York** Gompers, the father of American labor, collapsed in Mexico City but refused to be flown to Vera Cruz, insisting on returning by train to the U.S. border. "I wish to live until I arrive in my own country; if I die, I prefer to die at home." The president of the American Federation of Labor died eleven hours after reaching San Antonio, Texas. His final words were "God bless our American institutions. May they grow better day by day." He was taken to Washington, D.C., in a massive 1,200-pound bronze casket and lay in state in the headquarters of the A. F. of L. In New York, following his instructions, the casket was escorted by a military caisson drawn by six horses to the Elks Club, where his body was placed on a table on which also rested antlers, the symbol of the Elks, and a bible. Gompers was buried near Andrew Carnegie (see Business and Finance) and many other successful capitalists.

WILLIAM GREEN **(1873–November 21, 1952)** **South Lawn Cemetery, Coshocton, Ohio**   Leader of the United Mine Workers, president of the American Federation of Labor from 1924.

BILL HAYWOOD **(1869–May 18, 1928)** **Waldheim/Forest Home Cemetery, Forest Park, Illinois**   Big Bill Haywood, founder of the International Workers of the World, a radical labor union, moved to Moscow in 1921, styled himself as a political refugee "pending the revolution in America," and married a Russian office worker. When he died his ashes were divided into two parts, with one half buried in the Kremlin wall during a demonstration in Red Square. The other half was interred near the graves of the Haymarket victims, according to his wishes.

SIDNEY HILLMAN (1887–July 10, 1946) **Westchester Hills Cemetery, Hastings-on-Hudson, New York** Founder and leader of the Amalgamated Clothing Workers Union; his body was taken through the streets of New York's garment district as 350,000 members of the union stayed off the job out of respect.

MOTHER JONES (1830–November 30, 1930) **Union Miners' Cemetery, Mount Olive, Illinois** Agitator for coal miners' rights, Mary Harris Jones participated in many labor battles.

HELEN KELLER (1880–June 1, 1968) **Washington Cathedral, Washington, D.C.** Deaf and blind, she overcame these handicaps and became a national symbol of courage; spoke on behalf of the handicapped, world peace, and social reform.

MARTIN LUTHER KING, JR. (1929–April 4, 1968) **South View Cemetery, Atlanta, Georgia** The leader of the civil rights movement in the 1950s, was shot in Memphis while helping that city's sanitation men to form a union. His coffin was carried through the streets of Atlanta on a crude farm wagon pulled by two Georgia mules and followed by tens of thousands of mourners. The cart was made of rough planks of a faded green color, symbols of the Reverend King's identification with the poor. The funeral service included a taped excerpt from his last sermon, in which he asked for a short eulogy after death that would focus on his work for the poor rather than his awards and prizes. The graveyard, in which he was buried near his grandparents, had been founded in 1866 by six Negroes who were tired of taking their dead to the rear of the municipal cemetery. On his tombstone are the words of the spiritual—"Free at last, free at last, thank God Almighty, I'm free at last"—used by King in his famous speech during the March on Washington in 1963.

MEYER LONDON (1871–June 6, 1926) **Mount Carmel Cemetery, Glendale, Queens, New York** Socialist leader and congressman, killed by an automobile in New York City.

MALCOLM X (Malcolm Little) (1925–February 21, 1965) **Ferncliff Cemetery, Hartsdale, New York** As he was beginning to address a crowd at a Manhattan ballroom, Malcolm X was shot to death, possibly by dissidents within his Muslim group. He had remarked the week before that "I live like a man who is already dead." Bomb threats to the funeral home initiated heavy security, and each floral arrangement was carefully examined. The Black Muslim leader lay in a bronze coffin, which was taken to a Christian church, formerly a movie theater, adapted for the Muslim service. His body was wrapped in seven white shrouds, according to Muslim tradition, and could be seen through a glass lid. The funeral was carried live on television.

GEORGE MEANY (1894–January 10, 1980) **Gate of Heaven Cemetery, Silver Spring, Maryland**   First head of the AFL-CIO.

TOM MOONEY (1882–March 6, 1942) **Cypress Lawn Memorial Park, Colma, California**   Labor agitator sentenced to death for a 1916 bombing; his sentence was commuted to life imprisonment, and he was pardoned unconditionally in 1939.

LUCRETIA COFFIN MOTT (1793–November 11, 1880) **Friends Fair Hill Burial Ground, Philadelphia, Pennsylvania**   Abolitionist and suffragist, an organizer of the Seneca Falls Convention (1848).

CARRY NATION (1846–June 2 or 9, 1911) **Belton Cemetery, Belton, Missouri**   Temperance leader, devoted herself to smashing up saloons with an ax. Her gravestone reads: "Carry A. Nation/Faithful to the Cause of Prohibition/'She Hath Done What She Could.' "

WENDELL PHILLIPS (1811–February 2, 1884) **Granary Burying Ground, Boston, Massachusetts**   Lecturer for abolition, civil rights, and other controversial issues.

JACOB A. RIIS (1849–May 26, 1914) **Riverside Cemetery, Barre, Massachusetts**   Journalist, crusader for improvement of conditions for the urban poor; author of *How the Other Half Lives* (1890).

ELIZABETH CADY STANTON (1815–October 26, 1902)
Woodlawn Cemetery, Bronx, New York   Suffragist leader, one
of the conveners of the first women's rights convention in Seneca
Falls (1848).

LUCY STONE (1818–October 18, 1893) **Forest Hills Cemetery, Boston, Massachusetts**   The body of the women's rights
leader, one of the first to retain her maiden name after marriage,
lay in a coffin dressed in soft black silk with lace at the throat
and wrists, a gold pin, and her best cap. Her daughter placed her
favorite flower, lilies of the valley, in her hands. Two months
later she became the first person in Massachusetts to be cremated. Her ashes were placed in two urns and sealed with adhesive tape, on which her husband wrote her name. "Lucy
Stoners" was the name later given to women who kept their
maiden names after marriage.

SOJOURNER TRUTH (1797–November 26, 1883) **Oak Hill
Cemetery, Battle Creek, Michigan**   Born a slave, became a lecturer on abolition, women's rights, and temperance. She adopted
this name in preference to that given her by her master.

ROY WILKINS (1901–September 8, 1981) **Pinelawn Memorial Park and Cemetery, Farmingdale, Long Island, New York**
Head of the NAACP from 1965 to 1977.

WHITNEY M. YOUNG, JR. (1921–March 11, 1971) **Ferncliff Cemetery, Hartsdale, New York**   Executive director of National Urban League, 1961–71.

PRESIDENTS

JOHN ADAMS (1735–July 4, 1826) **First Unitarian Church, Quincy, Massachusetts** First U.S. vice-president, under Washington (1789–97), Second president (1797–1801), member of Continental Congress, suggested Washington as commander in chief. The dying Adams's last words were "Thomas Jefferson still lives." He had no way of knowing that Jefferson had died at 9:50 that morning.

JOHN QUINCY ADAMS (1767–February 23, 1848) **First Unitarian Church, Quincy, Massachusetts** Sixth president, diplomat, and political writer.

CHESTER A. ARTHUR (1830–November 18, 1886) **Albany Rural Cemetery, Albany, New York** Became twenty-first president upon the assassination of Garfield; supporter of civil service reform.

JAMES BUCHANAN (1791–June 1, 1868) **Woodward Hill Cemetery, Lancaster, Pennsylvania** The fifteenth president (1857–61) and the only bachelor; elected without a majority of the popular vote and attempted to strike a balance between extremist factions on both sides of the slave question. The Civil War began soon after he left office.

GROVER CLEVELAND (1837–June 24, 1908) **Princeton Cemetery, Princeton, New Jersey** The twenty-second and twenty-fourth president, lost the presidential election in between to Benjamin Harrison.

CALVIN COOLIDGE (1872–January 5, 1933) **Plymouth Cemetery, Plymouth, Vermont** Succeeded to the presidency upon the death of Warren G. Harding (1923); he was elected the following year to a full term. His public policies, favoring business, led to the stock market speculation that resulted in the crash of 1929.

DWIGHT DAVID EISENHOWER (1890–March 28, 1969) **Eisenhower Center, Abilene, Kansas** Oldest president to complete his term, Eisenhower was seventy years and ninety-eight days old when he left office in 1961. A distinguished military career culminated in his being named supreme commander of Allied Expeditionary Forces and directing the battle for Europe in World War II. After a period as president of Columbia University (1948–50) Eisenhower organized NATO, and in 1952 he resigned from the army to run for the presidency.

MILLARD FILLMORE (1800–March 8, 1874) **Forest Lawn Cemetery, Buffalo, New York** Thirteenth president, worked for compromise on slavery question.

JAMES A. GARFIELD (1831–September 19, 1881) **Lake View Cemetery, Cleveland, Ohio** The second president to be assassinated, Garfield was shot twice in the back by Charles J. Guiteau (see Criminals), a disappointed office seeker, at the railroad depot in Washington. He was taken immediately afterward to the White House, complaining of pain in the feet and ankles, resulting from damage to the spinal cord. A medical team decided that the bullet had lodged in Garfield's abdomen, and the doctors fell into disagreement. Garfield lingered for eighty days, during which his only official act was the signing of an extradition paper. After his death from blood poisoning, doctors discovered that the bullet had lodged in a different part of his body than they had imagined. Inept medical treatment was considered one of the causes of death. Doctors' bills totaled $85,000, of which the Senate authorized about $10,000, denouncing the physicians as quacks.

ULYSSES S. GRANT (1822–July 23, 1885) **General Grant National Memorial, New York, New York**   Four days after completing the manuscript of his memoirs (a best seller that earned his heirs $500,000) Grant died. Mark Twain had encouraged him to undertake the book to pay off his debts. Grant, who knew he was dying of throat cancer, remarked after a day's writing, "I have been adding to my book and to my coffin," but the doctors felt that the project kept him alive. Shortly before his death, no longer able to speak, Grant wrote a note to his son listing New York City as one of his choices for burial because "the people of that city befriended me in my need." The former president was interred in Riverside Park, where his wife made daily visits bringing white roses. The public objected to the fact that Grant's tomb was a mean-looking red brick vault, and in 1897 it was replaced by the imposing Doric structure that has become a New York landmark.

WARREN G. HARDING (1865–August 2, 1923) **Harding Memorial, Marion, Ohio**   Beset by the impending revelations of scandals reflecting improper actions by several cabinet members and high government officials, Harding died after a trip to Alaska. His administration has been revealed to have been one of the most corrupt in U.S. history. He and Florence Harding were the first presidential couple to die during a president's term of office.

BENJAMIN HARRISON (1833–March 13, 1901) **Crown Hill Cemetery, Indianapolis, Indiana**   The twenty-third president (1889–93), grandson of William Henry Harrison, received electoral majority though the larger popular vote went to Grover Cleveland, who defeated him in the following election.

WILLIAM HENRY HARRISON (1773-April 4, 1841)
William Henry Harrison Memorial State Park, North Bend, Ohio Harrison was the first president to expire while in office; the first to die in the White House and the first to lie in state there. He served the shortest term of any chief executive, from March 4, 1841, until his death the following month. On a cold and stormy inauguration day, Harrison, without hat or coat, led the parade on horseback, delivered a two-hour speech out-of-doors (the longest inaugural address ever), and attended three inaugural balls. Three weeks later he developed a severe chill and died of pneumonia.

RUTHERFORD B. HAYES (1822-January 17, 1893)
Rutherford B. Hayes State Memorial, Fremont, Ohio An election commission appointed by Congress gave Hayes the disputed presidential election over Samuel Tilden (see Government Leaders) by one electoral vote (1877). His administration marked the end of the Reconstruction era.

HERBERT HOOVER (1874-October 20, 1964)
Herbert Hoover National Historic Site, West Branch, Iowa Thirty-first president (1929-33), Hoover presided over the beginning of the Depression and determined that the economy would recover without federal intervention. He lost a bid for reelection in 1932 to Franklin D. Roosevelt. Hoover lived longer after his term of office than any other president: 31 years and 231 days.

ANDREW JACKSON (1767-June 8, 1845)
The Hermitage, Nashville, Tennessee "Old Hickory" lies next to his wife, Rachel, who died before he took office. His tombstone does not mention his presidency (1829-37), which has come to stand for the rise of popular democracy.

THOMAS JEFFERSON (1743-July 4, 1826)
Monticello, Charlottesville, Virginia Jefferson and his boyhood friend, Dabney Carr, made a pact that whoever died first would be buried by the other under their favorite oak tree on the Monticello estate. At Carr's death this pledge was upheld, and he became the first occupant of the small graveyard Jefferson himself laid out. The president's grave is marked by an obelisk and a self-composed epitaph that omits any reference to his term of office: "Here was

buried Thomas Jefferson, author of the Declaration of Independence, of the Statute of Virginia for Religious Freedom, and the Father of the University of Virginia."

ANDREW JOHNSON (1808–July 31, 1875) **Andrew Johnson Cemetery, Greeneville, Tennessee**   Reconstruction president, survived attempts of Congress to impeach him (1868). His monument, a tall column crowned by an American eagle, has a scroll symbolizing the U.S. Constitution, which Johnson considered his political Bible.

LYNDON BAINES JOHNSON (1908–January 22, 1973) **LBJ Ranch, Johnson City, Texas**   A longtime member of Congress, as president Johnson was able to obtain passage of the Civil Rights Act (1964).

JOHN FITZGERALD KENNEDY (1917–November 22, 1963) **Arlington National Cemetery, Arlington, Virginia**   The assassinated Kennedy was the first president whose parents survived him and the sixth to lie in state in the Capitol rotunda.

Some of the many visitors leave flowers at the Arlington grave site of President John F. Kennedy, who lies near the Custis-Lee mansion. (United States Army)

His coffin rested on the same black-draped catafalque that had been used to support the fallen Lincoln. A military procession bore Kennedy to Washington's St. Matthew's Cathedral, where the funeral was held, and then to Arlington, where he became the second president to be buried there. As commander in chief and a former naval officer, Kennedy was buried with full military honors.

ABRAHAM LINCOLN (1809–April 15, 1865) Oak Ridge Cemetery, Springfield, Illinois The first president to be assassinated, Lincoln died the day after he was shot by John Wilkes Booth (see Criminals) at Ford's Theatre in Washington. He suffered from a wound behind the ear that would have proven fatal even with modern medical treatment. A mustard plaster was applied to the fallen president from the neck to the ankles, but he never regained consciousness.

Lincoln's body lay in state in the Capitol rotunda and then was taken to his native Springfield on a twelve-day journey, the train stopping frequently for the grieving public to view it. By the time his body was buried it had been moved seventeen times since its removal from Ford's Theatre.

In 1876 a gang of thieves broke into Lincoln's tomb, planning to hold the body for ransom. They were apprehended and punished with a year in jail for lock breaking because there was no law against body snatching. The Illinois legislature quickly passed one, and Lincoln has lain undisturbed ever since.

JAMES MADISON (1751–June 28, 1836) Montpelier Estate, Montpelier Station, Virginia Fourth president of the U.S., political theorist, buried in family plot on his estate.

WILLIAM McKINLEY (1843–September 14, 1901) McKinley Memorial, Canton, Ohio McKinley was shot at the Pan-American Exposition in Buffalo by an anarchist who fired two shots from a pistol hidden in his handkerchief. Shortly before the gun went off the president had handed a little girl his lucky red carnation. McKinley was taken to an emergency hospital on the premises, but the doctor in charge was not there. Surgery was begun by a surgeon and a well-known gynecologist, without adequate light. The bullet could not be found and the doctors inserted no drainage tube, causing infection to result. Their bills totaled $45,000.

JAMES MONROE (1758–July 4, 1831) **Hollywood Cemetery, Richmond, Virginia** Fifth president, established Monroe Doctrine (1820).

FRANKLIN PIERCE (1804–October 8, 1869) **Old North Cemetery, Concord, New Hampshire** Died in obscurity in New England, shunned for his opposition to the Civil War.

JAMES KNOX POLK (1795–June 15, 1849) **State Capitol Grounds, Nashville, Tennessee** A week before his death, not long after his term ended, the eleventh president (1845–49) was baptized, fulfilling a promise he had made to a minister. Under his administration Oregon's northern boundary was established and the U.S. acquired California and the entire Southwest as a result of the Mexican War.

FRANKLIN DELANO ROOSEVELT (1882–April 12, 1945) **Franklin D. Roosevelt National Historic Site, Hyde Park, New York** FDR died of a cerebral hemorrhage at Warm Springs, Georgia, in the Little White House. A special solid-mahogany copper-lined casket was ordered from Atlanta, though the use of copper had been suspended during the war. The undertaker's workmen labored gratis through the night to hammer a solid-copper liner underneath the satin. Roosevelt's body, accompanied by Mrs. Roosevelt, traveled north to Washington on a slow train while mourners lined the tracks. Then it was carried on a caisson pulled by six white horses in a procession up Washington's Pennsylvania Avenue before making the final trip to his Hyde Park estate.

After funeral arrangements had been made, Roosevelt's own instructions regarding his death were found in a sealed envelope addressed to his son, James, who was overseas in the war. Mrs. Roosevelt refused to open the envelope, since it was not addressed to her, but its contents later revealed that the funeral had been carried out contrary to his wishes: the four-term president had specifically requested that there be no embalming, no Washington procession, and no mahogany coffin.

THEODORE ROOSEVELT (1858–January 6, 1919) **Young's Cemetery, Oyster Bay, Long Island, New York**   "Trustbuster" TR died in his sleep at his Oyster Bay estate.

WILLIAM HOWARD TAFT (1857–March 8, 1930) **Arlington National Cemetery, Arlington, Virginia**   Vigorous proponent of antitrust legislation; first president buried in Arlington.

ZACHARY TAYLOR (1784–July 9, 1850) **Springfield, Louisville, Kentucky**   Hero of the Mexican War; second president to die in the White House while in office.

HARRY S. TRUMAN (1884–December 26, 1972) **Harry S. Truman Library and Museum, Independence, Missouri**   Thirty-third president, made decision to drop atomic bomb on Japan; buried in the area where he grew up.

JOHN TYLER (1790–January 18, 1862) **Hollywood Cemetery, Richmond, Virginia**   First vice-president to become president because of death, he was buried without official governmental notice. Fifty years later, a grave-site monument was authorized by Congress.

MARTIN VAN BUREN (1782–July 24, 1862) **Kinderhook Cemetery, Kinderhook, New York**   Eighth president (1837–41), noted for his political acumen, secretary of state and then vice-president under Jackson. His administration suffered from economic crisis, but although Van Buren lost a bid for reelection, he remained active in political affairs.

GEORGE WASHINGTON (1732–December 14, 1799) **Mount Vernon Estate, Mount Vernon, Virginia**   Military hero and first president; died after catching a cold at Mount Vernon.

WOODROW WILSON (1856–February 3, 1924) **Washington Cathedral, Washington, D.C.**   World War I president, and the only chief executive buried in the nation's capital.

BUSINESS AND FINANCE

PHILIP DANFORTH ARMOUR (1832–January 6, 1901)
Graceland Cemetery, Chicago, Illinois Founder of the meat-packing firm, one of the first to use refrigerator cars to transport meat.

JOHN JACOB ASTOR (1763–March 29, 1848) **St. Thomas Church, New York, New York** Astor, a poor immigrant boy from Germany, made a fortune in the fur trade and in New York real estate and never lost his passion for money. In his final days he was so weak that he had to be fed on breast milk and tossed in a blanket ten minutes a day for exercise. Still, in the words of one friend, "his relish for wealth is as keen as ever." From the blanket where he was being tossed, he enjoined one of his rent collectors to collect from an impoverished widow. "Mr. Astor," the man pleaded, "she has had misfortunes and we must give her time." Astor would not hear of this excuse, so the agent went to the millionaire's son, who gave him money and told him to present it to the father as the widow's. "There," exclaimed the dying Astor as he grasped the coins, "I told you she would pay if you went the right way to work with her."

AUGUST BELMONT (1853–December 10, 1924) **Island Cemetery, Newport, Rhode Island**   Banker, leading sportsman, and founder of Belmont Race Track.

VINCENT BENDIX (1882–March 27, 1945) **Graceland Cemetery, Chicago, Illinois**   Industrialist, pioneer automobile and airplane manufacturer, founder of the Bendix Company.

NICHOLAS BIDDLE (1786–February 27, 1844) **St. Peter's Churchyard, Philadelphia, Pennsylvania**   Financier, president of the U.S. Bank from 1823 to 1836.

JOSEPH BERNARD BLOOMINGDALE (1842–November 21, 1904) **Linden Hills Cemetery, Maspeth, Queens, New York**   A founder of Bloomingdale's department store (1872).

"DIAMOND JIM" BRADY (1856–April 13, 1917) **Green-Wood Cemetery, Brooklyn, New York**   Amassing his fortune through his success as a salesman for a railroad-supply company, Brady indulged his love of jewels by assembling thirty complete sets of diamonds and other stones worth over a million dollars. "Diamond Jim" lay in his coffin decked out in all the stones of his favorite, number-one diamond set, but by state law it could not be buried with him, posing too much of a temptation to grave robbers. His request was to be cremated, but his executors interred him in the elaborate mausoleum he had already erected.

DAVID DUNBAR BUICK (1854–March 6, 1929) **Woodmere Cemetery, Detroit, Michigan**   Auto industrialist, started the Buick Motor Car Company.

ARDE BULOVA (1889–March 19, 1958) **JOSEPH BULOVA** (1851–November 18, 1935) **Woodlawn Cemetery, Bronx, New York**   Father and son, Joseph the founder, Arde the developer of the Bulova Watch Company.

ADOLPHUS BUSCH (1839–October 10, 1913) **Bellefontaine Cemetery, St. Louis, Missouri** With his father-in-law, Eberhard Anheuser, he founded Anheuser-Busch (1861) and developed the pasteurization of beer.

ANDREW CARNEGIE (1835–August 11, 1919) **Sleepy Hollow Cemetery, North Tarrytown, New York** Steel magnate; his philanthropies exceeded $300 million, including 2,800 libraries, foundations, and schools.

SAMUEL SHANNON CHILDS (1863–March 17, 1925) **Cemetery of the Basking Ridge Presbyterian Church, Basking Ridge, New Jersey** Founder of the Childs Restaurant chain (1888).

WALTER PERCY CHRYSLER (1875–August 18, 1940) **Sleepy Hollow Cemetery, North Tarrytown, New York** Industrialist, founded Chrysler Corporation and built the Chrysler Building in New York City (1930).

Auto magnate David Dunbar Buick lies beneath a simple yet immediately recognizable gravestone. (Sandra Shapiro)

JAY COOKE (1821–February 16, 1905) St. Paul's Churchyard, Elkins Park, Pennsylvania   Known as the financier of the Civil War; his failure in 1873 caused a financial panic.

PETER COOPER (1791–April 4, 1883) Green-Wood Cemetery, Brooklyn, New York   Built the first American steam locomotive (1830), invented the washing machine, manufactured the wire cables used for laying the Atlantic cable.

EZRA CORNELL (1807–December 9, 1874) Sage Chapel, Cornell University, Ithaca, New York   Organizer of Western Union Telegraph Company (1855), founder of Cornell University (1862).

CHARLES CROCKER (1822–August 14, 1888) Mountain View Cemetery, Oakland, California   Railroad tycoon, one of the leading figures in the financial development of the West.

HORACE ELGIN DODGE (1868–December 10, 1920) **JOHN FRANCIS DODGE** (1864–January 14, 1920) Woodlawn Cemetery, Detroit, Michigan   Horace was the engineering genius of the Dodge Company, John Francis its organizational wizard. The brothers died within months of each other and are in an enormous mausoleum of Egyptian motif guarded by two large sphinxes.

HERBERT HENRY DOW (1866–October 15, 1930) Midland Cemetery, Midland, Michigan   Chemist and first president of the Dow Chemical Company.

BENJAMIN NEWTON DUKE (1855–January 8, 1929) **JAMES BUCHANAN DUKE** (1856–October 10, 1925) Maplewood Cemetery, Durham, North Carolina   The brothers developed the American Tobacco Company; benefactors of Duke University.

ÉLEUTHÈRE IRÉNÉE DU PONT (1771–October 31, 1834) Du Pont Family Cemetery, Greenville, Delaware   Chief powder maker for the U.S. during the War of 1812 and founder of the Du Pont empire.

WILLIAM GEORGE FARGO (1818–August 3, 1881) **Forest Lawn Cemetery, Buffalo, New York** Founder of American Express (1844) and Wells Fargo (1851).

CYRUS WEST FIELD (1819–July 12, 1892) **Stockbridge Cemetery, Stockbridge, Massachusetts** Toward the end of his life the man responsible for the laying of the Atlantic cable was totally wiped out financially, back where he had started fifty years before. Gone were his railroad securities, stocks, and investments in coal, steel, and utilities. The inscription on his gravestone attests to the achievement that could not be destroyed: "Cyrus West Field/To Whose Courage, Energy and Perseverance/The World Owes the Atlantic Telegraph."

MARSHALL FIELD (1834–January 16, 1906) **Graceland Cemetery, Chicago, Illinois**   At his death Field was the richest merchant in the world and the largest individual taxpayer in the U.S. He lies near his only son, Marshall Field, Jr. (1868–November 27, 1905), who accidentally shot himself in the abdomen with a revolver.

JIM FISK (1838–January 7, 1872) **Prospect Hill Cemetery, Brattleboro, Vermont**   When his business partner, Edward S. Stokes, became an implacable rival for the love of Fisk's beautiful mistress, the tycoon had him wrongfully arrested for embezzlement. After several court cases and countercharges, Stokes had had enough and shot his nemesis in the lobby of a New York hotel, shouting, "I've got you now!" The high-living Colonel Fisk was laid out in the Opera House wearing his $2,000 uniform with white kid gloves, his sword at his side, and a gloriously waxed red mustache. As Fisk's barber passed by the coffin he gave the mustache a final twist, murmuring, "One more twirl, dearest of friends, for the last time." After Fisk was buried in his native Brattleboro the citizens collected $25,000 for a monument by sculptor Larkin Mead, who also did the Lincoln monument at Springfield, Illinois. At the corners of its large base are four almost bare nymphets representing railroading, shipping, the stage, and commerce, Fisk's great passions. One elderly Vermonter told biographer W. A. Swanberg, "Never saw a more appropriate monument. Fisk had trouble with naked women all his life, so they put four of 'em over his grave."

HARVEY SAMUEL FIRESTONE (1868–February 7, 1938) **Columbiana Cemetery, Columbiana, Ohio**   Founder of Firestone Tire and Rubber Company (1900). He planned his memorial, a Greek temple of sculptured granite with eight Doric columns symbolizing Firestone, his wife, and their six children.

EDSEL FORD (1893–May 26, 1943) **Woodlawn Cemetery, Detroit, Michigan**   Henry Ford's only child, the company's president from 1919 to 1943; a highly unsuccessful Ford car bore his name.

HENRY FORD (1863–April 7, 1947) **The Ford Cemetery, St. Martha's Episcopal Church, Detroit, Michigan** The man who founded the Ford Motor Company with twenty-eight thousand dollars died one of the richest individuals in the world. At two o'clock, when his funeral began, every industry in Michigan stopped its activities, the first such gesture. An individualist to the end, Ford had eschewed the elegant memorials of other auto magnates and chose to be buried in a plain grave in an old family cemetery located in a corner of his wheatfields. After the service Ford plant protection men erected a small, wooden sentry box alongside the family plot and assigned twenty-four-hour guards.

HENRY CLAY FRICK (1849–December 2, 1919) **Homewood Cemetery, Pittsburgh, Pennsylvania** Chairman of the Carnegie Steel Company, died on the same day the government took final steps to deport Alexander Berkman, a radical who had attempted to assassinate him in 1892.

KING CAMP GILLETTE (1855–July 9, 1932) **Forest Lawn Memorial Park, Glendale, California** Inventor of the safety razor and blade, founder of the Gillette Company (1901).

BERNARD F. GIMBEL (1885–September 29, 1966) **CHARLES GIMBEL** (1861–September 9, 1932) **ELLIS GIMBEL** (1865–March 17, 1950) **Mount Sinai Cemetery, Philadelphia, Pennsylvania** Three of the seven Gimbel brothers who started the department store.

STEPHEN GIRARD (1750–1831) **Founder's Hall, Girard College, Philadelphia, Pennsylvania** Merchant and banker who financed the War of 1812.

BENJAMIN FRANKLIN GOODRICH (1841–August 3, 1888) **Lake View Cemetery, Jamestown, New York** Founder of B. F. Goodrich Rubber Company (1876), the first firm to make solid rubber tires.

HETTY GREEN (1835–July 3, 1916) **Immanuel Cemetery, Bellows Falls, Vermont** Considered the greatest woman financier in the world, the "witch of Wall Street" was also celebrated for her miserliness and extreme greed. Although she was the richest woman in America, she lived in a cold-water flat, denied her son medical attention, refused to pay her taxes, and never gave a cent to any charity. Born a Quaker, she was baptized into the Episcopal faith, it is said, so that she could be buried for nothing in her husband's family plot. Her son celebrated her demise by buying his mistress a diamond-studded chastity belt for fifty thousand dollars and hiring a personal staff of fourteen young women, including two "masseuses" and a half dozen typists, although he owned only one typewriter.

JENNIE GROSSINGER (1892–November 20, 1972) **Ahavath Israel Cemetery, Liberty, New York** Developed her parents' hotel in the Catskill Mountains into a world-famous resort.

JAY GOULD (1836–December 2, 1892) **Woodlawn Cemetery, Bronx, New York** The railroad speculator was so hated because of his shady business practices that stock in his empire rose more than two points the day he died. He was buried in one of the first great mausoleums built in Woodlawn, an Ionic temple supported by granite columns. To prevent vandalism, the undertaker's assistants soldered the lid on the coffin; this nerve-wracking procedure took so long that Gould's son began to weep.

MEYER GUGGENHEIM (1828–March 15, 1905) **Salem Fields Cemetery, Brooklyn, New York** Built a mining fortune; also buried in the family plot: his sons Daniel (1856–September 28, 1930); Simon (1867–November 2, 1941), who was the sixth of his seven sons and the sixth to die; Solomon (1861–November 3, 1949); and a grandson, Harry (1890–January 22, 1971). Son Benjamin went down with the *Titanic*.

EDWARD HENRY HARRIMAN (1848–September 9, 1909) **Cemetery of St. John's Episcopal Church, Arden, New York** Railroad tycoon; owned and directed the Union Pacific, Illinois Central, Delaware and Hudson, Erie, Northern Pacific, and Georgia Central railroads.

HENRY JOHN HEINZ (1844–May 14, 1919) **Homewood Cemetery, Pittsburgh, Pennsylvania** Invented the slogan "57

Varieties" to describe the products of his food-processing company.

MILTON SNAVELY HERSHEY (1857–October 13, 1945) **Hershey Cemetery, Hershey, Pennsylvania** Founded Hershey Chocolate Corporation and built the town. His funeral was non-denominational, with a Catholic priest and five Protestant ministers officiating. Ten years earlier he had given each of the town's churches twenty thousand dollars to free them from debt.

CONRAD NICHOLSON HILTON (1887–January 3, 1979) **Calvary Hills Cemetery, Dallas, Texas** Hotelier, at his death owner of 125 hotels throughout the world and worth $100 million.

CHARLES ELMER HIRES (1851–July 31, 1937) **Westminster Cemetery, Bala-Cynwyd, Pennsylvania** In his drugstore he developed root beer out of sarsaparilla root.

JOHNS HOPKINS (1795–December 24, 1873) **Green Mount Cemetery, Baltimore, Maryland** Financier; his money built Johns Hopkins University and hospital.

MARK HOPKINS (1813–March 29, 1878) **Sacramento City Cemetery, Sacramento, California** A railroad tycoon and major power in the West, the somber Hopkins and his sedate wife led a quiet existence in an elegant mansion on San Francisco's Nob Hill. When he died, Mrs. Hopkins installed the body in a marble mausoleum costing $150,000 and not too long afterward married an interior decorator half her age. The Nob Hill mansion was later converted into the lively "in" hotel of the jazz age, scene of many goings-on Mark Hopkins definitely would not have approved of.

GEORGE ALBERT HORMEL (1860–June 5, 1946) **Oakwood Cemetery, Austin, Minnesota** Produced the first canned hams in the U.S.

HOWARD HUGHES (1905–April 5, 1976) **Glenwood Cemetery, Houston, Texas** The billionaire, once a popular Hollywood playboy, lived as a recluse for several decades, paralyzed by a fear of germs. To the end he fought suggestions that he reveal the whereabouts of his will, thereby assuring a plethora of claims and litigation that succeeded his death. When he died on a plane from Mexico to Houston he weighed ninety pounds, had shrunk two inches, and was a haunted, frightened shell of himself. "No one should have to die like that" was the pitying comment of an associate he had once tried to ruin.

H. L. HUNT (1889–November 29, 1974) **Sparkman-Hillcrest Memorial Park, Dallas, Texas** Oilman, one of the richest men in the world; his will said anyone who challenged it forfeited all rights to benefits.

COLLIS P. HUNTINGTON (1821–August 14, 1900) **Woodlawn Cemetery, Bronx, New York** When the flag on his steam launch fell from its holder three times, the railroad tycoon became apprehensive. "That flag won't stay up. Somebody must be going to die," commented Huntington, who at the time was in perfect health. A few days later he died in a choking fit. He had spent a quarter of a million dollars for a magnificent marble mausoleum, but superstitiously refused to look at the finished structure.

HENRY JOHN KAISER (1882–August 24, 1967) **Mountain View Cemetery, Oakland, California** Ruler of Kaiser Industries, a major shipbuilder during World War II.

JOHN HARVEY KELLOGG (1852–December 14, 1943) **WILL KEITH KELLOGG** (1860–October 6, 1951) **Oak Hill Cemetery, Battle Creek, Michigan** John Harvey, a physician, invented cornflakes. Will Keith began the W. K. Kellogg Company and manufactured them.

JOSEPH P. KENNEDY (1888–November 18, 1969) **Holyhood Cemetery, Brookline, Massachusetts** A success in banking, shipbuilding, and motion picture distribution, Kennedy was head of a political family (see Presidents, Government Leaders) and founder of philanthropic enterprises. He was chairman of the Securities and Exchange Commission (1934–35) and, as ambassador to Great Britain, supported Chamberlain's futile efforts at negotiation with Hitler.

HENRIETTA CHAMBERLAIN KING (1832–March 31, 1925) **Chamberlain Cemetery, Kingsville, Texas** Cattle rancher; she took over the failing King Ranch at the death of her husband, Richard, made it successful, and enlarged it to the size of Delaware.

JAMES L. KRAFT (1874–February 16, 1953) **Memorial Park Cemetery, Evanston, Illinois** Founder of Kraft Foods.

SAMUEL HENRY KRESS (1863–September 22, 1955) **Woodlawn Cemetery, Bronx, New York** Founder of the dime store chain; he gave nearly six hundred paintings and sculptures to the National Gallery of Art in 1939.

HENRY MARTYN LELAND (1843–March 26, 1932) **Woodmere Cemetery, Detroit, Michigan** Head of Cadillac and Lincoln Motor Companies; his small headstone is the least conspicuous of any of the auto magnates', many of whom preferred large mausoleums.

OSCAR FERDINAND MAYER (1859–March 11, 1955) **Rosehill Cemetery, Chicago, Illinois** Developer of major meat-packing firm.

ELMER HENRY MAYTAG (1883–July 20, 1940) **FREDERICK LOUIS MAYTAG** (1857–March 26, 1937) **Newton Union Cemetery, Newton, Iowa** Frederick Louis founded Maytag (1907); Elmer Henry made it a major manufacturer of washing machines.

J. PIERPONT MORGAN (1837–March 31, 1913) **Cedar Hill Cemetery, Hartford, Connecticut** Head of the country's largest banking house, possessed nearly $100 million at his death.

RANSOM ELI OLDS (1864–August 26, 1950) **Mt. Hope Cemetery, Lansing, Michigan** A father of the automotive industry; only person to have two cars named for him: the Oldsmobile and the REO (taken from his initials).

FRED PABST (1836–1904) **Forest Home Cemetery, Milwaukee, Wisconsin** President of the world's largest brewery (1892).

JAMES WARD PACKARD (1863–March 20, 1928) **Oakwood Cemetery, Warren, Ohio** Organized Packard Automobile Co. (1902).

POTTER PALMER (1826–May 4, 1902) **Graceland Cemetery, Chicago, Illinois** More than any other man, Palmer was responsible for the rebuilding of Chicago after the great fire. He and his wife, Bertha, were the city's social leaders, and when he died he left everything directly to her management, almost unheard of in those days. "A million dollars is enough for any woman," Marshall Field sniffed when he heard of it. Mrs. Palmer died sixteen years after her husband, having doubled his estate to twenty million dollars.

GEORGE SWINNERTON PARKER (1866–September 26, 1952) **Pine Grove Cemetery, Lynn, Massachusetts** Founder of Parker Brothers Games (1888), manufacturers of Monopoly.

GEORGE PEABODY (1795–November 4, 1869) **Harmony Grove Cemetery, Peabody, Massachusetts** The first great modern philanthropist, banker Peabody founded many institutions: libraries in four cities, three museums of science, the Peabody Education Fund for the South, and George Peabody College for Teachers in Nashville, Tennessee. He introduced this personal charity to London, where he lived, and the Peabody Homes for the poor housed eighteen thousand people there. Memorialized in Westminster Abbey. Both Britain and the U.S. honored his benevolent deeds.

JAMES CASH PENNEY (1875–February 12, 1971) **Woodlawn Cemetery, Bronx, New York** J. C. Penney Co. became a nationwide chain numbering 1,660 stores.

ALLAN PINKERTON (1819–July 1, 1884) **Graceland Cemetery, Chicago, Illinois** Pinkerton's National Detective Agency had a part in the solution of most major U.S. crimes from 1850 to 1885.

LYDIA E. PINKHAM (1819–May 17, 1883) **Pine Grove Cemetery, Lynn, Massachusetts** Manufacturer of Lydia E. Pinkham's compound, a popular nineteenth-century tonic for "female troubles."

CHARLES WILLIAM POST (1854–May 9, 1914) **Oak Hill Cemetery, Battle Creek, Michigan** Inventor of Grape-Nuts and Postum, founded the Postum Cereal Co. in 1897; killed himself because of stomach illness.

WILLIAM COOPER PROCTER (1862–May 2, 1934) **Spring Grove Cemetery, Cincinnati, Ohio** Manufacturer; president and chairman of the board of Procter and Gamble Co.

CHARLES REVSON (1906–August 24, 1975) **Ferncliff Cemetery, Hartsdale, New York** Builder of the Revlon Cosmetics empire, known for his skill at humiliating others. His wife, Lynn, whom he had left after giving her thirty thousand dollars in a tin can for their tenth anniversary, reciprocated by wearing everything he hated to his funeral.

WILLIAM MARSH RICE (1816–September 23, 1900) **Rice University, Center Campus Quadrangle, Houston, Texas** The Texas millionaire was chloroformed to death in his Madison Avenue mansion by his "legal adviser," who, in cahoots with Rice's secretary-valet, produced a bogus will making himself the old man's heir. The "adviser" had the body cremated so quickly that police became suspicious; the pair were arrested, informed on each other, and were the objects of a sensational trial.

JOHN DAVISON ROCKEFELLER, JR. (1874–May 11, 1960) Rockefeller Family Cemetery, North Tarrytown, New York **WILLIAM ROCKEFELLER** (1841–June 24, 1922) Sleepy Hollow Cemetery, North Tarrytown, New York Brothers who worked in the family oil-refining business, John D. developing philanthropies based on the family fortune, William becoming a successful stock market manipulator.

JOHN D. ROCKEFELLER, SR. (1839–May 23, 1937) Lake View Cemetery, Cleveland, Ohio By his own efforts Rockefeller accumulated more wealth than any other private citizen and also became the world's greatest philanthropist, surpassing Andrew Carnegie. The founder of Standard Oil got his start as a twelve-dollar-a-month clerk in Cleveland, and by the time he retired had accumulated one and a half billion dollars.

HENRY HUTTLESTON ROGERS (1840–May 19, 1909) Riverside Cemetery, Fairhaven, Massachusetts Financier and oil executive, he devised the concept of transporting oil by pipeline.

JACOB RUPPERT (1867–January 13, 1939) Kensico Cemetery, Valhalla, New York President of the Ruppert Brewery, one-time owner of the world-champion New York Yankees. The last person to see him alive was Babe Ruth (see Sports Figures), and "Babe" was just about his last word.

RUSSELL SAGE (1816–July 22, 1906) Oakwood Cemetery, Troy, New York Originally a successful grocer in Troy, Sage developed his fortune through banking and stock speculation and solidified it with investments in railroads and telegraph companies. The financier, who had a reputation as a skinflint, was said to be worth eighty million dollars at his death. Concerned about body kidnappers, the family buried him in a mahogany coffin placed inside a chilled-steel burglarproof outer coffin. It took more than twenty people to get the coffin into its final resting place, which was equipped with a burglar alarm.

HARLAND SANDERS (1890–December 16, 1980) **Cave Hill Cemetery, Louisville, Kentucky**   The Colonel was a senior citizen when he turned his prized chicken recipe into a successful fast-food chain.

RUDOLPH JAY SCHAEFER (1863–November 9, 1923) **Woodlawn Cemetery, Bronx, New York**   Brewing company executive, first to introduce bottled beer to the market.

CHARLES MICHAEL SCHWAB (1862–September 18, 1939) **Gate of Heaven Cemetery, Hawthorne, New York**   Steel magnate, made Bethlehem Steel the largest independent steel producer.

GEORGE WHITFIELD SCRANTON (1811–March 24, 1861) **Dunmore Cemetery, Dunmore, Pennsylvania**   Manufacturer, inventor of a process to smelt iron ore with anthracite coal (1842).

RICHARD WARREN SEARS (1863–September 28, 1914) **Rosehill Cemetery, Chicago, Illinois**   Founder of Sears, Roebuck and Co. (1893), pioneer mail-order company.

ALFRED P. SLOAN (1875–February 17, 1966) **Memorial Cemetery of St. John's Church, Cold Spring Harbor, Long Island, New York**   Chairman of General Motors Corp. (1937–1956), founder of the Sloan-Kettering Institute for Cancer Research (1945).

A. LELAND STANFORD (1824–June 21, 1893) **Stanford Family Mausoleum, Stanford University, Palo Alto, California**   The western railroad magnate founded Stanford University as a memorial to his son, who died at age fifteen of typhoid in Italy. Almost destroyed by the boy's death, Stanford got the idea for the university during a séance with a noted medium. Before he died he had become so heavy that his legs could not support his great weight. He was put on a rigorous diet of fried hashed meat and hot water, but this treatment failed. Stanford and his wife and son are in a mausoleum on the university campus; the students call them "the Holy Family."

CLEMENT STUDEBAKER (1831–November 27, 1901) Riverview Cemetery, South Bend, Indiana   His firm, one of the largest wagon and carriage manufacturers in the U.S., was transformed into the Studebaker Auto Company.

GUSTAVUS FRANKLIN SWIFT (1839–March 29, 1903) Mount Hope Cemetery, Chicago, Illinois   Founded Swift and Co., meatpacking firm (1885); important in development of refrigerated railroad car.

J. WALTER THOMPSON (1847–October 16, 1928) Woodlawn Cemetery, Bronx, New York   Began J. Walter Thompson advertising agency; made advertising important to the economy.

CHARLES LEWIS TIFFANY (1812–February 18, 1902) Green-Wood Cemetery, Brooklyn, New York   Head of Tiffany and Company; injured his hip at the age of ninety and died after trying to add a log to the fire rather than call a servant.

JOHN THOMAS UNDERWOOD (1857–July 2, 1937) Green-Wood Cemetery, Brooklyn, New York   Manufacturer of the typewriter (1883).

CORNELIUS VANDERBILT (1794–January 4, 1877) **WILLIAM HENRY VANDERBILT** (1821–December 8, 1885) **WILLIAM KISSAM VANDERBILT** (1849–July 12, 1920) Moravian Cemetery, New Dorp, Staten Island, New York   Cornelius, the "Commodore," built the family fortune on steamboats and railroads. William Henry, his son, and William Kissam, his grandson, consolidated the Vanderbilt holdings.

JOHN WANAMAKER (1838–December 12, 1922) Burial ground of the Church of St. James the Less, Philadelphia, Pennsylvania   Merchant, founder of the store bearing his name (1869).

FELIX M. WARBURG (1871–October 20, 1937) Salem Fields Cemetery, Brooklyn, New York   Financier and philanthropist, partner in Kuhn, Loeb & Co., international bankers, from 1897 to 1937. Instrumental in founding several Jewish charities and securing the first legislation for probation for juvenile offenders (1902).

MONTGOMERY WARD (1844–December 7, 1913) **Rosehill Cemetery, Chicago, Illinois**   Founder of the first mail-order business in the U.S. (1872).

THOMAS JOHN WATSON (1874–June 19, 1956) **Sleepy Hollow Cemetery, North Tarrytown, New York**   Created the international giant corporation, IBM; coined the motto "THINK."

FRANK WINFIELD WOOLWORTH (1852–August 8, 1919) **Woodlawn Cemetery, Bronx, New York**   By 1911, had built a network of over 1,000 five-and-ten-cent stores.

WILLIAM WRIGLEY, JR. (1861–January 26, 1932) **Forest Lawn Memorial Park, Glendale, California**   Made a popular product out of chewing gum, founded the firm bearing his name (1891).

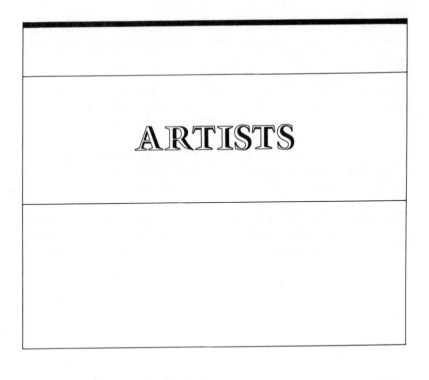

ARTISTS

JOHN JAMES AUDUBON (1785–January 27, 1851) **Trinity Cemetery, New York, New York** Artist of birds and wildlife, buried on land that was once part of his farm.

EDWARD BOEHM (1913–January 29, 1969) **St. Mary's Cemetery, Trenton, New Jersey** Creator of porcelains of birds noted for their delicacy and realism.

MATHEW B. BRADY (c. 1823–January 15, 1896) **Congressional Cemetery, Washington, D.C.** Photographer of the Civil War and a pioneer in the field.

ALEXANDER STIRLING CALDER (1870–January 7, 1945) **West Laurel Hill Cemetery, Bala-Cynwyd, Pennsylvania** Sculptor of civic monuments; father of artist Alexander Calder (see Address Unknown), famed for his mobiles.

ROBERT CAPA (1913–May 25, 1954) **Amawalk Friends Cemetery, Amawalk, New York** The photographer, who covered five wars in eighteen years, was killed by a mine near Thai Binh while covering the war in Indochina. He was awarded the Croix de Guerre with palm at the memorial service held in Lanessau Hospital Chapel in Hanoi.

GEORGE CATLIN (1796–December 23, 1872) **Green-Wood Cemetery, Brooklyn, New York** Painted 470 pictures of Indians and made 700 sketches.

RALPH CRAM (1863–September 2, 1942) **Chapel near St. Elizabeth's Episcopal Church, Sudbury, Massachusetts** Popularizer of the Gothic style in architecture; architect of the chapel at Princeton University, the Cathedral of St. John the Divine in New York City, the rebuilding of West Point.

NATHANIEL CURRIER (1813–November 20, 1888) **Green-Wood Cemetery, Brooklyn, New York** Half of the famous Currier and Ives team of lithographers and printers.

STUART DAVIS (1894–June 24, 1964) **Green River Cemetery, East Hampton, Long Island, New York** Abstract painter of jazz themes; his signature is chiseled on a polished black granite stone; buried near Jackson Pollock.

CHARLES DEMUTH (1883–October 23, 1935) **Lancaster Cemetery, Lancaster, Pennsylvania** Watercolorist notable for studies of flowers and fruit; early came under the influence of geometric shapes of industrial technology.

ASHER BROWN DURAND (1796–September 17, 1886) **Green-Wood Cemetery, Brooklyn, New York** Leader of the Hudson River School of landscape painting, he painted several presidents and was an engraver noted for reproducing Trumbull's *Signing of the Declaration of Independence.*

THOMAS EAKINS (1844–June 25, 1916) **Woodlands Cemetery, Philadelphia, Pennsylvania** Exponent of realism in American art; forced to resign (1886) from Pennsylvania Academy of

The grave of modern artist Stuart Davis is marked by his signature on black granite. (Elly Davis)

Fine Arts because of his insistence on using nude models. His most notable works include *The Surgical Clinic of Professor Gross* (1875) and *The Swimming Hole* (1883).

DANIEL CHESTER FRENCH (1850–October 7, 1931) **Sleepy Hollow Cemetery, Concord, Massachusetts**   Sculptor of the Minute Man statue at Concord Bridge and the Lincoln statue in the Lincoln Memorial.

CHARLES DANA GIBSON (1867–December 23, 1944) **Mount Auburn Cemetery, Cambridge, Massachusetts**   Creator of the popular "Gibson girl."

CASS GILBERT (1859–May 17, 1934) Fairlawn Cemetery, Ridgefield, Connecticut
Architect of New York's pioneering skyscraper, the sixty-story Woolworth Building (1913).

WILLIAM JAMES GLACKENS (1870–May 22, 1938) Cedar Hill Cemetery, Hartford, Connecticut
Illustrator and painter of contemporary scenes, he died on a visit with fellow painter John Prendergast.

ARSHILE GORKY (1904–July 21, 1948) North Cemetery, Sherman, Connecticut
Gorky hanged himself in a barn on his property after calling a neighbor and one of his art students. A first cousin of Maxim Gorky, the Russian writer, he was a pioneer in the development of abstract expressionism. The artist's recent troubles had included a car accident in which his neck had been broken and his painting arm paralyzed; his wife and children had left him, and he had undergone an operation for cancer.

HORATIO GREENOUGH (1805–December 18, 1852) Mount Auburn Cemetery, Cambridge, Massachusetts
An early American sculptor, did seated statue of Washington in a Grecian pose for the U.S. Capitol Building. The monument was so heavy that the floor shook and it had to be removed. Today it greets visitors to the Smithsonian Museum of Science and Technology.

WALTER GROPIUS (1883–July 5, 1969) Mount Auburn Cemetery, Cambridge, Massachusetts
The founder of the Bauhaus School in Germany and the father of modern architecture, requested a "fiesta" rather than a funeral service: "Cremate me but ask not for the ashes. The piety for cinders is a halfway thing; out with it. Wear no signs of mourning. It could be beautiful if all my friends of the present and of the past could get together for a fiesta à la Bauhaus—drinking, laughing, loving. Then I shall surely join in more than in life. It is more fruitful than graveyard orating. Love is the essence of everything." His friends held the party, but his ashes were buried rather than discarded.

CHILDE HASSAM (1859–August 27, 1935) Cedar Lawn Cemetery, East Hampton, Long Island, New York
American impressionist painter; *July 14th Rue Daunou* and *Fifth Avenue* are among his works.

LEWIS W. HINE (1874–November 3, 1940) **Ouleout Cemetery, Franklin, New York**   Photographer of the social ills of the Depression.

HANS HOFMANN (1880–February 17, 1966) **Snow Cemetery, Truro, Massachusetts**   Dominant American abstract expressionist of post-World War II era; his work is marked by his use of strong colors.

WINSLOW HOMER (1836–September 29, 1910) **Mount Auburn Cemetery, Cambridge, Massachusetts**   Landscape painter, noted for his interpretations of the sea.

EDWARD HOPPER (1882–May 16, 1967) **Oak Hill Cemetery, Nyack, New York**   Realistic artist, chiefly of city scenes.

HARRIET HOSMER (1830–February 21, 1908) **Mount Auburn Cemetery, Cambridge, Massachusetts**   Creator of widely reproduced Victorian statues: *Puck* and *Will-o'-the-Wisp.*

ALBERT KAHN (1869–December 8, 1942) White Chapel Memorial Cemetery, Troy, Michigan Industrial architect, modernized the concept of a factory. He was a pioneer in the use of reinforced concrete and steel; directed industrial building program in Soviet Union, 1928–32.

LOUIS KAHN (1901–March 17, 1974) Montefiore Cemetery, Philadelphia, Pennsylvania Leading modern architect of his time, he died of a heart attack and his body lay unclaimed for several days. He designed the capital at Dacca in Bangladesh, the Kimball Art Museum in Fort Worth, Texas, and the Yale Art Gallery.

ROCKWELL KENT (1882–March 13, 1971) Kent Estate, Au Sable Forks, New York Painter, wood engraver, lithographer, and writer, noted for his stark and exotic landscapes. He is buried on the grounds of his estate.

FRANZ KLINE (1910–May 13, 1962) Hollenbach Cemetery, Wilkes-Barre, Pennsylvania Abstract expressionist, noted for huge black-on-white canvases.

PIERRE CHARLES L'ENFANT (1754–June 14, 1825) Arlington National Cemetery, Arlington, Virginia Original designer of Washington, D.C.; his plan for the city is engraved on his tomb, overlooking the city.

JOHN MARIN (1872–October 1, 1953) Fairview Cemetery, Fairview, New Jersey Watercolorist of the Maine coast.

REGINALD MARSH (1898–July 3, 1954) Maple Hill Cemetery, Dorset, Vermont Realistic painter of everyday New York City scenes.

GRANDMA MOSES (1860–December 13, 1961) Maple Grove Cemetery, Hoosick Falls, New York Anna Mary Robertson, the self-taught American primitive painter who specialized in farm scenes, was seventy-six when she began to paint because she could no longer embroider.

BARNETT NEWMAN (1905–July 4, 1970) **Montefiore Cemetery, St. Albans, Queens, New York**   Abstract expressionist who devised new styles in composition, dividing the canvas with bands of color. In his later work he used large areas of primary color for his effects (*Who's Afraid of Red, Yellow and Blue IV*, 1969–70).

CHARLES WILLSON PEALE (1741–February 22, 1827) **Saint Peter's Churchyard, Philadelphia, Pennsylvania**   A prolific portrait painter during the Revolutionary era, he did sixty likenesses of Washington alone. When he died at eighty-six he had married three times and was looking forward to his fourth nuptials.

JACKSON POLLOCK (1912–August 11, 1956) **Green River Cemetery, East Hampton, Long Island, New York**   The innovative abstract painter, who did his work by squirting and dripping paint on a canvas that lay flat on the floor, died in an automobile accident. Pollock's wife, artist Lee Krasner, selected a huge boulder under a tree for his gravestone and placed a large bronze plaque on it with his dates and his signature, much enlarged.

The wife of artist Jackson Pollock chose this boulder to mark his grave in a cemetery near the artists' colony where he lived. (Elly Davis)

FREDERIC REMINGTON (1861–December 26, 1909) Evergreen Cemetery, Canton, New York   Painter and sculptor of the American West whose works nearly always included a horse; he wanted his epitaph to read "He Knew the Horse," but it records only his name and dates.

HENRY HOBSON RICHARDSON (1838–April 27, 1886) Walnut Hills Cemetery, Brookline, Massachusetts   The architect who developed the modified French/Spanish/Romanesque style called "Richardsonian."

NORMAN ROCKWELL (1894–November 8, 1978) Stockbridge Cemetery, Stockbridge, Massachusetts   Popular artist, known for his nostalgic paintings of homespun Americana.

MARK ROTHKO (1903–February 25, 1970) East Marion Cemetery, East Marion, Long Island, New York   A pioneer of abstract expressionist painting, Rothko slashed his elbows in a despondent mood. His death touched off a court battle regarding custody of his paintings and the honesty of his executors, who had turned his works over to a Manhattan art gallery. After six years of litigation, his daughter was granted financial compensation by the courts.

WILLIAM RUSH (1756–January 17, 1833) Christ Church Burial Ground, Philadelphia, Pennsylvania   First native American sculptor; his grave cannot be located precisely within the burial ground, although he is known to lie here.

AUGUSTUS SAINT-GAUDENS (1848–August 3, 1907) Saint-Gaudens Memorial, Cornish, New Hampshire   Sculptor of large public statuary; buried under a small marble temple in a pine grove on his estate.

BEN SHAHN (1898–March 14, 1969) Roosevelt Cemetery, Roosevelt, New Jersey   Painter and lithographer of social themes; did a series of twenty-three paintings on Sacco and Vanzetti (see Buried Abroad).

JOSEPH STELLA (1880–November 5, 1946) **Woodlawn Cemetery, Bronx, New York**   Pioneer of the modern art movement in America, he is best known for his painting of the Brooklyn Bridge.

GILBERT STUART (1755–July 9, 1828) **Central Burying Ground, Boston, Massachusetts**   Stuart, who painted George Washington and other founding fathers, made several fortunes but spent even more on drink and dissipation. He battled with his wife, tortured his children, and died in Boston both famous and bankrupt. Newspapers sang his praises and leading artists wore mourning for a month in his memory, but the funeral revealed his family's true feelings. Stuart's remains were hastily buried in a cut-rate coffin in a grave purchased from a tradesman. The number of the vault was permanently lost, and neither family, friends, nor anyone else could visit his grave. No monument or stone marks the irascible artist's last resting place.

LOUIS HENRY SULLIVAN (1856–April 14, 1924) **Graceland Cemetery, Chicago, Illinois**   Architect Sullivan was responsible for the beautification of the skyscraper; designed the Getty tomb, a designated architectural landmark in the cemetery where he is buried.

THOMAS SULLY (1783–November 5, 1872) **Laurel Hill Cemetery, Philadelphia, Pennsylvania**   Painter of two thousand portraits and five hundred historical pictures.

JOHN TRUMBULL (1756–November 10, 1843) **Yale University Art Gallery, New Haven, Connecticut**   His tomb is the art gallery building, which he designed and which was the first college art museum in the U.S. He donated his paintings to Yale in exchange for a stipend of one thousand dollars a year for life and the stipulation that he be buried in the art gallery. His crypt, beneath the gallery, is marked by a tablet: "Colonel John Trumbull, Patriot and Artist, friend and aide of Washington . . . To his country he gave his SWORD AND PENCIL." Trumbull is remembered for his epic pictures of the Revolution.

MAX WEBER (1881–October 4, 1961) **Mount Ararat Cemetery, Farmingdale, Long Island, New York** Known as the dean of modern art in America; Weber's style changed over the years from cubist-inspired to increasingly abstract.

STANFORD WHITE (1853–June 25, 1906) **Graveyard of St. James Episcopal Church, St. James, Long Island, New York** White, a partner in the architectural firm of McKim, Mead and White, is credited with designs for the New York *Herald* building, Washington Square arch, and the Century Club, all in New York City. A confirmed voluptuary, he kept three apartments designed for his pleasure, and in one of them debauched Evelyn Nesbit, a beautiful teenaged showgirl. Nesbit later wed the mentally unbalanced Harry K. Thaw, heir to a Pittsburgh fortune, who brooded about his wife's "ruin" at White's hands. Finally he shot White to death at the glamorous roof-garden dinner club of Madison Square Garden, which the architect had designed. Judged insane, Thaw was committed to a mental institution but escaped, demanded a new trial, and, due to his family's influence, was set free. In arranging White's funeral, his wife was as discreet as she had been toward his affairs. A special train was hired to take the family to the funeral, which began earlier than announced to avoid curious onlookers.

GRANT WOOD (1892–February 12, 1942) **Riverside Cemetery, Anamosa, Iowa** Leader of midwestern school of art, his most famous painting is *American Gothic.*

FRANK LLOYD WRIGHT (1869–April 9, 1959) **Unity Chapel, Spring Green, Wisconsin** One of the most influential modern architects, creater of organic architecture; after a simple funeral he was carried the half mile to the cemetery on a farm wagon.

RELIGIOUS LEADERS

FELIX ADLER (1851–April 24, 1933) **Mount Pleasant Memorial Park, Hawthorne, New York** Founder of the Ethical Culture Society (1876), a secularization of Judeo-Christian concepts.

RICHARD ALLEN (1760–March 26, 1831) **Mother Bethel African Methodist Episcopal Church, Philadelphia, Pennsylvania** Buried at the site where he founded the African Methodist Episcopal Church, Allen was the first bishop of one of the largest black religious denominations in the U.S. Born a slave, he organized the first Negro convention in Philadelphia, which adopted a platform denouncing slavery and encouraging abolitionist activity.

HENRY WARD BEECHER (1813–March 7, 1887) **Green-Wood Cemetery, Brooklyn, New York** The most respected and renowned Protestant minister of his day, Beecher preached virtue from the pulpit while involved in an affair with Elizabeth Tilton,

102

wife of his good friend Theodore Tilton. When the news got out the scandal shook the entire nation. Beecher's civil trial for adultery ended with a hung jury in 1875. He lies next to his wife, and the stone above them reads: "He thinketh no evil." Elizabeth Tilton is buried nearby in the same cemetery.

EVANGELINE CORY BOOTH (1865–July 17, 1950) **Kensico Cemetery, Valhalla, New York** Daughter of its founders, she became the Salvation Army's fourth general and the only woman to lead the International Army.

SAINT FRANCES XAVIER CABRINI (1850–December 22, 1917) **Saint Cabrini Chapel, Missionary Sisters of the Sacred Heart, New York, New York** The first American citizen to be canonized (1946), founder of schools, convents, and orphanages.

EDGAR CAYCE (1877–January 3, 1945) **Riverside Cemetery, Hopkinsville, Kentucky** Psychic counselor and faith healer, used extrasensory perception to make medical diagnoses.

RICHARD JAMES CUSHING (1895–November 2, 1970) **Portiuncula Chapel, Cardinal Cushing School and Training Center, Hanover, Massachusetts** The son of an immigrant Irish blacksmith, Cushing rose to become a prince of the church and a leader in the ecumenical movement. Noted for his accessibility, Cardinal Cushing requested that he be buried in a crypt facing the playground of this school, which he sponsored for retarded children, so that he could be "watching the children who are so close to me."

FATHER DIVINE (c. 1882–September 10, 1965) **Woodmont Palace Mission Estate, Gladwyne, Pennsylvania** Leader of a religious cult, the Peace Mission Movement; his followers believe him to be the personification of God.

ROSE PHILIPPINE DUCHESNE (1769–November 18, 1852) **Memorial Shrine of Blessed Philippine Duchesne, Academy of the Sacred Heart, St. Charles, Missouri** Missionary to the Indians.

MARY BAKER EDDY (1821–December 3, 1910) **Mount Auburn Cemetery, Cambridge, Massachusetts** As a child, the founder of Christian Science (1879) was beset by physical symptoms, which continued to plague her as an adult. Following the death of her first husband, her illnesses became so numerous that her family had to ply her with morphine and rock her to sleep like an infant. After she developed the principles of healing through faith and mental concentration her health was never poor again. As an old woman she slipped quietly into death, and the doctor who signed her death certificate remarked, "I do not recall ever seeing in death before a face which bore such a beautifully tranquil expression."

JONATHAN EDWARDS (1703–March 22, 1758) **Princeton Cemetery, Princeton, New Jersey** Calvinist theologian, defender of the doctrines of the Puritan tradition.

ANN LEE (1736–September 8, 1784) **Shaker Cemetery, Colonie, New York** Called Mother Ann, founder of the first Shaker Community (1776).

COTTON MATHER (1663–February 24, 1728) **Copp's Hill Burying Ground, Boston, Massachusetts** Theologian, descended from two Puritan divines, John Cotton and Increase Mather, and leader of the second generation of Puritans. Defended the court verdicts in the Salem witch hunts.

AIMEE SEMPLE McPHERSON (1890–September 27, 1944) **Forest Lawn Memorial Park, Glendale, California** Most widely known woman evangelist of her day; she had a nervous breakdown in 1930 and died from an overdose of barbiturates, ruled accidental.

THOMAS MERTON (1915–December 10, 1968) **Community Cemetery, Abbey of Gethsemani, Trappist, Kentucky** A Trappist monk, he wrote books about religion, including a best-selling autobiography, *The Seven Storey Mountain*; his interest in Zen Buddhism led him to a conference in Thailand, where he accidentally touched a faulty electric fan and was electrocuted.

REINHOLD NIEBUHR (1892–June 1, 1971) **Stockbridge Cemetery, Stockbridge, Massachusetts** Modern theologian, related religion to the social sciences and advocated "liberal realism."

G. BROMLEY OXNAM (1891–March 12, 1963) **Mount Auburn Cemetery, Cambridge, Massachusetts** Methodist bishop and president of the World Council of Churches.

SOLOMON SCHECHTER (1847–November 19, 1915) **Mount Hebron Cemetery, Flushing, Queens, New York** Scholar, founder of Conservative Judaism.

JUNIPERO SERRA (1713–August 28, 1784) **Basilica, Mision San Carlos Borromeo, Carmel, California**   Serra was a missionary who baptized more than six thousand Indians and established a string of missions along the coast of California. He died clasping the wooden cross he had brought from Spain and always kept with him. After death his body had to be protected from admirers who thought he was a saint and hoped to retrieve a lock of hair or a piece of clothing. To prevent desecration, his habit and handkerchiefs were cut up and distributed. His funeral procession wound twice around the plaza to give a chance to all who wanted the privilege of carrying the coffin.

ELIZABETH SETON (1774–January 4, 1821) **Seton Shrine Chapel, Emmitsburg, Maryland**   The first native American to be beatified (1963), Mother Seton was first buried near an oak tree on the Daughters of Charity property and then placed in a vault beneath the floor of the Mortuary Chapel. In 1962, prior to her beatification, her remains were exhumed, and in 1968 they were transferred to the altar of the new Seton Shrine Chapel.

FULTON J. SHEEN (1895–December 9, 1979) **Saint Patrick's Cathedral, New York, New York**   Catholic bishop, well-known radio and television figure.

JOSEPH SMITH (1805–June 27, 1844) **Joseph Smith Homesite, Nauvoo, Illinois**   Smith, founder of the Church of Jesus Christ of Latter-day Saints (1830) and leader of the Mormon community of Nauvoo, Illinois, had destroyed the printing presses of a Carthage newspaper that attacked him for polygamy. The governor demanded that Smith and his followers come to Carthage for trial, promising them protection. Joseph and his brother, Hyrum, surrendered, but feelings ran so high against the Mormons that the governor's promise proved worthless. A mob stormed the jail, instantly killing Hyrum. Joseph emptied his six-shooter into the crowd of assailants, then jumped from the jailhouse window, and died in the courtyard of gunshot wounds. Both brothers are buried near their original log cabin, the oldest structure in Nauvoo. The graves were kept secret until they were found in 1928 after an extensive search.

FRANCIS JOSEPH SPELLMAN (1889–December 2, 1967)

Saint Patrick's Cathedral, New York, New York   Cardinal Spellman lies in the crypt beneath the high altar where all New York's archbishops are interred. His requiem mass was the first for a cardinal to be conducted entirely in English, following the relaxation of rules governing the mass. As a symbol of the new ecumenism, the Greek Orthodox Primate of North and South America conducted in his honor the first Greek Orthodox service in a Roman Catholic Church since A.D. 1054.

Before his coffin was sealed, an illuminated scroll containing his biography and identification of his remains was placed inside. The scroll, one of the few modern examples of medieval illumination, was done in waterproof ink on nondeteriorating sheepskin.

BILLY SUNDAY (1863–November 6, 1935) Waldheim/Forest Home Cemetery, Forest Park, Illinois

Popular evangelist, said to have preached to more than eighty million people; the greatest single influence for Prohibition.

PAUL TILLICH (1886–October 22, 1965) Paul Tillich Park, New Harmony, Indiana

Left Germany (1933) because of opposition to Nazi regime; his theology embraced the ideas of psychology and existentialism as they illuminate Christian doctrine. His ashes are interred among the fir trees in the park. These trees, which he had loved as a boy, were ordered as a memorial from his native Germany.

ISAAC MAYER WISE (1819–March 26, 1900) Walnut Hills Cemetery, Evanston, Ohio

Transplanted Reform Judaism from Germany to the U.S.

STEPHEN S. WISE (1874–April 19, 1949) Westchester Hills Cemetery, Hastings-on-Hudson, New York

Exponent of Reform Judaism, founder of several important liberal organizations.

BRIGHAM YOUNG (1801–August 29, 1877) Mormon Pioneer Memorial, Salt Lake City, Utah

Founder of the Salt Lake City Mormon community, Young had between seventeen and twenty-five wives and fifty-six children. As he was dying of appendicitis he called out, "Joseph! Joseph! Joseph!" as if communicating with his close friend Joseph Smith, the Prophet and founder of Mormonism. Young was buried in a plain pine coffin with simple services and no mourning, since Mormon teachings hold that death is only a birth into a higher sphere. He lay in state in the Tabernacle, his coffin enclosed in an airtight metallic burial case with a glass insert over the face. Young designed his vault so that it is impossible to remove a single stone from the structure.

SCIENTISTS AND INVENTORS

CLEVELAND ABBE (1838–October 28, 1916) **Rock Creek Cemetery, Washington, D.C.** First official daily weather forecaster in the U.S.; called "Old Prob" because of his issuance of three weather probabilities a day.

LOUIS AGASSIZ (1807–December 14, 1873) **Mount Auburn Cemetery, Cambridge, Massachusetts** Naturalist, discovered that much of North America had once been covered by glaciers.

EDWIN HOWARD ARMSTRONG (1890–March 31, 1954) **Woodlawn Cemetery, Bronx, New York** The inventor of FM radio. Depressed because litigation with broadcasting companies took 90 percent of his time, he jumped from his thirteenth-floor apartment, leaving a note for his wife. He was found, fully clothed in hat, gloves, and overcoat, on a third-floor balcony. Armstrong's wife had left him because he refused to spend less time on research and inventions.

BENJAMIN BANNEKER (1731–October, 1806) **Westchester Grade School Grounds, Oella, Maryland**   Scientist Banneker had published an almanac with his own calculations for tides and weather but still there was doubt that a black man could achieve so much. Thomas Jefferson's arguments on behalf of his ability were used in the abolitionist cause and made the almanac a best-seller. As Banneker's casket was being lowered into the grave his house caught on fire and burned to the ground before help could arrive. The bible used at the funeral service and a few personal items were all that survived the day.

LUTHER BURBANK (1849–April 11, 1926) **Burbank Home, Santa Rosa, California**   Burbank, called the greatest plant breeder and wizard of horticulture, is buried in the yard of his old cottage under a cedar of Lebanon he had grown from seed. He chose the site, planning that the tree would serve as his monument. In his casket his wife placed his mother's picture, a favorite porcelain dog, two drawings made by his niece, and, in his pocket, a wooden whistle he used to call his dog, Bonita.

JOHN BURROUGHS (1837–March 29, 1921) **Burroughs Memorial Field, Roxbury, New York**   Naturalist and writer, buried beneath "boyhood rock," a rock that was his childhood favorite.

GEORGE WASHINGTON CARVER (c. 1864–January 5, 1943) **Tuskegee Institute, Tuskegee Institute, Alabama**   Agricultural scientist, educator, and botanist; his epitaph reads in part: "He could have added fortune to fame, but caring for neither, he found happiness and honor in being helpful to the world." Carver is buried alongside Booker T. Washington (see Social Scientists and Educators).

SAMUEL COLT (1814–January 9, 1862) **Cedar Hill Cemetery, Hartford, Connecticut**   Inventor of the revolving breech pistol (1835–36).

LEE DE FOREST (1873–June 30, 1961) **San Fernando Mission Cemetery, Mission Hills, California**   "Father of Radio," left an estate valued at $1,250 because he never received royalties for his more than three hundred inventions.

THOMAS A. DOOLEY (1927–January 18, 1961) **Calvary Cemetery, St. Louis, Missouri**   Medical missionary, established hospitals in Asia; died of cancer the day after his thirty-fourth birthday.

THOMAS ALVA EDISON (1847–October 18, 1931) **Glenmont, West Orange, New Jersey**   Edison, the quintessential inventor, once remarked, "I'm long on ideas but short on time. I only expect to live to be about 100." His inventions include telegraph apparatus, phonograph, incandescent lamp, electrical apparatus, and motion picture sound systems, and he held more than 1,300 U.S. and foreign patents. During his last years Edison complained of stomach difficulties and went on a variety of diets. The final one, to which he remained loyal to the end, was milk, interrupted only by an occasional orange. In 1919, when Edison began research on synthetic rubber, he limited himself to drinking two cups of milk every two hours from a special brown cow in Parsippany, New Jersey. Over the next years he suffered the symptoms of malnutrition, but he continued most of his activities as usual. His last few months provoked a national deathwatch, with a press room in his garage and daily medical bulletins for President Hoover.

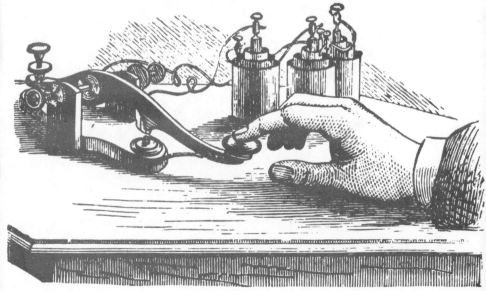

112

ENRICO FERMI (1901–November 28, 1954) **Oak Woods Cemetery, Chicago, Illinois** Nobel Prize–winning physicist (1938); leader of group that created the first man-made nuclear chain reaction.

ROBERT FULTON (1765–February 24, 1815) **Trinity Churchyard, New York, New York** Engineer, inventor, painter; developer of first commercially successful steamboat.

ROBERT GODDARD (1882–August 10, 1945) **Hope Cemetery, Worcester, Massachusetts** Physicist and rocket expert, fired the world's first liquid-fuel rocket (1926).

GEORGE WASHINGTON GOETHALS (1858–January 22, 1928) **West Point Cemetery, U.S. Military Academy, West Point, New York** Army major general, chief engineer of the Panama Canal, and later governor of the Canal Zone; requested burial at West Point, and services were held in the old cadet chapel just inside the cemetery.

CHARLES GOODYEAR (1800–July 1, 1860) **Grove Street Cemetery, New Haven, Connecticut** His efforts to discover a means of destroying the adhesive properties of rubber culminated in the vulcanization process (1839), which gives rubber elasticity and strength and allowed its use in the automotive industry.

KAREN HORNEY (1885–December 4, 1952) **Ferncliff Cemetery, Hartsdale, New York** Psychiatrist who emphasized environmental and cultural factors in determining personality.

ELIAS HOWE (1819–October 3, 1867) **Green-Wood Cemetery, Brooklyn, New York** Inventor of the first practical sewing machine (1844).

ALFRED C. KINSEY (1894–August 25, 1956) **Rose Hill Cemetery, Bloomington, Indiana** Zoologist, famous for his study of human sexual behavior; died while working on research on the sex lives of men in prisons.

CHARLES HORACE MAYO (1865–May 26, 1939) **WILLIAM J. MAYO** (1861–July 28, 1939) **Oakwood Cemetery, Rochester, Minnesota** Physicians and brothers, founded the Mayo Clinic, which became the medical mecca of the world. They died within months of each other and are buried next to each other.

CYRUS H. McCORMICK (1809–May 13, 1884) **Graceland Cemetery, Chicago, Illinois** Inventor of the first modern reaper (1834) and many other farm machines.

OTTMAR MERGENTHALER (1854–October 28, 1899) **Loudon Park Cemetery, Baltimore, Maryland** Patented the Linotype machine in 1884.

MARIA MITCHELL (1818–June 28, 1889) **Prospect Hill Cemetery, Nantucket, Massachusetts** Astronomer, first woman to be elected to the American Academy of Arts and Sciences. Toward the end she remarked, "Well, if this is dying, there is nothing very unpleasant about it."

SAMUEL F. B. MORSE (1791–April 2, 1872) **Green-Wood Cemetery, Brooklyn, New York** Developer of the electromagnetic recording telegraph (1840) and "Morse code."

JOHN MUIR (1838–December 24, 1914) **John Muir National Historic Site, Martinez, California** Called "John of the Mountains," "Guardian of the Yosemite," and "Naturalist of the Sierras," he was devoted to the wilderness of America. After Muir's death in the Mojave Desert, his body was taken to his Martinez home of thirty years and buried in a family cemetery. His grave was lined with boughs of *Sequoia gigantea*, the tree that he had popularized and planted near his home. Appropriately for the man who crusaded for the development of national parks and reservations, Muir's home and grave site are administered by the National Park Service.

GEORGE M. PULLMAN (1831–October 19, 1897) **Graceland Cemetery, Chicago, Illinois** Fearful of body kidnappers, the inventor of the sleeping car had ordered his coffin wrapped in tar paper, bolted with steel bolts, and embedded in a room-sized chamber filled with concrete and topped with bolted steel rails.

OTTO RANK (1884–October 31, 1939) **Ferncliff Cemetery, Hartsdale, New York** Psychiatrist, focused on birth trauma as the source of neuroses.

WALTER REED (1851–November 23, 1902) **Arlington National Cemetery, Arlington, Virginia** Physician, conqueror of yellow fever; his last words were "I leave so little."

ELMER A. SPERRY (1860–June 16, 1930) **Green-Wood Cemetery, Brooklyn, New York** Developer of the gyroscopic compass (1896–1910) and four hundred other inventions.

ELI WHITNEY (1765–January 8, 1825) Grove Street Cemetery, New Haven, Connecticut   Inventor of the cotton gin (1793) and a system of manufacturing interchangeable gun parts.

ORVILLE WRIGHT (1871–January 30, 1948) **WILBUR WRIGHT** (1867–May 30, 1912) Woodland Cemetery, Dayton, Ohio   Inventors of the first practical flying machine (1905).

SOCIAL SCIENTISTS AND EDUCATORS

FREDERICK LEWIS ALLEN (1890–February 13, 1954) **Forest Hills Cemetery, Boston, Massachusetts** The historian and journalist who used daily newspaper stories and cultural events to chronicle history in such popular books as *Only Yesterday* (1931).

CHARLES A. BEARD (1874–September 1, 1948) **MARY R. BEARD** (1876–August 14, 1958) **Ferncliff Cemetery, Hartsdale, New York** Historians and husband and wife, favored multi-disciplinary approach using economics, sociology, etc.; *The Rise of American Civilization* (1927).

MARY McLEOD BETHUNE (1875–May 18, 1955) **Bethune-Cookman College, Daytona Beach, Florida** Founder and president of Bethune-Cookman College (1923); founder of the National Council of Negro Women (1937).

NICHOLAS MURRAY BUTLER (1862–December 7, 1947) **Cedar Lawn Cemetery, Paterson, New Jersey** President of Columbia University (1902–45), helped establish Carnegie Endowment for International Peace (1925).

JOHN DEWEY (1859–June 1, 1952) **Dewey Memorial, University of Vermont, Burlington, Vermont** Educator, his theories were the basis for progressive education; until his wife's death Dewey's ashes were stored in the safe at the Community Church in New York, because she wanted to keep them nearby. Then both their ashes were buried in Vermont.

CHARLES WILLIAM ELIOT (1834–August 22, 1926) **Mount Auburn Cemetery, Cambridge, Massachusetts** President of Harvard during its transformation from a college into a university (1869–1909).

GEORGE WASHINGTON GALE (1789–September 13, 1861) **Hope Cemetery, Galesburg, Illinois** Educator and founder of colleges where students paid for their education with manual labor, Oneida Institute, Whitesboro, New York (1827), and Knox College (1837).

ROBERT MAYNARD HUTCHINS (1899–May 14, 1977) **Santa Barbara Cemetery, Santa Barbara, California** "Wonder boy" of higher education, became president of the University of Chicago at the age of thirty and later chancellor, spending twenty-one years establishing the school as the innovator of educational methods. Later he was president of the Fund for the Republic and the Center for the Study of Democratic Institutions.

WILLIAM JAMES (1842–August 26, 1910) **City of Cambridge Cemetery, Cambridge, Massachusetts** Philosopher and psychologist, accepted all religions as equal and equally acceptable.

ABBOTT L. LOWELL (1856–January 6, 1943) **Mount Auburn Cemetery, Cambridge, Massachusetts** President of Harvard for twenty-four years; funeral service was held at the Harvard Memorial Church in Harvard Yard, built during his tenure.

ANNE SULLIVAN MACY (1866–October 20, 1936) **Washington Cathedral, Washington, D.C.**   Teacher and companion of Helen Keller (see Social Reformers), near whom she is interred.

HORACE MANN (1796–August 2, 1859) **North Burial Ground, Providence, Rhode Island**   Educator, famed for his contributions to the quality of public education and teaching.

MARGARET MEAD (1901–November 15, 1978) **Buckingham Friends Cemetery, Lashaska, Pennsylvania**   Anthropologist, noted for her work on adolescent sexual patterns in different cultures, *Coming of Age in Samoa* (1928). Long associated with the American Museum of Natural History in New York; part of the museum park is now called Margaret Mead Green.

ALLAN NEVINS (1890–March 3, 1971) **Kensico Cemetery, Valhalla, New York**   Pulitzer Prize–winning biographer for *Grover Cleveland* (1932) and *Hamilton Fish* (1936), he synthesized social, economic, and political aspects of the Civil War period in a six-volume history, *The Ordeal of the Union* (1947–60); professor at Columbia University.

ALICE FREEMAN PALMER (1855–December 6, 1902) **GEORGE HERBERT PALMER** (1842–May 7, 1933) **Chapel, Wellesley College, Wellesley, Massachusetts**   Alice Palmer was president of Wellesley and a proponent of higher education for women. George Palmer, a professor of philosophy, substituted lectures for the recitation method of teaching.

FRANCIS PARKMAN (1823–November 8, 1893) **Mount Auburn Cemetery, Cambridge, Massachusetts**   Leading nineteenth-century historian, author of *The Oregon Trail* (1849).

EZRA STILES (1727–May 12, 1795) **Grove Street Cemetery, New Haven, Connecticut**   Theologian, educator, lawyer, and minister, president of Yale from 1778 to 1795.

WILLIAM GRAHAM SUMNER (1840–April 12, 1910) **Mount Auburn Cemetery, Cambridge, Massachusetts**   Sociologist and political economist, advocated free trade and opposed social reform.

M. CAREY THOMAS (1857–December 1, 1935) **M. Carey Thomas Library, Bryn Mawr College, Bryn Mawr, Pennsylvania**   Feminist and educator, organized Bryn Mawr College (1885); she is buried in the Cloisters, a colonnaded area in the center of the library that bears her name.

BOOKER T. WASHINGTON (c. 1858–November 14, 1915) **Tuskegee Institute, Tuskegee Institute, Alabama**   Founder of Tuskegee as an educational institution for blacks, stressed economic independence as the bulwark of civil rights.

EMMA WILLARD (1787–April 15, 1870) **Oakwood Cemetery, Troy, New York**   Established the Emma Willard School (1821), pioneered advanced education for women.

The Cloisters in the library at Bryn Mawr College where educator and feminist M. Carey Thomas is buried. (Judith Meyer Wallace)

WRITERS

HENRY ADAMS (1838–March 28, 1918) Rock Creek Cemetery, Washington, D.C. Adams, the writer and historian known for *The Education of Henry Adams* (1906), is buried in an unmarked grave next to that of his wife, according to his own wishes. But his wife's tomb is so famous that it could not have been from a desire to be left alone. Marian Adams committed suicide, and he commissioned a monument for her grave by the sculptor Augustus Saint-Gaudens (see Artists). Popularly known as *Grief*, it is a figure of no determined sex enshrouded in a cloak that gives it a sense of mystery. The statue was placed in a grove of trees for privacy, but it aroused controversy and curiosity because some considered it agnostic; tourists flocked to see it, disturbing Adams, who had planned to spend quiet moments there. Eleanor Roosevelt (see Government Leaders) is said to have spent time at the spot for comfort after she learned of Franklin D. Roosevelt's infidelity with Lucy Page Mercer.

121

Although writer Henry Adams's grave is unmarked, he lies near his wife, for whom he commissioned this Saint-Gaudens monument, popularly called Grief. *(Rock Creek Cemetery, Washington, D.C.)*

LOUISA MAY ALCOTT (1832–March 6, 1888) Sleepy Hollow Cemetery, Concord, Massachusetts Author of *Little Women* (1868); she is buried near two of her sisters who inspired characters in the book, Abigail May (Beth) and Anna Bronson (Meg). Her grave is decorated each Memorial Day to commemorate service as a Civil War nurse.

SHOLEM ALEICHEM (Solomon Rabinowitz) (1859–May 13, 1916) Mount Neboh Cemetery, Glendale, Queens, New York Popular Yiddish writer; his stories of Tevye the dairyman were turned into the hit musical *Fiddler on the Roof* (1964).

HORATIO ALGER, JR. (1832–July 18, 1899) Glenwood Cemetery, South Natick, Massachusetts Wrote popular books about poor boys who made good through perseverance.

NELSON ALGREN (1909–May 9, 1981) **Oakland Cemetery, Sag Harbor, Long Island, New York**   Chicago writer of realistic novels, well known for *The Man With the Golden Arm* (1949).

MAXWELL ANDERSON (1888–February 28, 1959) **Ferncliff Cemetery, Hartsdale, New York**   Dramatist, often wrote in verse, with historical themes: *What Price Glory?* (1924), *Winterset* (1935), and *Anne of the Thousand Days* (1948).

SHERWOOD ANDERSON (1876–March 8, 1941) **Roundhill Cemetery, Marion, Virginia**   On a South American cruise with his wife, Anderson was stricken suddenly and taken off the boat at Colon, Panama Canal Zone. The short-story writer and novelist, best known for *Winesburg, Ohio* (1919), died there. The cause of death turned out to be an hors d'oeuvre toothpick that had perforated his intestine. He had requested this inscription for his tombstone: "Life not death is the great adventure."

ROBERT CHARLES BENCHLEY (1889–November 21, 1945) **Prospect Hill Cemetery, Nantucket, Massachusetts**   A humorist and practical joker; Benchley's ashes were taken to the cemetery by his family in a long auto drive from New York City. When they got there, they found that the small bronze box with his name and dates was empty; the crematorium had neglected to fill it. "You know," his daughter remarked, "I can hear him laughing now."

JOHN BERRYMAN (1914–January 7, 1972) **Resurrection Cemetery, St. Paul, Minnesota**   Pulitzer Prize–winning poet (1964), professor and critic, committed suicide.

ANNE DUDLEY BRADSTREET (c. 1612–September 16, 1672) **First Burial Ground, North Andover, Massachusetts**   First colonial woman poet, died of consumption.

LOUIS BROMFIELD (1896–March 18, 1956) **Malabar Farm State Park, Lucas, Ohio**   Popular journalist and novelist, works include *Mrs. Parkington* (1943), *The Wild Country* (1948), and the nonfiction *Malabar Farm* (1948), about his farm, on which he chose to be buried.

WILLIAM CULLEN BRYANT **(1794–June 12, 1878) Roslyn Cemetery, Roslyn, Long Island, New York**   New England nature poet, known particularly for his early poems "Thanatopsis," "To a Waterfowl," and "The Yellow Violet"; later a journalist.

PEARL S. BUCK **(1892–March 6, 1973) Green Hills Farm, Perkasie, Pennsylvania**   First American woman to win a Nobel Prize for literature (1938), she was buried under an ash tree on her farm, facing east, without a religious service. Famous for her novel *The Good Earth* (1932); her tombstone has Chinese calligraphy depicting her maiden name: Precious Gem.

WILLA CATHER **(1876–April 24, 1947) Old Burying Ground, Jaffrey Center, New Hampshire**   Pulitzer Prize–winning author; these words from her novel *My Antonia* (1918) are on her tombstone: "That is happiness, to be dissolved into something complete and great."

RAYMOND CHANDLER **(1888–March 26, 1959) Mount Hope Cemetery, San Diego, California**   Mystery writer, creator of detective Philip Marlowe.

JAMES FENIMORE COOPER **(1789–September 14, 1851) Christ Churchyard, Cooperstown, New York**   First significant American novelist, known for *The Leatherstocking Tales*; died in the town named for him, of sclerosis of the liver.

STEPHEN CRANE **(1871–June 5, 1900) Evergreen Cemetery, Hillside, New Jersey**   Wrote about the reality of the slums, died in Germany of tuberculosis.

E. E. CUMMINGS **(1894–September 2, 1962) Forest Hills Cemetery, Boston, Massachusetts**   Poet, created his own syntax and rules of punctuation, wrote his name and works in lowercase letters.

CLARENCE DAY **(1874–December 28, 1935) Woodlawn Cemetery, Bronx, New York**   His sketches about his parents were adapted for the stage hits *Life with Father* and *Life with Mother*.

EMILY DICKINSON (1830–May 15, 1886) **West Cemetery, Amherst, Massachusetts** Reclusive poet, published little during her lifetime; her tombstone bears the prophetic words "Called Back," which she wrote in her last note to a cousin.

HILDA DOOLITTLE (H. D.) (1886–September 27, 1961) **Nisky Hill Cemetery, Bethlehem, Pennsylvania** Imagist poet.

JOHN DOS PASSOS (1896–September 28, 1970) **Yeocomico Churchyard, Westmoreland County, Virginia** Novelist, noted for his trilogy, *U.S.A.* (1937).

THEODORE DREISER (1871–December 28, 1945) **Forest Lawn Memorial Park, Glendale, California** Novelist, pioneer of naturalism, he was buried in his black lecture suit and black bow tie. His last wife put a sonnet she had written in the casket. Charlie Chaplin was among the one hundred mourners for the man whose work was challenged as immoral because those of easy virtue went unpunished. His most popular novel was *An American Tragedy* (1925), based on an actual murder trial.

PAUL LAURENCE DUNBAR (1872–February 9, 1906)
Woodland Cemetery, Dayton, Ohio   The poet, who wrote in Negro folk dialect, became sick with tuberculosis and died while reciting the Twenty-third Psalm with a minister. He was placed in a vault until the spring, when he was put in a plot near the road, near a pool, as he had requested. His mother planted a willow tree by the grave to fulfill his verse: "Lay me down beneaf de willers in the grass." In 1909 a boulder of Miami Valley granite with a bronze plaque designed by Tiffany was erected at the grave.

RALPH WALDO EMERSON (1803–April 27, 1882) **Sleepy Hollow Cemetery, Concord, Massachusetts**   Poet and leading spokesman for transcendentalism; his monument has his lines: "The passive master lent his land/to the vast Soul which o'er him planned." He also wrote the epitaph for his five-year-old son Waldo, buried here: "The hyacinthine boy for whom Morn well might break and April bloom."

WILLIAM FAULKNER (1897–July 6, 1962) **St. Peter's Cemetery, Oxford, Mississippi**   The Nobel Prize–winning novelist (1949) who created a geographical entity in his novels that reflects much of southern history: *The Sound and the Fury* (1929), *Light in August* (1932), *Intruder in the Dust* (1948), and *A Fable* (1954) are some of his works. He lies near four generations of Faulkners in the family plot marked "Falkner." His stone reads, "Beloved go with God."

F. SCOTT FITZGERALD (1896–December 21, 1940) **Saint Mary's Cemetery, Rockville, Maryland**   Chronicler of the Jazz Age in such books as *The Great Gatsby* (1925); originally he was refused burial in a Catholic cemetery because he had been a lapsed Catholic. He was moved here in 1975.

T. THOMAS FORTUNE (1856–June 2, 1928) **Eden Cemetery, Philadelphia, Pennsylvania**   Started the *New York Age* (1883), a distinguished black newspaper, coined the word "Afro-American."

ROBERT FROST (1874–January 29, 1963) **Old Bennington Cemetery, Bennington, Vermont**   Poet of New England life and character; his epitaph: "I had a lover's quarrel with the world." Grave is surrounded by those of soldiers from the Battle of Bennington, 1777.

ELLEN GLASGOW (1874–November 21, 1945) **Hollywood Cemetery, Richmond, Virginia**   Glasgow's novels describe Southern society in transition from postbellum to modern day; her work includes *Barren Ground* (1925), *In This Our Life* (1941). At her death the remains of her dogs were exhumed from her garden and placed in her casket. On her stone are words she selected from Milton's *Lycidas*: "Tomorrow to fresh Woods, and Pastures New."

PAUL GOODMAN (1911–August 2, 1972) **Stratford Center Cemetery, Stratford, New Hampshire**   Poet, novelist, and social commentator in such books as *Growing Up Absurd* (1960) and *Compulsory Mis-education* (1964).

EDGAR A. GUEST (1881–August 5, 1959) **Woodlawn Cemetery, Detroit, Michigan**   Popular poet of sentimental verses.

EDWARD EVERETT HALE (1822–June 10, 1909) **Forest Hills Cemetery, Boston, Massachusetts**   Novelist, clergyman, published *Man Without a Country* (1863) anonymously.

DASHIELL HAMMETT (1894–January 10, 1961) **Arlington National Cemetery, Arlington, Virginia**   Mystery writer, creator of Sam Spade; buried in the national cemetery for his services in World Wars I and II.

LORRAINE HANSBERRY (1930–January 2, 1965) **Beth El Cemetery, Croton-on-Hudson, New York**   First black woman to have a play produced on Broadway: *A Raisin in the Sun* (1959); died of cancer.

MOSS HART (1904–December 20, 1961) **Ferncliff Cemetery, Hartsdale, New York**   Playwright, collaborator on a string of successful musicals and comedies, including *The Man Who Came to Dinner* (1939).

NATHANIEL HAWTHORNE (1804–May 18 or 19, 1864)
Sleepy Hollow Cemetery, Concord, Massachusetts   Novelist,
known for *The House of the Seven Gables* (1851) and *The Scarlet
Letter* (1850); died on a trip to the White Mountains with Franklin
Pierce (see Presidents), former president. The manuscript of an
unfinished novel was laid in his coffin.

DuBOSE HEYWARD (1885–July 16, 1940) St. Philip's
Churchyard, Charleston, South Carolina   Author of *Porgy* (1925),
on which Gershwin's opera *Porgy and Bess* is based.

OLIVER WENDELL HOLMES, SR. (1809–October 7, 1894)
Mount Auburn Cemetery, Cambridge, Massachusetts   Physi-
cian, essayist, and poet; father of noted jurist (see Supreme Court
Justices).

WILLIAM INGE (1913–June 10, 1973) Old Mount Hope Cem-
etery, Independence, Kansas   Playwright, noted for *Come Back
Little Sheba* (1950) and *Picnic* (1953); committed suicide in his
Mercedes Benz in his garage.

WASHINGTON IRVING (1783–November 28, 1859) Sleepy
Hollow Cemetery, North Tarrytown, New York   Early American
writer, creator of "Rip Van Winkle" (1820) and "The Legend of
Sleepy Hollow" (1820).

HENRY JAMES (1843–February 28, 1916) City of Cambridge
Cemetery, Cambridge, Massachusetts   Novelist and longtime
resident of Britain; James's work includes *The Portrait of a Lady*
(1881), *The Bostonians* (1886), *The Aspern Papers* (1888), and *The
Golden Bowl* (1904). After his death and cremation in London,
his sister-in-law smuggled his ashes into the U.S. to avoid possible trouble with customs during wartime. His tombstone reads:
"Henry James, O.M./Novelist-Citizen/of Two countries/Interpre-
ter of his/Generation on both/sides of the Sea."

RANDALL JARRELL (1914–October 14, 1965) New Garden
Friends Cemetery, Greensboro, North Carolina   Poet and critic.

FRANCIS SCOTT KEY (1779–January 11, 1843) **Mount Olivet Cemetery, Frederick, Maryland** Author of the words to "The Star-spangled Banner," lies under an American flag that is never lowered.

OLIVER LA FARGE (1901–August 2, 1963) **National Cemetery, Santa Fe, New Mexico** Won Pulitzer Prize for *Laughing Boy* (1930), a story about Navaho life.

SINCLAIR LEWIS (1885–January 10, 1951) **Greenwood Cemetery, Sauk Centre, Minnesota** First American to win the Nobel Prize in literature (1930); his ashes were scattered in a grave in his home town along with many of his novels, which include *Main Street* (1920), *Elmer Gantry* (1927), and *Cass Timberlane* (1945).

VACHEL LINDSAY (1879–December 5, 1931) **Oak Ridge Cemetery, Springfield, Illinois** Lindsay, the poet famous for declaiming his work, which imitated the sounds of bells and other inanimate objects, was mentally ill and committed suicide. He arranged pictures of his wife and children in a circle on the dining room table with two lighted candles, fixed a place for himself with pillows and a blanket, and drank a bottle of Lysol. At the time his death was reported as heart failure, but his wife told poet Edgar Lee Masters that it was an attack of epilepsy. She later confessed the truth to Masters and he revealed it in his biography of his friend. Lindsay was buried on a slope of the cemetery near Lincoln's tomb (see Presidents).

HENRY WADSWORTH LONGFELLOW (1807–March 24, 1882) **Mount Auburn Cemetery, Cambridge, Massachusetts** Poet; his long narratives describe historical American events in verse: *Evangeline* (1847), *Song of Hiawatha* (1855), *Paul Revere's Ride* (1861).

AMY LOWELL (1874–May 1, 1925) **Mount Auburn Cemetery, Cambridge, Massachusetts** Imagist poet and critic.

JOHN P. MARQUAND (1893–June 16, 1960) **Sawyer's Hill Burying Ground, Newburyport, Massachusetts** Wrote satirical novels set among aristocratic New England society, such as *The Late George Apley* (1937) and *Point of No Return* (1949).

EDGAR LEE MASTERS (1869–March 5, 1950) **Petersburg Oakland Cemetery, Petersburg, Illinois**   Wrote the *Spoon River Anthology* (1915) and other poems.

CARSON McCULLERS (1917–September 29, 1967) **Oak Hill Cemetery, Nyack, New York**   Novelist, wrote of outcasts, *A Member of the Wedding* (1946); died after lying in a coma for forty-seven days following a stroke.

CLAUDE McKAY (1890–May 22, 1948) **Calvary Cemetery, Woodside, Queens, New York**   At his death, McKay was a long time distant from Harlem, the setting and inspiration for his poems and novels of the 1920s. He had wanted to be buried from Harlem and his body was sent there from Chicago, but it arrived too late for the funeral services, which were conducted in a Harlem church without him.

HERMAN MELVILLE (1819–September 28, 1891) **Woodlawn Cemetery, Bronx, New York**   Novelist, author of *Moby Dick* (1851); buried next to his wife under a tall oak; his stone has an unrolled scroll and quill pen carved on it. Psychics came here to get vibrations about the whereabouts of the Lindbergh baby.

H. L. MENCKEN (1880–January 29, 1956) **Loudon Park Cemetery, Baltimore, Maryland** Critic of American language and society.

GRACE METALIOUS (1924–February 25, 1964) **Smith Meeting House Cemetery, Gilmanton, New Hampshire** Gilmanton did not welcome the notoriety that ensued after novelist Metalious published her steamy best-seller about illicit sex in a small town (*Peyton Place*, 1956). For years there was no love lost between the erratic writer and her neighbors; it was not her intention to rest among them for eternity. Metalious's deathbed will stipulated that her body be given to Dartmouth Medical School, but the school refused the donation because of her family's objections. The New Hampshire Supreme Court authorized a funeral and burial in Gilmanton.

EDNA ST. VINCENT MILLAY (1892–October 19, 1950) **Steepletop, Austerlitz, New York** First woman to receive the Pulitzer Prize for poetry (1923); buried on the grounds of her home, which has become a writers' colony; grave is in an azalea grove in a birch forest.

MARGARET MITCHELL (1900–August 16, 1949) **Oakland Cemetery, Atlanta, Georgia** Author of one book, *Gone With the Wind* (1936), the biggest best-seller in U.S. history up to its time.

CLEMENT CLARKE MOORE (1779–July 10, 1863) **Trinity Cemetery, New York, New York** Poet, author of "A Visit from St. Nicholas" (1823); each Christmas Eve, carolers visit his grave.

MARIANNE MOORE (1887–February 5, 1972) **Evergreen Cemetery, Gettysburg, Pennsylvania** Poet who delighted in the mundane; editor of *The Dial* (1925–29). Her *Collected Poems* won a 1951 Pulitzer Prize.

CHRISTOPHER MORLEY (1890–March 28, 1957) **Roslyn Cemetery, Roslyn, New York** Novelist and essayist, founder and editor of the *Saturday Review of Literature* (1924–40).

OGDEN NASH (1902–May 19, 1971) **Little River Cemetery, North Hampton, New Hampshire**   Witty poet and punster; his collections include *I'm a Stranger Here Myself* (1938) and *Bed Riddance* (1970).

FRANK NORRIS (1870–October 25, 1902) **Mountain View Cemetery, Oakland, California**   Novelist, used literature to illuminate social problems: *The Octopus* (1901), *The Pit* (1903).

FLANNERY O'CONNOR (1925–August 3, 1964) **Memory Hill Cemetery, Milledgeville, Georgia**   Novelist; her characters combine the grotesque and the humorous; died after ten years as an invalid with lupus.

CLIFFORD ODETS (1906–August 14, 1963) **Forest Lawn Memorial Park, Glendale, California**   Dramatist; his work expressed the social protest of the 1930s in such plays as *Waiting for Lefty* (1935) and *Golden Boy* (1937).

JOHN O'HARA (1905–April 11, 1970) **Princeton Cemetery, Princeton, New Jersey**   Short-story writer and novelist: *Appointment in Samarra* (1934), *Butterfield 8* (1935); his stone is inscribed: "Better/Than Anyone Else/He Told the Truth/About his Time/He was/A Professional/He wrote/Honestly and Well."

O. HENRY (William Sydney Porter) (1862–June 5, 1910) **Riverside Cemetery, Asheville, North Carolina**   Short-story writer, known for his ironic endings.

EUGENE O'NEILL (1888–November 27, 1953) **Forest Hills Cemetery, Boston, Massachusetts**   Only U.S. playwright to receive the Nobel Prize (1936); plays include *Anna Christie* (1922), *Strange Interlude* (1928), and *Long Day's Journey into Night* (1956).

MAXWELL PERKINS (1884–June 17, 1947) **Lakeview Cemetery, New Canaan, Connecticut**   Editor and supporter of Thomas Wolfe and F. Scott Fitzgerald.

EDGAR ALLAN POE (1809–October 7, 1849) **Westminster Presbyterian Churchyard, Baltimore, Maryland** Poe's life, obsessed with the macabre, ended with appropriate mystery in Baltimore. He was said to have been kidnapped and doped by hoodlums who led him on election day from one polling place to another to vote numerous times. His poor health caused him to collapse from the strain, and he died shortly afterward. A marker commemorates his burial behind the church from October 9, 1849, to November 17, 1875; later he was moved to the Poe family plot.

EMILY POST (1872–September 25, 1960) **St. Mary's Cemetery, Tuxedo Park, New York** Author of best-selling etiquette book.

AYN RAND (1905–March 6, 1982) **Kensico Cemetery, Valhalla, New York** Founder of the philosophy of objectivism, which espouses "rational selfishness." Her philosophy is reflected in her popular books *The Fountainhead* (1943) and *Atlas Shrugged* (1957).

QUENTIN REYNOLDS (1902–March 17, 1965) **Holy Cross Cemetery, Brooklyn, New York** Writer, reported from Berlin in the 1930s, became war correspondent during World War II. Books include *London Diary* (1941), *I, Willie Sutton* (1953), *The Battle of Britain* (1953), *Minister of Death, the Eichmann Story* (1960).

JAMES WHITCOMB RILEY (1849–July 22, 1916) **Crown Hill Cemetery, Indianapolis, Indiana** Hoosier poet, buried at the highest point of the cemetery, an elegantly simple Greek temple above his grave.

MARY ROBERTS RINEHART (1876–September 22, 1958) **Arlington National Cemetery, Arlington, Virginia** Mystery writer, author of *The Circular Staircase* (1908).

EDWIN ARLINGTON ROBINSON (1869–April 6, 1935) **Gardiner Cemetery, Gardiner, Maine** Naturalist poet; his New England characters might be modeled on Gardiner; hemlock and laurel from the MacDowell Colony (see Musicians) covered his coffin.

THEODORE ROETHKE (1908–August 1, 1963) **Oakwood Cemetery, Saginaw, Michigan**   Poet; his work reflects his midwestern roots; suffered a heart attack while swimming in a pool with his friends nearby but oblivious to his danger.

CARL SANDBURG (1878–July 22, 1967) **Carl Sandburg Birthplace, Galesburg, Illinois**   *Remembrance Rock*, the title of the poet's only novel, refers to a park in which a rock, surrounded by four cedar trees, rests on soil from great historic sites: Plymouth Rock, Valley Forge, Gettysburg, and the Argonne in France, to commemorate World War I. The idea of remembrance was duplicated in the backyard of the poet's birthplace, with soil from every place Sandburg had lived and his parents' birthplaces in Sweden. Sandburg requested that after death his ashes be mixed with this soil. There is no tombstone. The rock has at its base a quote from the novel: "For it could be a place to come and remember."

DELMORE SCHWARTZ (1913–July 11, 1966) **Cedar Park Cemetery, Paramus, New Jersey**   Poet and editor of the *Partisan Review*; he suffered a heart attack while taking out the garbage, and his body lay unclaimed for two days in a morgue.

WALLACE STEVENS (1879–August 2, 1955) **Cedar Hill Cemetery, Hartford, Connecticut**   Modern poet noted for his subtle verse; *Harmonium* (1923) and *The Man with the Blue Guitar* (1937) are among his collections. Also was insurance company executive.

HARRIET BEECHER STOWE (1811–July 1, 1896) **Andover Chapel Cemetery, Phillips Academy, Andover, Massachusetts**   Author of *Uncle Tom's Cabin* (1852); wreath on her coffin from the black citizens of Boston was signed "The Children of Uncle Tom."

BOOTH TARKINGTON (1869–May 19, 1946) **Crown Hill Cemetery, Indianapolis, Indiana**   Novelist, best known for *Alice Adams* (1921) and *Seventeen* (1917).

SARA TEASDALE (1884–January 29, 1933) **Bellefontaine Cemetery, St. Louis, Missouri** A poet noted for her sensitivity and eccentricity, Teasdale lived a reclusive life and considered herself an invalid. She found it difficult to say good-bye and usually simply turned away and left the room. Suffering a severe depression, she saved up her sleeping pills and took them all at once just before taking a bath. As she requested, her tombstone reads "Sara Teasdale Filsinger," although she had divorced her husband in 1929.

HENRY DAVID THOREAU (1817–May 6, 1862) **Sleepy Hollow Cemetery, Concord, Massachusetts** Poet, essayist, naturalist; *Walden* (1854) describes his solitary experiences; buried opposite Nathaniel Hawthorne.

JAMES THURBER (1894–November 2, 1961) **Green Lawn Cemetery, Columbus, Ohio** Humorist, cartoonist, contributor to *The New Yorker* (1927–52).

WALLACE THURMAN (1902–December 22, 1934) **Silver Mount Cemetery, Staten Island, New York** Bohemian writer; his satirical works about the Harlem Renaissance disturbed both blacks and whites. He died of tuberculosis in a city hospital on New York's Welfare Island.

MARK TWAIN (Samuel Langhorne Clemens) (1835–April 21, 1910) **Woodlawn Cemetery, Elmira, New York** Popular author, creator of *Tom Sawyer* (1876) and *Huckleberry Finn* (1885). Elmira was his summer home.

MARK VAN DOREN (1894–December 10, 1972) **Cornwall Hollow Cemetery, Cornwall, Connecticut** Poet and teacher; wrote critical studies of Dryden (1920) and Hawthorne (1949) and several anthologies. His volumes of poetry include *Collected Poems, 1922–1938*, which won the Pulitzer Prize in 1939.

NOAH WEBSTER (1758–May 28, 1843) **Grove Street Cemetery, New Haven, Connecticut** Lexicographer and philologist, noted for his dictionary (1828).

WALT WHITMAN (1819–March 26, 1892) **Harleigh Cemetery, Camden, New Jersey** Poet whose free-verse *Leaves of Grass* (1855) had a revolutionary impact on American literature; his own design for his vault of rough stone was inspired by William Blake's poem *The Gates of Paradise.*

JOHN GREENLEAF WHITTIER (1807–September 7, 1892) **Union Cemetery, Amesbury, Massachusetts** Quaker poet (*Snow-Bound*, 1866), crusading abolitionist.

THORNTON WILDER (1897–December 7, 1975) **Mount Carmel Cemetery, Hamden, Connecticut** Playwright, best known for *Our Town* (1938).

WILLIAM CARLOS WILLIAMS (1883–March 4, 1963) **Hillside Cemetery, Lyndhurst, New Jersey** Modern poet, physician; noted especially for his five-volume poem *Paterson* (1946–58).

EDMUND WILSON (1895–June 12, 1972) **Pleasant Hill Cemetery, Wellfleet, Massachusetts** Literary and social critic, influential editor; among his books are *Axel's Castle* (1931), *To the Finland Station* (1940), *Scrolls from the Dead Sea* (1955).

THOMAS WOLFE (1900–September 15, 1938) **Riverside Cemetery, Asheville, North Carolina** Novelist, author of *You Can't Go Home Again* (1940), buried in his birthplace with his family: died of tuberculosis of the brain.

ALEXANDER WOOLLCOTT (1887–January 23, 1943) **Hamilton College Cemetery, Clinton, New York** Drama critic Woollcott, a man of acerbic wit and impeccable English usage, was stricken by a fatal heart attack while on a radio panel show. Unable to speak, he wrote "I AM SICK" on a piece of paper. Fellow panelist Rex Stout knew immediately that something was seriously wrong. "A healthier Woollcott would have printed: 'I AM ILL.'" Woollcott was buried at his alma mater, in the cemetery he termed "the last dormitory."

EXPLORERS AND SETTLERS

JOHN CAPEN "GRIZZLY" ADAMS (1812–October 25, 1860) Bay Path Cemetery, Charlton, Massachusetts   Adams was a respectable New England cobbler until he went west in 1849, made himself a suit of buckskin, and became a hunter of, and also friend to, grizzly bears. People said grizzlies could not be tamed, but Adams and his grizzly friends became familiar figures in the Rockies, on the streets of San Francisco, and in performances with P. T. Barnum. When Adams became mortally ill, Barnum ordered a buckskin hunting suit for his successor, but the mountain man outfoxed him by requesting that he be buried in the brand-new outfit. After his death, Barnum hired the best stonecutter in the area to carve a picture of Adams and his favorite bear, Gentle Ben, on the stone.

DANIEL BOONE (1734–September 26, 1820) Frankfort Cemetery, Frankfort, Kentucky   Explorer, pioneer, and guide, opened development of the Kentucky region; his daring exploits have given him the status of a legendary figure.

137

P. T. Barnum ordered this folk carving for the grave of hunter "Grizzly" Adams. It shows him with his favorite bear, Gentle Ben. (Ed Deane. Courtesy Bruce H. Lamprey)

JIM BRIDGER (1804–July 17, 1881) **Mount Washington Cemetery, Independence, Missouri**   Scout, explorer, and mountain man, he loved the untamed wilderness. Toward the end of his life, when his vision failed, he would say, "I wish I war back thar among the mountains again. A man kin see so much farther in that country." On his grave, an old friend put a memorial that shows his importance to the opening of the West: "Celebrated as hunter, trapper, fur trader and guide—Discovered Great Salt Lake in 1824, the South Pass 1827, Visited Yellowstone Lake and Geysers 1830. Founded Fort Bridger 1843. Opened Overland Route by Bridger's Pass to Great Salt Lake. . . ."

RICHARD E. BYRD (1888–March 11, 1957) **Arlington National Cemetery, Arlington, Virginia**   First man to fly across the North Pole (1926) and the South Pole (1929).

CALAMITY JANE (MARTHA JANE CANARY) (c. 1852–August 1, 1903) **Mount Moriah Cemetery, Deadwood, South Dakota**   "Bury me next to Wild Bill," murmured the pioneer scout as she lay dying. After the biggest funeral ever seen in Deadwood, her request was honored. She lies next to Wild Bill Hickok, the man she claimed was her lover and perhaps one of her twelve "husbands."

KIT CARSON (1809–May 23, 1868) **Kit Carson Cemetery, Taos, New Mexico** The old frontiersman died lying on buffalo robes on the floor of a house at Fort Lyon on the Arkansas River. After several weeks of a limited diet, he had demanded a heavy dinner of his favorite buffalo steak and a bowl of coffee followed by a smoke, although he was warned it could be fatal. It was. He was buried with military honors in Taos. The only flowers available were white paper flowers from the women's bonnets, which were put in his rough-planked coffin.

JESSE CHISHOLM (1806–March 4, 1868) **Jesse Chisholm Gravesite, Geary, Oklahoma** Chisholm, who was part Chero-

Trailbreaker Jesse Chisholm lies in an unmarked site in an old Indian burial ground. This tribute to his hospitality was erected later.

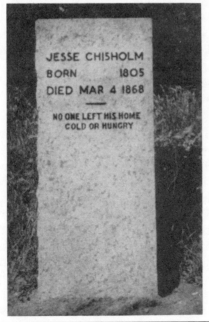

kee, laid out the 220-mile trail running from the Mexican border to Abilene that became the one great highway for ranchers driving cattle northward. He died of ptomaine poisoning after eating some bear stew and was buried in an old Indian burying ground in Left-Hand Spring. The plot was unmarked, as were all Indian graves, but a monument was put up in 1938 to the man who expressed the highest ideals of western hospitality: "No one left his home cold or hungry."

WILLIAM CLARK (1770–September 1, 1838) **Bellefontaine Cemetery, St. Louis, Missouri**   With Meriwether Lewis, led expedition to the Northwest Territory (1804–06).

WILLIAM "BUFFALO BILL" CODY (1846–January 10, 1917) **Buffalo Bill Memorial Museum and Grave, Lookout Mountain, Colorado**   Hunter, scout, star of his own Wild West Show.

HENRY T. P. COMSTOCK (1820–September 27, 1870?) **Sunset Hills Cemetery, Bozeman, Montana**   His name was attached to the most famous mining strike in history, the Comstock Lode, but Comstock, like most prospectors, sold out at the first chance. His claim, the Ophir Mine, later produced millions for its owners. Fortune never again smiled on Comstock. Finally, down to his last penny, he committed suicide. His grave was unmarked for many years until a subscription fund was raised for a large headstone.

JULIEN DuBUQUE (1762–March 24, 1810) **Julien DuBuque Monument Preserve, Dubuque, Iowa**   The founder of Dubuque, Iowa, was the first white man to settle permanently in the state. He was first buried on a bluff overlooking the Mississippi and was soon joined by his Indian friend and father-in-law, Chief Peosta. When DuBuque's remains were disinterred in 1897 for reburial in a twenty-eight-foot-high memorial tower, Peosta's bones were removed and wired together, and his skeleton was placed on a pedestal. The bones of DuBuque's Indian bride, Petosta, were shown in the Indian artifacts section of a museum until complaints about the display of both Indians caused them to be removed and buried about fifty feet from DuBuque's grave.

WYATT EARP (1848–January 13, 1929) **Hills of Eternity Cemetery, Colma, California**   Famed western law officer of frontier days, spent his last years in a small Los Angeles cottage. William S. Hart and Tom Mix (see Entertainers) were among his pallbearers.

JOHN C. FREMONT (1813–July 13, 1890) **Rockland Cemetery, Sparkill, New York**   Known as the "Pathfinder," he mapped out the Oregon Trail and the South Pass in the Rockies.

MATTHEW A. HENSON (1866–March 9, 1955) **Woodlawn Cemetery, Bronx, New York**   Accompanied Peary and planted the U.S. flag at the North Pole (1909).

WILD BILL HICKOK (1837–August 2, 1876) **Mount Moriah Cemetery, Deadwood, South Dakota**   The western hero was a dead shot with a pistol and had killed some twenty-one men, all in fair fights. On August 2, 1876, he joined a poker game in Deadwood's Saloon No. 10 and, contrary to his usual practice, sat with his back to the door. In the middle of the game, Jack McCall shot Bill Hickok in the back of the head with a .45 pistol. Wild Bill fell over the table, dying instantly, while his hand—a pair of black aces, a pair of black eights, and a jack of diamonds—fell to the floor. This combination is still known as the "deadman's hand." An iron fence protects his grave, which was once marked by a rough sandstone obelisk about six feet tall with a bust of Wild Bill on top.

MERIWETHER LEWIS (1774–October 11, 1809) **Meriwether Lewis Park, near Hohenwald, Tennessee**   The young explorer who, with William Clark, found a land route to the Pacific was found dead in an isolated frontier cabin and was thought to have killed himself, although some suspicion fell on his "hosts." His body was buried in a clearing near the house, in a coffin of hewn oak planks fastened with iron nails made by a nearby smith. In 1848 the state erected a monument on the site; it is a broken column, symbolizing his early death.

CHARLES A. LINDBERGH (1902–August 26, 1974) **Kipahulu Hawaiian Churchyard, Kipahulu, Maui, Hawaii**   As soon as New York doctors told him he was dying, the famed aviator made arrangements to return to Maui, his favorite home. With only days to live, he made plans for his burial, requesting daily reports on the digging of his grave, which was hewn out of rock. He ordered the simplest coffin possible, made of eucalyptus wood, and burial in khaki trousers and a plain shirt. At each of the four corners of Lindbergh's grave plumeria plants mark the burial place of gibbons he had owned. His epitaph is taken from his writings: "If I take the wings of morning and dwell in the uttermost parts of the sea."

Monument to explorer Meriwether Lewis. A broken column was often used to symbolize an early death. (National Park Service)

JACQUES MARQUETTE (1637–May 18, 1675) **Fr. Marquette Monument, St. Ignace, Michigan**   Missionary, explored the Mississippi River; died near the mouth of the Marquette River and was buried at the mission he had founded. Two hundred years later (1877) his remains were unearthed and reburied.

WILLIAM BARCLAY "BAT" MASTERSON (1853–October 25, 1921) **Woodlawn Cemetery, Bronx, New York**   Noted marshal of the west, worked in Tombstone and Dodge City, ultimately joined the New York City police force.

ROBERT E. PEARY (1856–February 20, 1920) **Arlington National Cemetery, Arlington, Virginia**   Led first expedition to reach the North Pole (1909).

ZEBULON MONTGOMERY PIKE (1779–April 27, 1813) **Military Cemetery, Sackets Harbor, New York**   Explorer Pike, who never did reach the summit of the Colorado peak named for him, died in the East during the War of 1812; he was buried in a cemetery outside Fort Tompkins, preserved in a hogshead of whiskey, according to legend. Because of flooding, the entire graveyard was moved in 1909 and the bones were reinterred. A whiskey-filled casket with a glass top was unearthed, and as it was moved the glass broke and the body immediately disintegrated. A marker was later erected at what is believed to be Pike's grave.

JUAN PONCE DE LEON (c. 1460–1521) **Metropolitan Cathedral, San Juan, Puerto Rico**   Discovered Florida while searching for the legendary fountain of youth (1513); also explored Puerto Rico.

WILEY POST (1899–August 15, 1935) **Fairlawn Cemetery, Oklahoma City, Oklahoma**   The aviator, who had flown around the northern part of the earth in a record 8 days, 15 hours, and 51 minutes in 1931, died in a plane crash near Point Barrow, Alaska. This accident was a double tragedy because Post's passenger was the raconteur Will Rogers (see Entertainers). Post was flown home and lay in the State Capitol building as airplanes circled slowly overhead, trailing crepe streamers, and visitors paid their respects. When his body was removed from the Capitol the planes dipped low and dropped the streamers and wreaths.

JOHN SWAIN SLAUGHTER (1845–February 8, 1945) **Boot Hill Graveyard, Tombstone, Arizona**   Born a slave, he became a well-known cowboy and once fought a one-round boxing match with world champion John L. Sullivan and lost, commemorated by a tablet at his grave site erected by black soldiers.

JOHN STEWART (?–1823) **Old Mission Church Cemetery, Upper Sandusky, Ohio**   Black missionary to the Wyandotte Indians in Ohio.

JOHN SUTTER (1803–June 18, 1880) **Lititz Moravian Cemetery, Lititz, Pennsylvania**   A pioneer in the settlement of California; gold was first discovered on his property, Fort Sutter. Gold fever seized everyone when word of the find got out; his land was overrun by squatters and his enterprises were ruined. With only a small pension from the state of California, he moved to Lititz, and spent the rest of his life petitioning the federal government for compensation for his acreage. At his death, the Moravian Brethren broke with their tradition and allowed him, a non-Moravian, to be buried in their cemetery, as he had wished. When Mrs. Sutter died seven months later they made another exception to their custom, which segregates the graves of the Sisters from those of the Brothers by a wide grassy aisle, and allowed her to lie in the same vault as her husband.

MARCUS WHITMAN (1802–November 29, 1847) **NARCISSA WHITMAN** (1808–November 29, 1847) **Whitman National Monument, Walla Walla, Washington**   Protestant missionaries to the Indians, the Whitmans were prominent in opening up the Pacific Northwest to settlement. They were massacred by the Cayuse at their mission and buried in a shallow grave nearby. Ironically, a Catholic missionary, one of their antagonists, happened by and was the only clergyman available to perform a funeral ceremony. The bodies of the Whitmans were moved to the present site on the fiftieth anniversary of the massacre and marked by a marble slab with the names of all the victims of the uprising.

GOVERNMENT LEADERS

DEAN ACHESON (1893–October 12, 1971) **Oak Hill Cemetery, Washington, D.C.** Secretary of state under Truman, a primary developer of cold war foreign policy.

SAMUEL ADAMS (1722–October 2, 1803) **Granary Burying Ground, Boston, Massachusetts** Signer of the Declaration of Independence and Boston Tea Party firebrand.

STEPHEN F. AUSTIN (1793–December 27, 1836) **State Cemetery, Austin, Texas** A leader in the fight for Texan independence from Mexico.

BERNARD M. BARUCH (1870–June 20, 1965) **Flushing Cemetery, Flushing, Queens, New York** After building a fortune through speculation in stocks before he was thirty, Baruch became national defense adviser in the First and Second World Wars.

THOMAS HART BENTON (1782–April 10, 1858) **Bellefontaine Cemetery, St. Louis, Missouri**   Missouri senator, championed agrarian interests.

JAMES G. BLAINE (1830–January 27, 1893) **Blaine Memorial Park, Augusta, Maine**   Republican politician and diplomat, influential in launching the Pan-American movement.

WILLIAM E. BORAH (1865–January 19, 1940) **Morris Hill Cemetery, Boise, Idaho**   Isolationist senator, led the fight against joining the League of Nations.

WILLIAM JENNINGS BRYAN (1860–July 26, 1925) **Arlington National Cemetery, Arlington, Virginia**   Leader of agrarian and free silver forces, three-time loser for the presidency; he is one of the few pacifists buried in the military cemetery.

RALPH BUNCHE (1904–December 9, 1971) **Woodlawn Cemetery, Bronx, New York**   U.N. diplomat, first black to win the Nobel Peace Prize (1950, for his efforts at mediating peace in the Middle East as head of U.N. Palestine Commission).

AARON BURR (1756–September 14, 1836) **Princeton Cemetery, Princeton, New Jersey**   Vice-president (1801–1805), tried for treason in 1807 and acquitted; killed Alexander Hamilton after challenging him to a duel.

JOHN C. CALHOUN (1782–March 31, 1850) **St. Philip's Churchyard, Charleston, South Carolina**   States'-righter Calhoun died convinced that he had failed to save either the Union or the South. Free passage to his funeral in Charleston was granted by railroad and steamship companies, and thousands came to pay their respects. They threw gold cloth roses on the coffin until the bier and the floor around it were a carpet of flowers. During the Civil War a company of soldiers guarded the tomb around the clock. When fighting came within earshot of Charleston, the sexton of St. Philip's dug up the body and reburied it at night beneath the church to avoid its desecration by northern troops.

HENRY CLAY (1777–June 29, 1852) **Lexington Cemetery, Lexington, Kentucky**   Called the "Great Compromiser," as senator made significant attempts to mediate between North and South.

DE WITT CLINTON (1769–February 11, 1828) **Green-Wood Cemetery, Brooklyn, New York** Governor of New York (1817–21, 1825–28), responsible for promoting idea of the Erie Canal.

JAMES M. COX (1870–July 15, 1957) **Woodland Cemetery, Dayton, Ohio** Politician, newspaper publisher, and governor of Ohio.

RICHARD DALEY (1902–December 20, 1976) **Holy Sepulchre Cemetery, Worth, Illinois** Mayor and boss of Chicago, especially visible during the 1968 Democratic National Convention, when Yippies invaded the city.

JEFFERSON DAVIS (1808–December 6, 1889) **Hollywood Cemetery, Richmond, Virginia** As many as 150,000 attended the funeral of the president of the Confederacy in New Orleans,

The body of Jefferson Davis was moved to Richmond's Hollywood Cemetery to rest with other Confederate heroes. (Hollywood Cemetery)

and fourteen Confederate generals were his pallbearers. In 1893 the governor of Virginia convinced his widow that all great southerners were buried in Virginia and Davis was taken on a funeral train to Richmond, given a full-scale military funeral, and buried not far from the graves of presidents Madison and Tyler. His tombstone reads: "Jefferson Davis/At Rest/An American Soldier/ And Defender of the Constitution/(1808–89)."

CHARLES G. DAWES (1865–April 23, 1951) **Rosehill Cemetery, Chicago, Illinois** Coolidge's vice-president, winner of Nobel Peace Prize (1925) for advancing the League of Nations.

THOMAS E. DEWEY (1902–March 16, 1971) **Pawling Cemetery, Pawling, New York** Three-term Republican governor of New York, twice unsuccessful candidate for president.

EVERETT McKINLEY DIRKSEN (1896–September 7, 1969) **Glendale Memorial Gardens, Pekin, Illinois** Known for a baroque oratorial style and honey-dipped voice, Dirksen lay in state in the Capitol Rotunda on the same wooden catafalque used for Lincoln, who was also an Illinois Republican.

STEPHEN A. DOUGLAS (1813–June 3, 1861) **Douglas Monument Park, Chicago, Illinois** Politician and orator, noted for his debates with Abraham Lincoln (1858). Called "the little giant"; his 100-foot-high monument is topped by a bronze statue.

JOHN FOSTER DULLES (1888–May 24, 1959) **Arlington National Cemetery, Arlington, Virginia** Secretary of state (1953–59), primary developer of policy of containment that sought to limit expansion of Soviet control to other countries. He is buried at one of the highest points in Arlington, looking across to the Lincoln Memorial and the Washington Monument.

MIRIAM "MA" FERGUSON (1875–June 25, 1961) **State Cemetery, Austin, Texas** Elected governor of Texas (1924) in place of her husband, who had been impeached for corruption; one of the first woman governors.

HAMILTON FISH (1808–September 6, 1893) **Cemetery of St. Philip's Church, Highlands, Garrison, New York**   Politician, diplomat, fought corruption in the Grant administration.

JAMES FORRESTAL (1892–May 22, 1949) **Arlington National Cemetery, Arlington, Virginia**   Forrestal resigned as secretary of defense two months before he plunged to his death from the sixteenth floor of the Bethesda Naval Hospital. Undergoing treatment for paranoia and extreme depression, he had imagined communist plotters everywhere. The inscription on his tombstone notes that he served "In the Cause of Good Government."

BENJAMIN FRANKLIN (1706–April 17, 1790) **Christ Church Burial Ground, Philadelphia, Pennsylvania**   As a young man, Franklin jotted down the following epitaph to amuse his friends:

> The Body of
> B. Franklin, Printer,
> Like the Cover of an old Book,
> Its Contents torn out,
> And stript of its Lettering & Gilding,
> Lies here, Food for Worms.

> But the Work shall not be lost;
> For it will, as he believe'd
> appear once more
> In a new and more elegant Edition
> Corrected and improved
> By the Author.

Franklin's grave is marked, as he instructed, with only his name and that of his wife, but the youthful epitaph can be found inscribed on a tablet nearby.

ALBERT GALLATIN (1761–August 13, 1849) **Trinity Churchyard, New York, New York**   Second secretary of the treasury (1801–14), longest to hold that position.

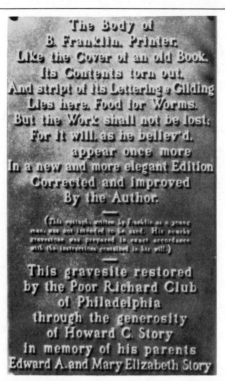

A youthful Benjamin Franklin wrote this epitaph as a joke. It was not used but is on a plaque near his actual burial site. (Christ Church, Philadelphia, Pennsylvania)

ELBRIDGE GERRY (1744–November 23, 1814) **Congressional Cemetery, Washington, D.C.** Gerry, vice-president under Madison, died on the way to the Capitol fulfilling his injunction that "It is the duty of every citizen though he may have but one day to live, to devote that day to the good of his country." The term "gerrymander" comes from his support of a partisan redistricting bill.

ELLA T. GRASSO (1919–February 5, 1981) **Saint Mary's Cemetery, Windsor Locks, Connecticut** First woman governor elected in her own right without succeeding her husband.

ALEXANDER HAMILTON (1755–July 12, 1804) **Trinity Churchyard, New York, New York** After his son fell in a duel, the former secretary of the treasury resolved never to participate in one. Aaron Burr, Hamilton's archenemy, called him out over a reputed slur, and Hamilton reluctantly journeyed to the dueling site in Weehawken, New Jersey. He raised and lowered his gun several times, as if to try its position, and remarked, "I beg your pardon for delaying you but the direction of the light renders it necessary." Then he put on his spectacles and announced he was ready to begin. Burr's unchallenged bullet penetrated his liver, inflicting a mortal wound.

JOHN HANCOCK (1737–October 8, 1793) **Granary Burying Ground, Boston, Massachusetts** First signer of the Declaration of Independence, Revolutionary leader.

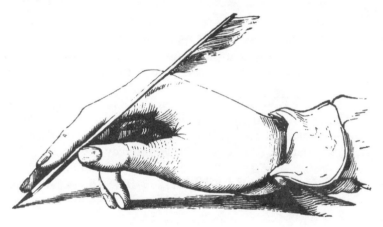

JOHN HAY (1838–July 1, 1905) **Lake View Cemetery, Cleveland, Ohio** As secretary of state (1896–1905) devised Open Door Policy toward China.

PATRICK HENRY (1736–June 6, 1799) **Red Hill Shrine, Brookneal, Virginia** Orator ("Give me liberty, or give me death") and Revolutionary leader; his tablet reads: "His fame is his best epitaph."

J. EDGAR HOOVER (1895–May 2, 1972) **Congressional Cemetery, Washington, D.C.** Powerful, longtime head of the Federal Bureau of Investigation (1924–72).

SAMUEL HOUSTON (1793–July 26, 1863) **Oakwood Cemetery, Huntsville, Texas**   Commanded Texas forces in victory over Mexico; on his monument is a tribute from Andrew Jackson: "The world will take care of Houston's fame."

CORDELL HULL (1871–July 23, 1955) **Washington Cathedral, Washington, D.C.**   Secretary of state and an organizer of the U.N.

HUBERT H. HUMPHREY (1911–July 14, 1978) **Lakewood Cemetery, Minneapolis, Minnesota**   Senator, vice-president, leading liberal, defeated by Richard M. Nixon for presidency in 1968.

JOHN JAY (1745–May 14, 1829) **John Jay Cemetery, Rye, New York**   Statesman, diplomat; he bequeathed two hundred dollars to the poor rather than have an elaborate funeral.

ROBERT F. KENNEDY (1925–June 6, 1968) **Arlington National Cemetery, Arlington, Virginia**   Attorney general, New York senator; assassinated during campaign for Democratic presidential nomination. Brother of John F. Kennedy (see Presidents).

ROBERT M. LA FOLLETTE (1855–June 18, 1925) **Forest Hill Cemetery, Madison, Wisconsin**   Leader of Republican Progressives, senator.

FIORELLO H. LAGUARDIA (1882–September 20, 1947) **Woodlawn Cemetery, Bronx, New York**   Popular mayor of New York City (1933–45).

ROBERT R. LIVINGSTON (1746–February 25, 1813) **St. Paul's Episcopal Church, Tivoli, New York**   Diplomat, administered oath of office to Washington at first inaugural.

HENRY CABOT LODGE (1850–November 9, 1924) **Mount Auburn Cemetery, Cambridge, Massachusetts**   Conservative Republican senator (1893–1924) opposed U.S. entry into the League of Nations and World Court. Before entering politics had a career as editor and biographer.

HUEY P. LONG (1893–September 10, 1935) **State House grounds, Baton Rouge, Louisiana** Governor, then senator, and the state's unchallenged dictator, Long was assassinated in his five-million-dollar statehouse by a young physician. After the shots rang out, pandemonium reigned, and all attention focused on the doctor, who was gunned down with sixty-one bullet holes in his body. Long, virtually unnoticed, staggered down the imposing staircase and fell into the arms of a commissioner, who took him to the hospital in a cab. His only remark during the journey was "I wonder why he shot me."

JOSEPH R. McCARTHY (1908–May 2, 1957) **Cemetery of St. Mary's Roman Catholic Church, Appleton, Wisconsin** Senator, led witch hunt for subversives in government.

JOHN W. McCORMACK (1892–November 22, 1980) **St. Joseph Cemetery, Boston, Massachusetts** First Roman Catholic Speaker of the House (1962–71).

HENRY MORGENTHAU, JR. (1891–February 6, 1967) **Mount Pleasant Memorial Park, Hawthorne, New York** Secretary of treasury, (1934–45), raised funds to finance the New Deal.

GOUVERNEUR MORRIS (1752–November 6, 1816) **St. Anne's Episcopal Churchyard, Bronx, New York** Revolutionary diplomat and financial expert, planned decimal system of coinage.

WAYNE MORSE (1900–July 22, 1974) **Rest Haven Memorial Park, Eugene, Oregon** Liberal senator, an early opponent of Vietnam war.

GEORGE W. NORRIS (1861–September 3, 1944) **Memorial Park, McCook, Nebraska** Senator, influential in creation of Tennessee Valley Authority (1933).

THOMAS PENDERGAST (1872–January 26, 1945) **Calvary Cemetery, Kansas City, Missouri** Democratic boss of Kansas City and the state until he was convicted of income tax evasion and sent to prison.

ADAM CLAYTON POWELL, JR. (1908–April 4, 1972) **Woodlawn Cemetery, Bronx, New York** Prominent black congressman and minister; excluded from the House for alleged improprieties (1967).

JOHN RANDOLPH (1773–May 24, 1833) **Hollywood Cemetery, Richmond, Virginia** States' rights advocate; originally buried on his Roanoke plantation facing west, at his request, to keep an eye on compromiser Henry Clay.

SAM RAYBURN (1882–November 16, 1961) **Willow Wild Cemetery, Bonham, Texas** When he died, the chair of the Speaker of the House was draped in black and flowers were placed on the desk in front of it. He had held the post twice as long as anyone previously (1940–47, 1949–53, 1955–61) and was responsible for the passage of much New Deal legislation.

NELSON A. ROCKEFELLER (1908–January 26, 1979) **Rockefeller Family Cemetery, North Tarrytown, New York** Used his share of the Rockefeller fortune to assemble a distinguished art collection and for philanthropic ends; he pursued a career in public service and politics. Governor of New York (1958–73) and vice-president of the U.S. by appointment (1974–77), Rockefeller died of a heart attack while alone with a young assistant with whom it was rumored he was having an affair. Because of these compromising circumstances, there were questions about the speed with which medical help was called and misleading stories concerning his death were originally given to the press.

ELEANOR ROOSEVELT (1884–November 7, 1962) **Franklin D. Roosevelt National Historic Site, Hyde Park, New York** Humanitarian, diplomat, first of the modern First Ladies.

ELIHU ROOT (1845–February 7, 1937) **Hamilton College Cemetery, Clinton, New York** Holder of several cabinet posts, senator, winner of Nobel Peace Prize (1912) for his efforts toward international peace.

NELLIE TAYLOE ROSS (1876–December 19, 1977) **Lakeview Cemetery, Cheyenne, Wyoming** First woman to be inaugurated as state governor (1925).

EDMUND RUFFIN (1795–June 18, 1865) **"Marlbourne Estate," Hanover County, Virginia** One of the most vehement secessionists, he fired the first shot on Fort Sumter; he committed suicide after the Civil War.

CARL SCHURZ (1829–May 14, 1906) **Sleepy Hollow Cemetery, North Tarrytown, New York** Came to U.S. in 1852 from Germany and supported Lincoln's political career. He voluntarily resigned his diplomatic post to participate in the Civil War. Later an influential senator (1869–75), writer, and editor.

WILLIAM H. SEWARD (1801–October 15, 1872) **Fort Hill Cemetery, Auburn, New York** Secretary of state under Lincoln; responsible for purchase of Alaska.

ALFRED E. SMITH (1873–October 4, 1944) **Calvary Cemetery, Woodside, Queens, New York** Four-time governor of New York and first Roman Catholic to run for president (1928).

EDWIN M. STANTON (1814–December 24, 1869) **Congressional Cemetery, Washington, D.C.** Secretary of war during Civil War.

ALEXANDER HAMILTON STEPHENS (1812–March 4, 1883) **Liberty Hall, Alexander H. Stephens Memorial State Park, Crawfordville, Georgia** Vice-president of Confederacy; tombstone reads: "Non sibi, sed aliis," Latin for "Not for himself, but for others."

THADDEUS STEVENS (1792–August 11, 1868) **Shreiner's Cemetery, Lancaster, Pennsylvania** A powerful congressman during Reconstruction and a champion of equal rights for blacks, Stevens chose to be buried in a small graveyard and explained why on his tombstone: "I repose in this quiet and secluded spot, not from any natural preference for solitude, but, finding other cemeteries limited by charter rules as to race, I have chosen this that I might illustrate in my death the principles which I advocated through a long life—Equality of Man before his Creator."

ADLAI E. STEVENSON (1900–July 14, 1965) **Evergreen Memorial Cemetery, Bloomington, Illinois**   Governor of Illinois, two-time Democratic candidate for president; his funeral was held in Washington Cathedral.

HENRY L. STIMSON (1867–October 20, 1950) **Memorial Cemetery of St. John's Church, Cold Spring Harbor, Long Island, New York**   Cabinet officer under four presidents, made deciding recommendation to Truman to drop the atom bomb.

CHARLES SUMNER (1811–March 11, 1874) **Mount Auburn Cemetery, Cambridge, Massachusetts**   Senator, abolitionist, leader of radical Republicans during Reconstruction; his funeral procession, over a mile long, included many blacks.

ROBERT A. TAFT (1889–July 31, 1953) **Indian Hill Episcopal-Presbyterian Churchyard, Cincinnati, Ohio**   Called "Mr. Republican," senator from 1939 to 1953; sponsored Taft-Hartley Labor Act (1947) regulating labor disputes. Noted for his stands against international alliances and in favor of conservative economic policies.

SAMUEL TILDEN (1814–August 4, 1886) **Presbyterian Church Cemetery, New Lebanon, New York**   Democratic presidential candidate (1876), lost by one electoral vote to Rutherford B. Hayes (see Presidents) in a controversial election.

WILLIAM M. TWEED (1823–April 12, 1878) **Green-Wood Cemetery, Brooklyn, New York**   The boss of New York City's Tammany Hall political machine, Tweed was undone by the cartoons of Thomas Nast, which led to an investigation of his misdeeds. He died in the Ludlow Street Jail, where he had been imprisoned for a year. He lay in state on the bed in jail, his three-hundred-pound body dressed in a white nightshirt and kept on ice until the funeral was arranged.

ARTHUR H. VANDENBERG (1884–April 18, 1951) **Oakhill Cemetery, Grand Rapids, Michigan**   Senator, committed isolationist, later architect of a bipartisan policy for international cooperation.

HENRY A. WALLACE (1888–November 18, 1965) **Glendale Cemetery, Des Moines, Iowa**   Vice-president under Franklin D. Roosevelt (1941–45), Progressive Party presidential candidate (1948).

DANIEL WEBSTER (1782–October 24, 1852) **Governor Winslow Cemetery, Marshfield, Massachusetts**   Senator, orator, devoted to the survival of the Union.

WENDELL L. WILLKIE (1892–October 8, 1944) **East Hill Cemetery, Rushville, Indiana**   Proponent of "One World" internationalism, Republican presidential candidate (1940).

SPORTS FIGURES

FORREST C. ALLEN (1885–September 19, 1974) **Oak Hill Cemetery, Lawrence, Kansas** Thirty-nine-year coach of the University of Kansas: basketball became an official Olympic event (1936) as a result of his efforts; called "Phog" for his foghorn voice.

MAX BAER (1909–November 21, 1959) **St. Mary's Cemetery and Mausoleum, Sacramento, California** Madcap Maxie, heavyweight champion (1934–35), died of a heart attack while shaving.

WALTER CAMP (1859–March 14, 1925) **Evergreen Cemetery, New Haven, Connecticut** Father of American football, he drew up the original rules and created the eleven-player team; Yale's first coach (1888), he selected the first all-American team and continued to do so for thirty-six years.

TY COBB (1886–July 16, 1961) **Rose Hill Cemetery, Royston, Georgia** Created or equaled more major league baseball records than any other player, batted over .300 in seventeen consecutive seasons.

MAUREEN CONNOLLY (1934–June 21, 1969) **Sparkman-Hillcrest Memorial Park, Dallas, Texas** After she became, in 1953, the first woman to win the Grand Slam—the U.S. Open, Wimbledon, the Australian Open, and the French Open—her tennis career ended the following year when her leg was injured in a riding accident and never healed properly. "Little Mo" died at age thirty-four of cancer and was buried on the opening day of Wimbledon, where flags were flown at half-staff in her honor.

JIM CORBETT (1866–February 18, 1933) **Cypress Hills Cemetery, Brooklyn, New York** Heavyweight champion from 1892 to 1897, Gentleman Jim raised boxing from a brawl to a sport.

ELY CULBERTSON (1891–December 27, 1955) **Meetinghouse Hill Cemetery, Brattleboro, Vermont** Introduced the bidding system, which replaced auction bridge.

DWIGHT DAVIS (1879–November 28, 1945) **Arlington National Cemetery, Arlington, Virginia** Tennis player and donor of the Davis Cup, as well as diplomat and cabinet officer.

DIZZY DEAN (1911–July 17, 1974) **Bond Cemetery, Bond, Mississippi** Fastball pitcher for St. Louis Cardinals (1930–37), Dean became a colorful sports commentator on radio and television, noted for his unique descriptions of the games.

JACK DEMPSEY (1862–November 2, 1895) **Mount Calvary Cemetery, Portland, Oregon** Dempsey, the first middleweight champion (1884, '86, '87, and '90), not the modern heavyweight, was called "The Nonpareil" and after his death was the subject of numerous tales. One of the most persistent was that he had been buried in an unmarked grave and totally neglected. A local reporter wrote a poem about this sad situation, and it was rumored that Dempsey's friends financed a tombstone with the poem inscribed on it. Actually, Dempsey's grave was marked all along; "John E. Dempsey" is the inscription on the stone his wife erected shortly after his burial.

RALPH DePALMA (1883–March 31, 1956) **Holy Cross Cemetery, Los Angeles, California** Winner of more races than any other driver, 2,557 out of 2,889.

ABNER DOUBLEDAY (1819–January 26, 1893) **Arlington National Cemetery, Arlington, Virginia** Credited with being the originator of baseball.

BOB FITZSIMMONS (1862–October 22, 1917) **Graceland Cemetery, Chicago, Illinois** Won the heavyweight boxing championship from Corbett (1897) and lost to Jeffries (1899).

JAMES "SUNNY JIM" FITZSIMMONS (1874–March 11, 1966) **Holy Cross Cemetery, Brooklyn, New York** Best-known horse trainer of all time, had 2,275 winners that brought in $13,082,911.

FRANKIE FRISCH (1898–March 12, 1973) **Woodlawn Cemetery, Bronx, New York** Played with the New York Giants and St. Louis Cardinals, with a lifetime batting average of .316.

LOU GEHRIG (1903–June 2, 1941) **Kensico Cemetery, Valhalla, New York** Called the "Pride of the Yankees," Gehrig set a record of 2,130 consecutive games played. Fans sorrowed when at the height of his career he was stricken with amyotrophic lateral sclerosis, a rare disease affecting the spinal cord, and died at the age of thirty-seven. His services featured no eulogy, for, in the words of the minister, "We need none because you all knew him."

WARREN GILES (1896–February 7, 1979) **Riverside Cemetery, Moline, Illinois** President of the National League, raised that organization to baseball dominance.

LEFTY GROVE (1900–May 23, 1975) **Frostburg Memorial Park, Frostburg, Maryland** Pitcher, 300-game winner.

WALTER C. HAGEN (1892–October 6, 1969) **Holy Sepulchre Cemetery, Southfield, Michigan** Often called the father of professional golf, he won the most Professional Golf Association championships.

HANOVER (1884–99) **University of Kentucky, Lexington, Kentucky** Famous racehorse; skeleton is on display.

RAY HARROUN (1879–January 19, 1968) **Anderson Memorial Park, Anderson, Indiana** Won the first Indianapolis auto race in 1911 at 74.59 mph on a two-and-a-half-mile track.

FREEMAN HATCH (1820–89) **Evergreen Cemetery, Eastham, Massachusetts** His epitaph reads: "In 1852 he became famous making the astonishing passage in a clipper ship Northern Light from San Francisco to Boston in 76 days 8 hours an achievement won by no mortal before or since."

JOHN W. HEISMAN (1869–October 3, 1936) **Rhinelander Cemetery, Rhinelander, Wisconsin** College football coach; high point of his career was with Georgia Tech (1914–18), where his teams went thirty-three games undefeated and in 1916 registered a record 222–0 victory over Cumberland.

A granite baseball marks the grave of William A. Hulbert, founder of the National League. (National Baseball Hall of Fame and Museum, Inc.)

GIL HODGES (1924–April 2, 1972) **Holy Cross Cemetery, Brooklyn, New York** First baseman of the Brooklyn Dodgers (1943–61), later manager of the New York Mets.

WILLIAM A. HULBERT (1832–April 10, 1882) **Graceland Cemetery, Chicago, Illinois** Founder of the National League. His grave is marked by a large granite baseball.

JAMES J. JEFFRIES (1875–March 3, 1953) **Inglewood Park Cemetery, Inglewood, California** Heavyweight champion (1899–1905), retired undefeated.

JACK JOHNSON (1878–June 10, 1946) **Graceland Cemetery, Chicago, Illinois** The first American black to hold the heavyweight boxing title (1908–15). Johnson was killed when his car hit an abutment. His tombstone bears the comment made when he was found: "Johnson—Is In Terrible Shape." The upkeep of his grave has been supported by the Boxing Writers Association and *Ring* magazine since the discovery that it was not well cared for.

BOBBY JONES (1902–December 18, 1971) **Oakland Cemetery, Atlanta, Georgia** Called "Emperor Jones," he won a record thirteen U.S. and British golf championships between 1923 and 1930.

KENESAW MOUNTAIN LANDIS (1866–November 25, 1944) **Oak Woods Cemetery, Chicago, Illinois** Baseball's first commissioner (1920–44).

EMANUAL LASKER (1868–January 11, 1941) **Shearith Israel Cemetery, Glendale, Queens, New York** World champion chess player for twenty-seven years, 1894–1921.

BENNY LEONARD (1896–April 18, 1947) **Mount Carmel Cemetery, Glendale, Queens, New York** World lightweight champion (1917–25), died in the ring while refereeing a match.

LEXINGTON (1850–July 1, 1875) **Smithsonian Museum of Natural History, Osteology Hall, Washington, D.C.** Champion racehorse, and sire to many others, including Preakness; he was

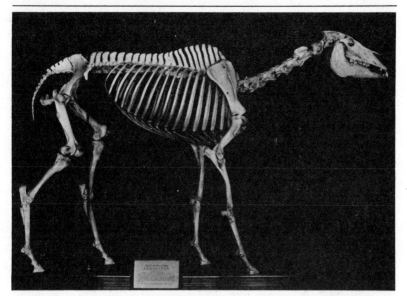

Lexington, champion racehorse and sire, has a permanent address at the Smithsonian Museum of Natural History. (Smithsonian Institution)

first buried in front of the Kentucky stables housing his "harem" of brood mares. After his owner donated Lexington's bones to the museum, he was disinterred and his skeleton mounted for exhibit.

SONNY LISTON (c. 1932–c. December 29, 1970) **Paradise Memorial Gardens, Las Vegas, Nevada** Liston's body was discovered on January 5, 1971, and the coroner estimated that the boxer had been dead for about a week. His death, attributed to narcotics, apparently occurred when he fell over backward while putting on his shoes, breaking the footboard of the bed. The television set was still on in the room, which contained a rattlesnake tail and a .38-caliber revolver. An ex-convict who never had learned to read or write, Liston suffered only one loss in thirty-four bouts before beating Floyd Patterson for the heavyweight title in 1962 with a knockout in the first round.

VINCE LOMBARDI (1913–September 3, 1970) **Mount Olivet Cemetery, Middletown, New Jersey** Coach of Green Bay Packers football team (1959–69), led them to Super Bowl championships in 1967 and 1968.

JOE LOUIS (1914–April 12, 1981) **Arlington National Cemetery, Arlington, Virginia**   When the twelve-year (1937–49) heavyweight champion died, his body lay in state at Caesar's Palace in Las Vegas, where he had been employed during the last ten years of his life. The boxing ring of the hotel was the pulpit for his funeral service. Frank Sinatra commented, "It's kind of nice to know the man who never rested on canvas now sleeps on clouds." Restrictions for burial in Arlington were waived by the president for the quiet son of an Alabama sharecropper who had been an army sergeant in World War II but did not see action. Three rifle volleys were fired across his coffin, and "Taps" was played.

CONNIE MACK (1862–February 8, 1956) **Holy Sepulchre Cemetery, Philadelphia, Pennsylvania**   Began career as catcher in 1886, then managed and later owned the Philadelphia Athletics (1901–54), who won nine pennants and five world championships between 1902 and 1931.

MAN O' WAR (1917–47) **Kentucky Horse Park, Lexington, Kentucky**   Set five world records in his two-year career as a racehorse; leading sire of all time. He was the first horse ever to be embalmed and the first to have a funeral. The horse lay in state in a natural oak casket lined with the yellow-and-black racing silks of the Rudle stable. A bugler sounded "Taps" as he was lowered into the ground.

ROCKY MARCIANO (1923–August 31, 1969) **Lauderdale Memorial Gardens and Mausoleum, Fort Lauderdale, Florida**   On the evening before his forty-sixth birthday, Marciano died when his plane crashed into the only oak tree in an Iowa cornfield. The only heavyweight champion ever to complete a professional career without a loss, he had won the heavyweight championship from Jersey Joe Walcott in 1952.

JOHN J. McGRAW (1873–February 25, 1934) **New Cathedral Cemetery, Baltimore, Maryland**   Manager of the New York Giants (1902–32), winner of three world baseball championships and ten National League pennants.

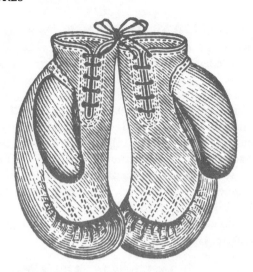

PAUL MORPHY (1837–July 10, 1884) **Saint Louis Cemetery #1, New Orleans, Louisiana**   After a brilliant beginning as chess master, Morphy's life disintegrated, as a result, some said, of the nervous strains of chess competition. He died of congestion of the brain attributed to bathing in cold water after a long walk in the heat.

WILLIAM A. MULDOON (1845–June 3, 1933) **Kensico Cemetery, Valhalla, New York**   Claimed the world wrestling championship, was called the "Iron Duke."

JAMES NAISMITH (1861–November 28, 1939) **Lawrence Memorial Park Cemetery, Lawrence, Kansas**   Invented basketball (1891), using two peach baskets and a soccer ball.

BARNEY OLDFIELD (1878–October 4, 1946) **Holy Cross Cemetery, Los Angeles, California**   Originally a bike racer, he won the Detroit 5-Mile Classic (1903) in 5 minutes 28 seconds; at his death he was a teacher of driving safety.

OLD HENRY CLAY (1837–Spring 1867) **Smithsonian Museum of Natural History, Washington, D.C.**   Called "Father of American Trotting Horses" because of his activities as a sire.

CHARLES WILLIAM PADDOCK (1900–July 21, 1943)
U.S. Government Cemetery, Sitka, Alaska   Called the world's
fastest human, the first to break ten seconds for the hundred-yard
dash; died in a plane crash while in the Marines.

BENNY "KID" PARET (1938–April 3, 1962) **Our Lady of
Mercy Cemetery, Miami, Florida**   Paret died a few days after he
was knocked unconscious by Emile Griffith in the twelfth round
of a championship match. Films revealed that the knockout had
come after a series of two-handed punches following ten consecutive right uppercuts to the chin. Paret was unable to fall at first
because the blows were pinning him to the corner post, which
propped him up on his feet. He was buried in Miami as an expression of his anti-Castro sympathies.

BRIAN PICCOLO (1943–June 16, 1970) **St. Mary's Cemetery,
Evergreen Park, Illinois**   The story of Piccolo's life and death
was made into a poignant movie, *Brian's Song* (1972), which recorded his filling in for Gail Sayers on the Chicago Bears football
team when Sayers had a knee operation. When Piccolo developed
cancer, Sayers went to the hospital with the trophy he himself
had received for the most courageous athlete of the year and gave
it to Piccolo.

BILL PICKETT (c. 1860–April 2, 1932) **near White Eagle Monument, Ponca City, Oklahoma**   The originator of bulldogging, or
steer wrestling, Pickett perfected a unique style: he would leap
up from his horse, grab the steer around the neck or by the horns,
and sink his teeth into the animal's upper lip. After a number of
years he lost his teeth and changed his style. He died after being
kicked by a horse.

VINCENT RICHARDS (1903–September 28, 1959) **Woodlawn Cemetery, Bronx, New York**   Only Olympic tennis champion in history, won the singles the only time it was included in
the Olympic Games (1924).

JACKIE ROBINSON (1919–October 24, 1972) **Cypress Hills
Cemetery, Brooklyn, New York**   The grandson of a slave, Robin-

son became, in 1947, the first black player in the major leagues. His quiet bravery when harassed by fans and teammates, plus his top-notch skills, earned him the National League's Rookie of the Year award and Most Valuable Player in 1949. After his death, his body was taken in a funeral procession through the black communities of Harlem and Bedford-Stuyvesant, where thousands lined the streets. He is buried just a few miles from where he triumphed at Ebbets Field.

KNUTE ROCKNE (1888–March 31, 1931) **Highland Cemetery, South Bend, Indiana**   Rockne died at the height of his career in a plane crash on the way to Hollywood, where he was to make a talking picture. After hearing the news, Will Rogers (see Entertainers) told jokes about Rockne for twenty-five minutes with tears streaming down his face at a meeting they were both to have attended. His funeral was the first to be covered with an international radio hookup, coast to coast and then by shortwave overseas. The body was carried by members of his Notre Dame football team, where he had coached for thirteen years. Chosen the greatest all-time coach; between 1918 and 1930 his team had lost only twelve games, and he never had a losing year. As a player he developed the forward pass in 1913, and as a coach he perfected the shift play, initiated the use of a second team to tire the opposition, and devised the diagonal runs of defensive linemen, called "stunting" or "looping." His death was voted sports story of the year.

BARNEY ROSS (1909–January 18, 1967) **Rosemont Park Cemetery, Chicago, Illinois**   Lightweight champion (1933) and welterweight champion (1934), was never knocked out.

RUFFIAN (1972–75) **Belmont Park Race Track, Elmont, Queens, New York**   In a match race with a stallion, thoroughbred racing's great filly broke her leg and was destroyed with millions watching on television. She was buried about thirty yards past the finish line at Belmont, beneath the flagpole in the infield of the racetrack. Her funeral featured the largest floral piece ever for a horse, a horseshoe made of 1,362 white carnations, eight and a half feet high and eight feet wide.

GEORGE HERMAN "BABE" RUTH (1895–August 16, 1948) **Gate of Heaven Cemetery, Hawthorne, New York** The death of the record home-run hitter moved the nation almost as much as President Franklin D. Roosevelt's (see Presidents) had three years earlier. Seventy-five thousand people filed into Yankee Stadium to pay their respects to the most popular ball player of all time. Among the pallbearers at his funeral on a scorching hot day were teammates Joe Dugan and Waite Hoyt. "Christ," Dugan confided through dry lips, "I'd give a hundred bucks for a cold beer." Hoyt, glancing at the coffin, shot back, "So would the Babe."

TERRY SAWCHUK (1929–May 31, 1970) **Mount Hope Cemetery, Pontiac, Michigan** Goal tender for the New York Rangers hockey team with a record 103 shutouts; died after an injury suffered while wrestling with a teammate off the ice.

TOM SHARKEY (1873–April 17, 1953) **Golden Gate National Cemetery, San Bruno, California** A heavyweight contender of the 1890s, called "Sailor Tom" because he had a battleship tattooed on his chest.

TRIS SPEAKER (1888–December 8, 1958) **Fairview Cemetery, Hubbard, Texas** Known as the "gray Eagle" of the outfield, played with Boston Red Sox (1907–15) and Cleveland Indians (1916–26).

AMOS ALONZO STAGG (1862–March 17, 1965) **Parkview Cemetery, Stockton, California** Honored as both player and coach (University of Chicago) in the Football Hall of Fame, the "Grand Old Man of Football" was an active coach for fifty-seven years. He developed the turtleback play and the spiral forward pass, invented the tackling dummy, and started the numbering of players.

CASEY STENGEL (1891–September 29, 1975) **Forest Lawn Memorial Park, Glendale, California** The manager of the New York Yankees and then the New York Mets, he was famed for his creative use of the English language. "Well, God is certainly getting an earful tonight," wrote columnist Jim Murray on the day of the garrulous Stengel's death. At the services many mourners, recalling Stengel's convoluted insights, could scarcely contain their laughter, a tribute Stengel would have probably appreciated.

JOHN L. SULLIVAN (1858–February 2, 1918) **Old Calvary Cemetery, Boston, Massachusetts**   On the day of his death, the last bare-knuckles heavyweight champion (1882–92) fainted but refused to go to bed, saying he could be his own doctor. He began preparations for a bath and died ten minutes later. After a life of drunken rampages, Sullivan had given up drinking on the day his hero, Theodore Roosevelt (see Presidents), was inaugurated president. Roosevelt was unable to make it to the funeral; Jim Corbett, who had beaten Sullivan for the title, was a pallbearer.

GOOSE TATUM (c. 1919–January 18, 1967) **Fort Bliss National Cemetery, El Paso, Texas**   Joined the Globetrotters Basketball Club in 1942 and averaged twenty-five points a game.

JIM THORPE (1888–March 28, 1953) **Jim Thorpe Monument, Jim Thorpe, Pennsylvania**   After the great sports hero's death, the towns of Mauch Chunk and East Mauch Chunk obtained his body for burial and voted to change their names to Jim Thorpe, Pennsylvania. By interring Thorpe, the Chunks hoped to establish a national shrine and attract tourists to help them out of an economic depression. Thorpe's body was placed in a twenty-ton pink marble mausoleum costing fifteen thousand dollars, and a foundation was started to build a museum and hospital in his honor. But plans went awry when the longed-for tourists failed to appear. "All we got was a dead Indian," commented John H. Otto, disappointed leader of the move to enshrine Thorpe.

HONUS WAGNER (1874–December 6, 1955) **Jefferson Memorial Park, Pleasant Hills, Pennsylvania**   Finest fielding shortstop (Pittsburgh Pirates, 1900–17) of baseball's first half century.

GEORGE WEISS (1895–August 13, 1972) **Evergreen Cemetery, New Haven, Connecticut**   During his tenure as general manager (1947–60), the New York Yankees won ten pennants and seven World Series.

JESS WILLARD (1881–December 15, 1968) **Forest Lawn Memorial Park, Glendale, California**　At death, the longest-lived heavyweight champion, 86 years, 351 days.

BABE DIDRIKSON ZAHARIAS (1914–September 27, 1956) **Forest Lawn Memorial Park, Beaumont, Texas**　All-around champion athlete, won Open golf championship, 1948, 1950, 1954, two track medals at the 1932 Olympics; she died of cancer.

MUSICIANS

LOUIS "SATCHMO" ARMSTRONG (1900–July 6, 1971) **Flushing Cemetery, Flushing, Queens, New York** Jazz trumpet player without peer; his many hits include "When the Saints Go Marchin' In" (1938), "A Kiss to Build a Dream On" (1950), and "Hello Dolly" (1964). "My life has been my music," he once said.

BÉLA BARTÓK (1881–September 26, 1945) **Ferncliff Cemetery, Hartsdale, New York** Modern Hungarian composer who utilized folk music themes in his work for piano, violin, and orchestra, such as *Music for Strings, Percussion and Celesta* (1936). Emigrated to the U.S. in 1940.

BIX BEIDERBECKE (1903–August 6, 1931) **Oakdale Cemetery, Davenport, Iowa** Jazz cornetist and composer, the first white musician to have a serious influence on the development of jazz.

CONNEE BOSWELL (1908–October 11, 1976) **Ferncliff Cemetery, Hartsdale, New York**   She and her sisters, Vet and Martha, were a hit singing group of the 1940s.

MAYBELLE "MOTHER" CARTER (1909–October 23, 1978) **Woodlawn East Memorial Park, Hendersonville, Tennessee**   Matriarch of the Carter Family, first group to be named to the Country Music Hall of Fame.

PATSY CLINE (1932–March 5, 1963) **Shenandoah Memorial Park, Winchester, Virginia**   One of the most popular country music singers; her career lasted only five years before she was killed in a plane crash. Among her biggest hits was "Walkin' After Midnight" (1957); elected to the Country Music Hall of Fame in 1973.

GEORGE M. COHAN (1878–November 5, 1942) **Woodlawn Cemetery, Bronx, New York**   At the great showman's requiem mass, a secular song was played for the first time on the grand organ of St. Patrick's Cathedral. "Over There," the popular Cohan tune, was played slowly in funeral-march tempo, triggering a flood of tears from the audience. Cohan, who was songwriter, performer, playwright, and producer, is buried alongside his mother, father, and sister, the quartet that reached vaudeville success together as "The Four Cohans."

NAT "KING" COLE (1919–February 16, 1965) **Forest Lawn Memorial Park, Glendale, California**   First black singer of romantic songs to acquire a following equal to that of Sinatra or Como.

JOHN COLTRANE (1926–July 17, 1967) **Pinelawn Memorial Park and Cemetery, Farmingdale, Long Island, New York**   Modern jazz saxophonist; his funeral, held at St. Peter's Lutheran Church, Manhattan's "jazz church," featured avant-garde jazz composed especially for it.

JIMMY DORSEY (1904–June 12, 1957) **Annunciation Cemetery, Shenandoah, Pennsylvania**   Saxophonist; with his brother,

Tommy, led the Dorsey Brothers Band, one of the most important of the Big Band era. The pair had a falling-out in the mid-1930s, and Tommy formed his own band.

TOMMY DORSEY (1905–November 26, 1956) **Kensico Cemetery, Valhalla, New York** Sweet mellow trombonist; his hits with his band include "Song of India" (1937), "Boogie Woogie" (1938), "Swing Low, Sweet Chariot" (1941), and "Deep River" (1941). Among the many musicians who started with him are Buddy Rich and Charlie Shavers.

NELSON EDDY (1901–March 6, 1967) **Hollywood Memorial Park Cemetery, Los Angeles, California** Singer, noted for his film appearances with Jeanette MacDonald; he sang his hit "Rose Marie" about seven thousand times.

DUKE ELLINGTON (1899–May 24, 1974) **Woodlawn Cemetery, Bronx, New York** Composer, pianist, orchestra leader, and major influence on the development of jazz.

CASS ELLIOTT (1941–July 29, 1974) **Hollywood Memorial Park Cemetery, Los Angeles, California** Sweet-voiced hefty singer with the Mamas and the Papas (1963–67); she choked to death on a sandwich.

ARTHUR FIEDLER (1894–July 10, 1979) **St. Joseph Cemetery, Boston, Massachusetts** Conductor of the Boston Pops for fifty years.

STEPHEN C. FOSTER (1826–January 13, 1864) **Allegheny Cemetery, Pittsburgh, Pennsylvania** The composer of such favorites as "Old Folks at Home" and "Jeanie with the Light Brown Hair" ended his days alone in poverty in New York City, haunting music stores, where few people remembered him. At the height of his career he had earned $1,300 dollars a year, but he had no royalty interest in his songs. Foster died in the charity ward of Bellevue Hospital; in his pants pocket was found a slip of paper reading, "Dear friends and gentle hearts." The Pennsylvania Railroad carried the funeral party home free of charge, and friends played his most beloved compositions at the grave site.

RUDOLPH FRIML (1879–November 13, 1972) **Forest Lawn Memorial Park, Glendale, California**   Composer of *Rose Marie* (1924) and thirty other popular operettas.

AMELITA GALLI-CURCI (1882–November 26, 1963) **Cypress View Mausoleum, San Diego, California**   Great coloratura.

GEORGE GERSHWIN (1898–July 12, 1937) **Temple Israel Cemetery, Hastings-on-Hudson, New York**   Composer of *Rhapsody in Blue* (1924) and *Porgy and Bess* (1925), died of a brain tumor.

LOUIS MOREAU GOTTSCHALK (1829–December 18, 1869) **Green-Wood Cemetery, Brooklyn, New York**   Composer; titles of his work reflect his New Orleans background and inspiration: "Le Banjo," "La Morte," "Radreuse," "Tarantella," "Tremole Étude."

W. C. HANDY (1873–March 28, 1958) **Woodlawn Cemetery, Bronx, New York**   Composer, first to publish blues music; his most famous hit, "St. Louis Blues," was played at his funeral.

LIL HARDIN (1898–August 27, 1971) **Lincoln Cemetery, Chicago, Illinois**   Jazz pianist and one of the most influential women in jazz; led an all-girl band and, later, an all-male band. Married to Louis Armstrong from 1924 to 1938, she died after taking part in a concert in his memory.

LORENZ HART (1895–November 22, 1943) **Mount Zion Cemetery, Maspeth, Queens, New York**   Known as Broadway's "Laureate of Lyrics," Richard Rodgers's partner for twenty years for such shows as *Jumbo* (1934) and *On Your Toes* (1937).

JIMI HENDRIX (1942–September 18, 1970) **Greenwood Memorial Park, Renton, Washington**   A year before his death from a drug overdose the rock singer said, "I tell you when I die I'm not going to have a funeral, I'm going to have a jam session. And, knowing me, I'll probably get busted at my own funeral." His funeral took place in a simple Baptist church far from the hyped-up world of rock.

VICTOR HERBERT (1859–May 26, 1924) **Woodlawn Cemetery, Bronx, New York**   Composer of operettas such as *Babes in Toyland* (1903) and *Naughty Marietta* (1910).

BILLIE HOLIDAY (1915–July 17, 1959) **St. Raymond's Cemetery, Bronx, New York**   "Lady Day" died in a New York hospital while under arrest for the possession of narcotics. The blues singer's drug habit had already cost her dearly: her cabaret license was revoked in 1947 after she was arrested and committed to a federal rehabilitation facility. Although she had not appeared onstage for several years, Holiday was buried wearing her favorite pink lace stage gown and pink gloves.

BUDDY HOLLY (1936–February 3, 1959) **City of Lubbock Cemetery, Lubbock, Texas**   Major singer and guitarist of early rock 'n' roll, worked out the distinctive country rock sound called rockabilly; his biggest success was "Peggy Sue" (1957). Holly was killed in a plane crash with two other performers.

JOSÉ ITURBI (1895–June 28, 1980) **Holy Cross Cemetery, Los Angeles, California**   Spanish-born concert pianist, noted for his performances of Mozart and Beethoven; appeared in such Hollywood musicals as *The Midnight Kiss* (1949), also performed at the Hollywood Bowl.

CHARLES EDWARD IVES (1874–May 19, 1954) **Wooster Cemetery, Danbury, Connecticut**   Composer, innovated use of atonal structure.

MAHALIA JACKSON (1911–January 27, 1972) **Providence Memorial Park, Metairie, Louisiana**   Gospel singer whose renditions of old and new spirituals became classics of soul. "I Will Move on Up a Little Higher," written by her, sold two million copies as a single.

SPIKE JONES (1911–May 1, 1965) **Holy Cross Cemetery, Los Angeles, California**   Bandleader of the 1940s, added offbeat sound effects to popular songs.

SCOTT JOPLIN (1868–April 1, 1917) **St. Michael's Cemetery, Astoria, Queens, New York**   Although recognized as a great ragtime composer, Joplin died penniless and friendless and was buried without ceremony or gravestone. His music includes "The Entertainer," adapted by Marvin Hamlisch for the hit movie *The Sting* (1973), but Joplin never received any royalties for any of his works. In 1974 the American Society of Composers and Performers placed a bronze plaque on the bare site that reads: "Scott Joplin, American Composer."

JEROME KERN (1885–November 11, 1945) **Ferncliff Cemetery, Hartsdale, New York**   Composer, his songs were featured in 104 stage and screen productions over forty years.

FRITZ KREISLER (1875–January 29, 1962) **Woodlawn Cemetery, Bronx, New York**   A child prodigy on the violin, he became known as the world's highest-paid concert violinist and one of the most popular; also published two hundred works as a composer.

MARIO LANZA (1921–October 7, 1959) **Holy Cross Cemetery, Los Angeles, California**   Tenor, by age twenty-nine was world-famous for his appearance in the film biography *The Great Caruso* (1951).

OSCAR LEVANT (1906–August 14, 1972) **Westwood Memorial Park, Los Angeles, California**   Pianist and wit, parodied his own neuroses.

GUY LOMBARDO (1902–November 5, 1977) **Pinelawn Memorial Park and Cemetery, Farmingdale, Long Island, New York**   Popular orchestra leader, with his Royal Canadians a New Year's Eve perennial.

EDWARD MᴀᴄDOWELL (1861–January 23, 1908) **MacDowell Colony, Peterborough, New Hampshire**   The composer of "To a Wild Rose" and other masterpieces had a nervous collapse three years before his death and never recovered his mental capacities. His grave on an open hilltop of his property carries an inscription from one of his works, "From a Log Cabin," which unconsciously foretold his own stagnant end:

> A house of dreams untold
> It looks out over the whispering tree-tops
> And faces the setting sun.

Today the Peterborough farm is the 500-acre MacDowell Colony, fulfilling the composer's ambition to build a creative environment where artists, musicians, and writers could work alongside one another.

THELONIOUS MONK (1918–February 17, 1982) **Ferncliff Cemetery, Hartsdale, New York**   Jazz pianist and composer; his wry and angular melodies constitute a striking contribution to the modern jazz repertory.

GRACE MOORE (1901–January 26, 1947) **Forest Hills Cemetery, Chattanooga, Tennessee**   Opera star; more successful with the public than the critics, she appeared in such screen vehicles as *One Night of Love* (1934); killed in a plane crash while entertaining U.S. troops overseas.

HELEN MORGAN (1900–October 8, 1941) **Holy Sepulchre Cemetery, Worth, Illinois**   Torch singer of 1920s.

RED NICHOLS (1905–June 28, 1965) **Forest Lawn Memorial Park, Glendale, California** Cornetist and bandleader of the Five Pennies.

IGNACE JAN PADEREWSKI (1860–June 29, 1941) **Arlington National Cemetery, Arlington, Virginia** The Polish pianist, composer, and statesman is one of the few foreigners known to be interred in the national cemetery. He rests there "temporarily" until Poland is once again free of foreign domination. The musician/patriot, first premier of the ruined Polish Republic, died in New York at the very time German and Russian troops were overrunning his country. President Roosevelt offered burial at Arlington, and Paderewski was entombed beneath the Mast of the Maine Monument with a nineteen-gun salute. When his remains are returned to Poland his heart will remain here. Although the hearts of several great Polish patriots lie in Warsaw Cathedral, the musician wanted his to remain in the country that had given sanctuary to himself and his hopes.

GREGOR PIATIGORSKY (1903–August 6, 1976) **Westwood Memorial Park, Los Angeles, California** Noted cellist.

EZIO PINZA (1892–May 8, 1957) **Putnum Cemetery, Greenwich, Connecticut** The bass opera singer was buried in this cemetery because of its proximity to a schoolyard; he loved the sounds of children playing.

ROSA PONSELLE (1897–May 25, 1981) **Druid Ridge Cemetery, Pikesville, Maryland** Operatic soprano, called "Caruso in petticoats."

COLE PORTER (1892–October 16, 1964) **Mount Hope Cemetery, Peru, Indiana** Composer, lyricist, whose work is marked by wit and sophistication; his popular Broadway shows include *Gay Divorcée* (1932), *Panama Hattie* (1940), *Something for the Boys* (1943), *Kiss Me, Kate* (1948), *Can-Can* (1953), *Silk Stockings* (1955).

ELVIS PRESLEY (1935–August 16, 1977) Graceland, Memphis, Tennessee The "King" of rock 'n' roll between 1956 and 1963, Presley captivated audiences with his delivery of such songs as "Heartbreak Hotel," "Love Me Tender," and "Hound Dog." The aftermath of Presley's death, like that of other great idols, was a crowd affair. One thousand people kept vigil outside his Memphis mansion, Graceland. Two were killed by a hit-and-run driver as souvenir hustlers hawked "In Memoriam" T-shirts. The singer was laid out in a cream-colored suit, silver tie, light blue shirt, diamond stickpin, and diamond cuff links. He was interred in a mausoleum in Memphis's Forest Hill Memorial Cemetery near the grave of his mother. About two weeks after the funeral, four men were arrested for attempting to steal the body and hold it for ransom. Elvis was reinterred with his mother in an elaborate garden on the grounds of the estate.

SERGEI RACHMANINOFF (1873–March 29, 1943) Kensico Cemetery, Valhalla, New York Russian pianist, composer, and conductor; his grave has become a place of pilgrimage for music lovers and musicians. His compositions include concertos, *Prelude in C Sharp Minor* (1892) for piano, *Rhapsody on a Theme of Paganini* (1934) for piano and orchestra.

TEX RITTER (1907–January 2, 1974) Oak Bluff Memorial Park, Port Neches, Texas Singing cowboy.

PAUL ROBESON (1898–January 23, 1976) Ferncliff Cemetery, Hartsdale, New York Black bass-baritone and actor, remembered for performances in *The Emperor Jones* (1924) and *Show Boat* (1928), and for his political activism.

JIMMIE RODGERS (1897–May 26, 1933) Oak Grove Cemetery, Meridian, Mississippi The "Singing Brakeman" was one of country music's most adored entertainers, recording a total of 111 songs. "My time ain't long," the tuberculosis-ridden performer said to friends before he arrived in New York for his last recording sessions. He was so weak that a cot had to be put into the studio, and he died a short time later. As the train carrying the former railroad man pulled into the station of his native Meridian, the engineer pulled his whistle to a low moan.

RICHARD RODGERS (1902–December 30, 1979) **Ferncliff Cemetery, Hartsdale, New York**   Composer for musical theater, collaborated with Lorenz Hart and Oscar Hammerstein II.

SIGMUND ROMBERG (1887–November 9, 1951) **Ferncliff Cemetery, Hartsdale, New York**   Composer of more than two thousand songs and seventy-eight musicals.

LILLIAN ROTH (1910–May 12, 1980) **Mount Pleasant Memorial Park, Hawthorne, New York**   Torch singer; her struggle with alcoholism was made into a movie, *I'll Cry Tomorrow* (1955).

ERNESTINE SCHUMANN-HEINK (1861–November 17, 1936) **Greenwood Memorial Park, San Diego, California**   Acclaimed as the world's greatest Wagnerian contralto, she was beloved by the public because of her performances for U.S. troops during World War I. Called the "mother of the doughboys," and an honorary officer of the American Legion, Schumann-Heink was reading a telegram from a former soldier just before she died. It was one of hundreds that came to her bedside from all over the country. The funeral featured full military honors, and "Taps" was sounded as she was lowered into her grave.

BESSIE SMITH (1895–September 26, 1937) **Mount Lawn Cemetery, Sharon Hill, Pennsylvania**   Controversy still surrounds the death of the great blues singer, who never made a poor recording ("Careless Love," 1925; "Dyin' by the Hour," 1927; "Kitchen Man," 1929; "Need a Little Sugar in My Bowl," 1931). Her death appears to have been hastened by the cruelties of segregation—after her car crashed in Tennessee there was an interminable wait before an ambulance arrived. Smith's son claimed that she was refused admission to the town's white hospital, and by the time she arrived at the poorly equipped black one she had lost too much blood to survive. Smith was broke when she died, but insurance paid for a grand send-off in glittering evening gown and silvery metallic coffin. For thirty-three years the singer's grave remained unmarked, until a Philadelphia housewife wrote to a newspaper about it and a fund-raising drive began. Money came from two main sources: rock star Janis Joplin, a Smith devotee, and Juanita Green, a registered nurse who as a child had scrubbed Bessie's kitchen floor. Columbia Records' publicity department created the inscription for the stone, which reads: "The Greatest Blues Singer in the World Will Never Stop Singing—Bessie Smith—1895–1937." Janis Joplin did not attend the dedication ceremony, probably to keep attention from focusing on herself; a few months later she, too, was dead.

JOHN PHILIP SOUSA (1854–March 6, 1932) Congressional Cemetery, Washington, D.C. Known for a quarter of a century as the "March King," he was buried in the uniform of a lieutenant commander of the naval reserve, with full military honors to the accompaniment of his own martial music.

HELEN TRAUBEL (1899–July 28, 1972) Westwood Memorial Park, Los Angeles, California Wagnerian soprano, appeared in nightclub act with popular comedians.

RICHARD TUCKER (1914–January 8, 1975) Mount Lebanon Cemetery, Glendale, Queens, New York The tenor was the first singer to have his funeral services in the Metropolitan Opera House in its history. In October 1975, Cardinal Cooke, a close friend, conducted a memorial mass at Saint Patrick's Cathedral for Tucker, the first ever said there for a Jew.

DINAH WASHINGTON (1924–December 14, 1963) Burr Oak Cemetery, Alsip, Illinois "Queen of the Blues," died of overdose of drugs.

KURT WEILL (1900–April 3, 1950) Mount Repose Cemetery, Haverstraw, New York Composer of several of the twentieth century's most popular operas. With Bertolt Brecht, wrote *Mahagonny* (1927) and *Threepenny Opera* (1928). In the United States he wrote *Lady in the Dark* (1941) and *Street Scene* (1947).

PAUL WHITEMAN (1891–December 29, 1967) Cemetery of the First Presbyterian Church of Ewing, Trenton, New Jersey Orchestra leader, popularized jazz music.

HANK WILLIAMS (1923–January 1, 1953) Oakwood Annex, Montgomery, Alabama   The "King of the Hillbillies," who could not read music although he composed many country-and-western hits, died in the back of an automobile, probably intoxicated. His monument is a slab of Vermont granite standing on a two-step pedestal with the opening notes of "I Saw the Light" across the top. At the base is a marble replica of Hank's cowboy hat, and etched into the stone of the base are the covers of the sheet music of Williams's hits. On the back is a poem entitled "Thank You Darling" by Williams's wife, Audrey, who had divorced him less than a year before.

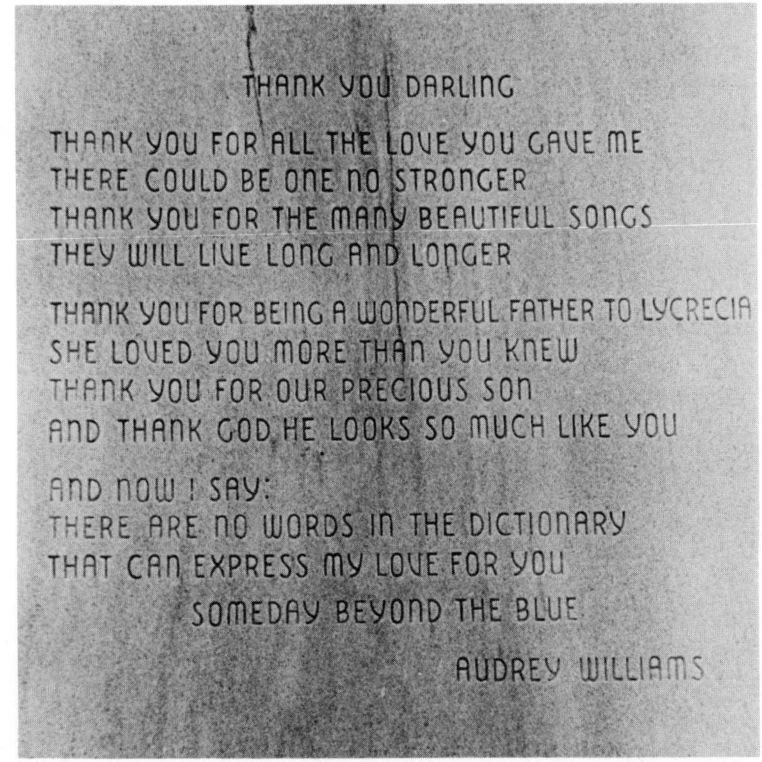

THANK YOU DARLING

THANK YOU FOR ALL THE LOVE YOU GAVE ME
THERE COULD BE ONE NO STRONGER
THANK YOU FOR THE MANY BEAUTIFUL SONGS
THEY WILL LIVE LONG AND LONGER

THANK YOU FOR BEING A WONDERFUL FATHER TO LYCRECIA
SHE LOVED YOU MORE THAN YOU KNEW
THANK YOU FOR OUR PRECIOUS SON
AND THANK GOD HE LOOKS SO MUCH LIKE YOU

AND NOW I SAY:
THERE ARE NO WORDS IN THE DICTIONARY
THAT CAN EXPRESS MY LOVE FOR YOU
        SOMEDAY BEYOND THE BLUE

                    AUDREY WILLIAMS

Hank Williams's ex-wife expressed her feelings in this poem engraved on the back of his gravestone. (Penny Weaver, Country Music Magazine*)*

Gravestone of country music star Hank Williams includes the opening of his hit song, "I Saw the Light," and a marble replica of his cowboy hat. (Penny Weaver, Country Music Magazine*)*

JOURNALISTS

JAMES GORDON BENNETT, SR. (1795–June 1, 1872) **Green-Wood Cemetery, Brooklyn, New York** Founder of the New York *Herald*, the first paper to use foreign and war correspondents.

MEYER BERGER (1898–February 8, 1959) **Riverside Cemetery, Saddle Brook, New Jersey** New York *Times* reporter, discovered the "other side" of the news in a column devoted to the human-interest angle.

NELLIE BLY (Elizabeth Cochrane Seaman) 1867–January 27, 1922) **Woodlawn Cemetery, Bronx, New York** Reporter for the New York *World*, she traveled around the world in 72 days, 6 hours, 11 minutes, breaking the record of Jules Verne's fictional hero, Phileas Fogg.

ABRAHAM CAHAN (1860–August 31, 1951) **Mount Carmel Cemetery, Glendale, Queens, New York** Founder of the *Jewish*

Daily Forward, socialist leader and labor activist. Funeral services were held in the *Forward* building, where he had been editor for forty years.

BOB CONSIDINE (1906–September 25, 1975) **Gate of Heaven Cemetery, Hawthorne, New York** Political reporter, columnist, ghostwriter.

JEANNETTE LEONARD GILDER (1849–January 17, 1916) **Bordentown Cemetery, Bordentown, New Jersey** Member of literary family, she became an agent, in her day called a "literary broker."

RICHARD WATSON GILDER (1844–November 18, 1909) **Bordentown Cemetery, Bordentown, New Jersey** Editor of the *Century*, poet, founder of the Authors' Club.

HORACE GREELEY (1811–November 29, 1872) **Green-Wood Cemetery, Brooklyn, New York** Famous for his exhortation: "Go West, young man, go West!", Greeley devoted his energies and his newspaper, *The Tribune*, to the campaign against slavery. He ran for president in 1872; the combination of emotional blows from his decisive loss and his wife's death a few days before the election drove him insane, and he died later that month.

WILLIAM RANDOLPH HEARST (1863–August 14, 1951) **Cypress Lawn Memorial Park, Colma, California** In ill health toward the end of his life, the powerful newspaper tycoon moved out of his San Simeon estate and went to live in the house of his mistress of thirty years, Marion Davies (see Entertainers). His health declined over four years, until he weighed only 125 pounds; when he died his widow took charge of the funeral ceremonies, having the body removed from the house while Davies slept. Hearst left a publishing empire that included eighteen newspapers in twelve cities (among them the San Francisco *Examiner*) and nine magazines (such as *Cosmopolitan* and *Good Housekeeping*).

MARGUERITE HIGGINS (1920–January 3, 1966) **Arlington National Cemetery, Arlington, Virginia** Only woman reporter covering Korean War, won Pulitzer Prize (1951).

HEDDA HOPPER (1890–February 1, 1966) **Rose Hill Cemetery, Altoona, Pennsylvania** Hollywood gossip columnist, noted for her outrageous hats.

CHET HUNTLEY (1911–March 20, 1974) **Sunset Hills Cemetery, Bozeman, Montana** Noted television newscaster, covered major events on the *Huntley-Brinkley Report* for fifteen years.

DOROTHY KILGALLEN (1913–November 8, 1965) **Gate of Heaven Cemetery, Hawthorne, New York** Hollywood and Broadway gossip columnist.

HENRY R. LUCE (1898–February 28, 1967) **Luce Family Cemetery, Roman Catholic Abbey of Our Lady of Mepkin, Moncks Corner, South Carolina** Founder of *Time* (1923), *Fortune* (1930), *Life* (1936), and *Sports Illustrated* (1954).

S. S. McCLURE (1857–March 21, 1949) **Hope Cemetery, Galesburg, Illinois** Publisher of *McClure's Magazine*, fostered muckraker journalism. On the day of his burial, Galesburg was struck by the worst cyclone in its history.

ROBERT R. McCORMICK (1880–April 1, 1955) **Cantigny estate, Wheaton, Illinois** Powerful national and international figure, the publisher of the Chicago *Tribune* was buried in his World War I uniform beneath an elm tree near his home.

JOSEPH MEDILL (1823–March 16, 1899) **Graceland Cemetery, Chicago, Illinois** Founder and part owner of the Chicago *Tribune* (1854–74).

BILL NYE (1850–February 22, 1896) **Calvary Churchyard, Fletcher, North Carolina** Humorist and journalist, wrote for the New York *World* after gaining his reputation with the Laramie, Wyoming, *Boomerang*, which he founded and edited (1881–84).

LOUELLA PARSONS (1881–December 9, 1972) **Holy Cross Cemetery, Los Angeles, California** Influential Hollywood gossip columnist.

ELEANOR "CISSY" MEDILL PATTERSON (1884–July 24, 1948) **Graceland Cemetery, Chicago, Illinois** Editor-publisher of the *Washington-Times-Herald*; powerful and sometimes eccentric member of a publishing family.

JOSEPH MEDILL PATTERSON (1879–May 26, 1946) **Arlington National Cemetery, Arlington, Virginia** Founder of New York *Daily News* (1919), America's most successful tabloid.

WESTBROOK PEGLER (1894–June 24, 1961) Gate of Heaven Cemetery, Hawthorne, New York   Controversial columnist, won Pulitzer Prize (1941) for his exposé of labor union corruption.

JOSEPH PULITZER (1847–October 29, 1911) Woodlawn Cemetery, Bronx, New York   Pulitzer lay in state in the library of his home with his right hand across his chest, clasping a copy of his newspaper, the *World*. He had made it the nation's biggest daily, crusading against government corruption and big business. His will financed a School of Journalism at Columbia University and the Pulitzer Prizes in journalism, literature, and music.

ERNIE PYLE (1900–April 18, 1945) National Memorial Cemetery of the Pacific, Honolulu, Hawaii   War correspondent Pyle, who wrote about the experiences of the average GI Joe, was killed in fighting on the Japanese-held island Ie Shima during World War II. The GIs buried him with his helmet on the shore of the China Sea with a marker inscribed: "At This Spot/The 77th Infantry Division/Lost a Buddy/Ernie Pyle/18 April 1945." Later, Pyle was moved to Hawaii.

WHITELAW REID (1837–December 15, 1912) Sleepy Hollow Cemetery, North Tarrytown, New York   Succeeded Horace Greeley as editor of the New York *Tribune*.

GRANTLAND RICE (1880–July 13, 1945) Woodlawn Cemetery, Bronx, New York   Regarded as one of the nation's finest sportswriters, wrote column for the New York *Tribune* (1914–30).

ED SULLIVAN (1902–October 13, 1974) Ferncliff Cemetery, Hartsdale, New York   Broadway columnist and host of popular television variety show (1948–71).

IDA M. TARBELL (1857–January 6, 1944) Woodlawn Cemetery, Titusville, Pennsylvania   Muckraking reporter, wrote exposé of Standard Oil.

HENRY VILLARD (1835–November 11, 1900) Sleepy Hollow Cemetery, North Tarrytown, New York   After a successful career as a reporter covering the Civil War, Villard became a financier, directing companies that merged into General Electric. He gained control of the New York *Evening Post* and put it in the charge of his son, Oswald. Villard was buried near the grave of another son, five-year-old Hilgard, who had driven in the golden spike that symbolized the completion of his father's Northern Pacific Railroad.

OSWALD G. VILLARD (1872–October 1, 1949) **Sleepy Hollow Cemetery, North Tarrytown, New York**   Editor of *The Nation* (1918–1932), influential liberal journal.

WILLIAM ALLEN WHITE (1868–January 29, 1944) **Maplewood/Memorial Lawn Cemeteries, Emporia, Kansas**   Owner and editor of the Emporia *Gazette*, symbol of outstanding small-town journalism.

WALTER WINCHELL (1897–February 20, 1972) **Greenwood Memorial Park, Phoenix, Arizona**   America's most powerful newspaper columnist in the 1930s and 1940s; noted for his breezy style and inventive, staccato language.

JOHN PETER ZENGER (1697–July 28, 1746) **Trinity Churchyard, New York, New York**   Colonial printer, acquitted in libel suit (1734–35) that established principle of freedom of the press in the U.S. He is said to have been buried in Trinity, but the actual grave site has never been found.

COLONISTS AND PATRIOTS

ABIGAIL ADAMS (1744–October 28, 1818) **First Unitarian Church, Quincy, Massachusetts** First lady, wife of John Adams (see Presidents) and mother of John Quincy Adams (see Presidents), outspoken advocate of equal rights for women.

JOHN ALDEN (1599–September 12, 1687) **Old Burying Ground, South Duxbury, Massachusetts** Pilgrim father, according to legend wed Priscilla Mullens after failing to win her heart for Miles Standish.

ETHAN ALLEN (1738–February 12, 1789) **Greenmount Cemetery, Burlington, Vermont** The free-spirited Allen, who captured Fort Ticonderoga from the British during the Revolution, spent his final years attacking conventional religion and drinking excessively. The stone erected after his funeral frankly noted that "His spirit tried the Mercies of his God in Whom he firmly

Trusted." Sometime during the 1850s this marker disappeared. Some explained that it had been shattered by lightning because of Allen's blasphemy, others that it was simply stolen. In the late 1800s the Vermont legislature appropriated a new monument made of Barre granite and standing forty-two feet high. When it came time to erect this imposing memorial, the story goes, not the slightest trace of the old iconoclast's coffin could be found. This mystery has never been solved. The monument stands today in Greenmount, and General Allen is probably somewhere close by, at least in spirit.

CRISPUS ATTUCKS (c. 1723–March 5, 1770) Granary Burying Ground, Boston, Massachusetts A runaway slave, he was the first Continental soldier to fall in the Boston Massacre. Attucks's body rested in Boston's famed Faneuil Hall until he and four other victims were buried in a single grave in a funeral that witnessed an outpouring of civic emotion. Many patriot leaders praised him, including John Adams, who wrote to a friend, "The world has heard from Crispus Attucks, and more important, the English-speaking world will never forget his noble daring and his excusable rashness in the holy cause of liberty."

WILLIAM BRADFORD (1589–May 19, 1657) Burial Hill, Plymouth, Massachusetts Governor of Plymouth Colony (1621–32); an obelisk honors his memory, although there is no precise evidence of his burial.

GEORGE ROGERS CLARK (1752–February 13, 1818) Cave Hill Cemetery, Louisville, Kentucky Frontiersman and army officer, protected Northwest Territory from British control.

GEORGE CLINTON (1739–1812) Old Dutch Churchyard, Kingston, New York First governor of New York State (1777–1795) and vice-president under Jefferson and Madison.

BARBARA FRITCHIE (1766–December 18, 1862) Mount Olivet Cemetery, Frederick, Maryland Civil War hero; though advanced in years, she defended the Union flag against Confederate troops.

THOMAS HOOKER (1586–July 19, 1647) **Center Congregational Churchyard, Hartford, Connecticut** Clergyman and one of the drafters of the Connecticut constitution (1639), first great document of American freedom.

MARY JEMISON (1743–September 10, 1833) **Letchworth State Park, Castile, New York** Famed as the "White Woman of the Genesee," she was adopted by the Senecas at the age of fifteen

Statue of pioneer Mary Jemison, the "White Woman of the Genesee," shows her in the Indian garb she usually wore. (Genesee Region, New York State Office of Parks, Recreation and Historic Preservation)

after they massacred her family. She lived as an Indian for more than thirty years, raised a family among them, and was originally buried on the Seneca reservation. In 1910 Jemison's body was removed to the Letchworth Valley she had loved. A statue in the state park shows her as she looked when she first arrived there, dressed in Indian clothing, with her oldest son on her back.

WILLIAM JOHNSON (1715–July 11, 1774) **N. Market Street, Johnstown, New York**   Sir William commanded garrisons in upper New York and was instrumental in driving France from North America during the French and Indian Wars.

DOLLEY MADISON (1768–July 12, 1849) **Montpelier Estate, Montpelier Station, Virginia**   Remembered for her skills as First Lady and hostess, she rescued Gilbert Stuart's portrait of George Washington from the White House when the British burned the capital during the War of 1812. Later in life Dolley became a dowager queen whose age was never mentioned, especially at her birthday parties. Congress voted her a seat on the floor of the House whenever she chose to attend, the first time such a privilege had been granted to a woman. James Madison's widow was buried in Washington's Congressional Cemetery in a funeral procession that was the largest up to that time to honor a woman. Some years later she was moved to the side of her husband on the grounds of their former estate.

GEORGE MASON (1725–October 7, 1792) **Gunston Hall Plantation, Lorton, Virginia**   In 1776 he framed the Declaration of Rights and the major part of the constitution of Virginia; Jefferson used his work as the basis for the Declaration of Independence.

ROBERT MORRIS (1734–May 8, 1806) **Churchyard of Christ Church, Philadelphia, Pennsylvania**   Financier and signer of the Declaration of Independence, Morris personally financed a large part of the Revolutionary War effort. But in his last years his immense fortune was lost and he endured three years in debtors' prison. Five years after discharge, still penniless, he wrote a will regretting the loss of his wealth, which he had hoped to distribute to those family members "that should outlive me."

PRISCILLA MULLENS (1602?–?) **Old Burying Ground, South Duxbury, Massachusetts**   Wife of John Alden; Miles Standish's thwarted love for her is immortalized in Longfellow's poem "The Courtship of Miles Standish" (1858).

REBECCA NURSE (1620–June 19, 1692) **Backyard, 149 Pine Street, Danvers, Massachusetts**   At the age of seventy-one Nurse was accused of torturing some girls with witchcraft. Even though a jury found her innocent, the judge requested them to reconsider because of the girls' suffering. Nurse was hanged as a Salem "witch" and buried in an unmarked grave on the homestead. A monument was erected in 1885 that reads in part: "O Christian Martyr! who for truth could die, When all about thee owned the hideous Lie! The world, redeemed from Superstition's sway, Is breathing freer for thy sake to-day."

PAUL REVERE (1735–May 10, 1818) **Granary Burying Ground, Boston, Massachusetts**   Famed for his ride in April 1775 to warn the colonists of the British attack on Concord, Massachusetts.

BETSY ROSS (1752–January 30, 1836) **Mount Moriah Cemetery, Philadelphia, Pennsylvania**   Credited by legend with making the first American flag.

BENJAMIN RUSH (1746–April 19, 1813) **Christ Church Burial Ground, Philadelphia, Pennsylvania**   Physician, signer of the Declaration of Independence, and founder of the first free dispensary in America.

JOHN RUTLEDGE (1739–July 23, 1800) **St. Michael's Churchyard, Charleston, South Carolina**   Patriot, advocate of home rule for the colonies.

HAYM SALOMON (1740–January 6, 1785) **Congregation Mikve Israel Burial Ground, Philadelphia, Pennsylvania**   "Financier of the Revolution," he gave most of his fortune to the new government and was never repaid.

DANIEL SHAYS (c. 1747–September 29, 1825) **Union Cemetery, Conesus, New York**   Revolutionary soldier; disgruntled

after the war, he led farmers in "Shays's Rebellion" against the Massachusetts government.

ROGER SHERMAN (1721–July 23, 1793) **Grove Street Cemetery, New Haven, Connecticut**   Only patriot to sign all four great state papers: Declaration of Independence, Articles of Association, Articles of Confederation, and the Constitution.

MILES STANDISH (c. 1584–October 3, 1656) **Old Burying Ground, South Duxbury, Massachusetts**   Military leader of Plymouth Colony, unrequited lover of Priscilla Mullens.

PETER STUYVESANT (c. 1610–February, 1672) **St. Mark's Church-in-the-Bowery, New York, New York**   The quick-tempered last governor of New Netherland surrendered the colony to the English in 1644 from his farm, or "Bowerie," as the Dutch called it, in lower Manhattan. Eight years later he died in that same house and his body was carried four steps out the door to burial in the family chapel he had built. Today, as St. Mark's Church-in-the-Bowery, the expanded chapel is the oldest site of continuing worship in New York City.

PEREGRINE WHITE (1620–1704) **Governor Winslow Cemetery, Marshfield, Massachusetts**   First child born to English parents in New England.

ROGER WILLIAMS (c. 1603–January/March 1683) **Roger Williams Memorial, Providence, Rhode Island**   Founder of Rhode Island, colony dedicated to religious toleration.

JOHN WINTHROP (1588–March 26, 1649) **King's Chapel Burying Ground, Boston, Massachusetts**   Served as governor of Massachusetts Bay Colony twelve times from 1629 to 1648.

CRIMINALS

ALBERT ANASTASIA **(1903–October 25, 1957) Green-Wood Cemetery, Brooklyn, New York** Master killer for Murder, Inc., gunned down while having a haircut in a Manhattan hotel.

KATE "MA" BARKER **(1872–January 16, 1935) Williams Cemetery, Welch, Oklahoma** "Ma" masterminded the criminal deeds of her sons: Lloyd (1896–1949), Arthur (1899–June 13, 1939), Fred (1902–January 16, 1935), and Herman (1894–September 10, 1927). She was found dead after a shoot-out with the FBI, her machine gun clutched to her bosom.

CLYDE BARROW **(1909–May 23, 1934) Western Heights Cemetery, Dallas, Texas BONNIE PARKER (1910–May 23, 1934) Crown Hill Memorial Park, Dallas, Texas** After murdering and robbing their way across the Southwest, the outlaw duo went down in a barrage of bullets in an ambush by Texas Rangers. A crowd of six thousand gathered at the scene and fought to get close to the car where the bodies lay. Its doors were pulled off their hinges, and one man wanted to amputate Barrow's finger, but the crowd prevented it. Bonnie's gray silk stocking, spattered with blood and bits of brain, went to a more successful souvenir hunter. Bonnie's mother ignored her daughter's wish to be buried with her lover: "Now that she's dead, she's all mine. I don't want her buried with Clyde. He had her while she was alive."

WILLIAM H. BONNEY, "BILLY THE KID" (1859–July 14, 1881) **Old Fort Sumner Military Cemetery, Fort Sumner, New Mexico**   A prodigy among outlaws, the Kid reportedly had killed twenty-one people by the time he reached that age. Lawman Pat Garrett and his posse finally trapped the Kid on a New Mexico ranch. Billy whispered, *"Quien es?"* into the darkness as he backed into the bedroom, where the waiting lawman fired two shots, killing him instantly. Pretty Deluvina Maxwell buried him at the ranch in a borrowed white shirt five sizes too large. The coffin was placed under a tender marker, ordered by Deluvina: *"Duerme Bien, Querido"* (Sleep well, beloved). To avoid curiosity seekers, the body was later moved to a common grave near Fort Sumner, where the Kid now lies with two of his old gang; the word "pals" was added to their headstone sometime after burial. The Kid's headstones have been stolen frequently through the years; one was recovered in 1981 in California.

JOHN WILKES BOOTH (1838–April 26, 1865) **Green Mount Cemetery, Baltimore, Maryland**   For four years after he was killed by federal troops for the murder of Abraham Lincoln (see Presidents), Booth's body was kept in Washington, D.C., while his family pleaded for its return. Finally, in 1869, the remains were shipped to Baltimore, where, despite the fact that feeling still ran high, the family "drove openly" to Green Mount. The Episcopal clergyman who performed the service did not know who he was burying and was later dismissed by his congregation. Booth lies in an unmarked grave, in accordance with President Andrew Johnson's order. Even after the burial, rumors about the assassin abounded. One report stated that he was actually interred near the old Washington, D.C., jail, where all traces of the grave had been obliterated; other stories claimed that the body had been sunk in the Potomac River or secretly buried on an island twenty-seven miles from the capital.

LIZZIE BORDEN (1860–June 1, 1927) **Oak Grove Cemetery, Fall River, Massachusetts**   She lies near the father and step-mother she was accused of hacking to death with an ax.

AL CAPONE (1899–January 25, 1947) **Mount Carmel Cemetery, Hillside, Illinois**   Chicago's gang lord died a few years after his release from Alcatraz Prison suffering the final stage of syph-ilis. "Al is nutty as a fruitcake," one of his lieutenants replied in answer to a query about whether he would resume gang lead-ership. Capone was buried in consecrated ground in Mount Olivet Cemetery, although the archbishopric had forbidden a requiem mass or elaborate graveside ceremony. His headstone, a marble shaft, noted his name and dates in Italian. The burial site was so trampled by tourists that the family had the body moved to Mount Carmel, along with other Capone graves, leaving the headstone in Mount Olivet to fool visitors.

FRANK COSTELLO (1893–February 18, 1973) **St. Michael's Cemetery, Astoria, Queens, New York**   Powerful underworld fig-ure of the 1930s and '40s.

KID CURRY (Harvey Logan) (1865–June 29, 1903) **Glen-wood Cemetery, Glenwood Springs, Colorado**   The most feared killer in Butch Cassidy's (see Buried Abroad) "Wild Bunch," he ended his own life after being trapped by a sheriff's posse.

LEON CZOLGOSZ (1873–October 29, 1901) **Fort Hill Cem-etery, Auburn, New York**   After President McKinley's (see Pres-idents) assassin died in the electric chair at New York's Auburn Prison, the authorities strong-armed his brother into turning the body over to them, arguing that Czolgosz could not get a decent burial anywhere outside. Instead of "decent" burial, prison offi-cials disintegrated the body and the coffin by pouring acid on them, claiming this would prevent enraged citizens from snatch-ing the corpse. The story goes that the grave site was guarded for some days by correction officers until the acid had done its work and then was left unmarked. Czolgosz's brother, meantime, lost a business opportunity—a museum had offered him five thou-sand dollars to display the body.

BOB DALTON (1868–October 5, 1892) GRAT DALTON (1864–October 5, 1892) Elmwood Cemetery, Coffeyville, Kansas

Adeline Younger Dalton was the mother of nine sons and four daughters. Four of the sons became notorious outlaws—the Dalton Gang—the others, respectable citizens. On October 5, 1892, Bob Dalton led the gang, including his brothers Grat and Emmet, in a raid on the bank in Coffeyville, Kansas. The townsfolk were prepared, and Bob and Grat were killed in bloody fighting, along with two other gang members. The bullet-riddled corpses lay in the town square for several days as thousands of gawkers looked

Lawmen display the bodies of two of the Dalton Brothers after their deaths in the raid at Coffeyville, Kansas. (Western History Collections, University of Oklahoma Library)

them over and a carnival atmosphere prevailed. Bob and Grat were finally buried in Elmwood. Their brother Frank (1860–November 27, 1888), a deputy U.S. Marshal, already lay in that cemetery, having been killed four years earlier while apprehending a bootlegger. Mrs. Younger tried to have her outlaw sons buried beside the virtuous Frank, but Coffeyville's indignant citizens wouldn't hear of it.

JACK "LEGS" DIAMOND (1896–December 18, 1931)
Mount Olivet Cemetery, Maspeth, Queens, New York Bootlegger Diamond was wounded so many times in his career that even his fellow criminals marveled at his ability to survive, but a bullet finally got him.

JOHN DILLINGER (1903–July 22, 1934) Crown Hill Cemetery, Indianapolis, Indiana
After America's most-wanted criminal was gunned down by the FBI in a Chicago movie theater, his sister told neighbors she wanted no pictures taken at the funeral; they obliged by smashing the cameras of newspapermen. A month later, Dillinger's father received permission to disinter the body, to take advantage, some thought, of a ten-thousand-dollar offer to exhibit it. He actually wanted to check reports that his son's brain had been illegally removed and destroyed in the course of medical examination. This was true, but the senior Dillinger eventually decided not to take any action against Cook County authorities and not to remove the body of his offspring.

CHARLES ARTHUR "PRETTY BOY" FLOYD (1901–October 22, 1934) Akins Cemetery, Akins, Oklahoma
Popular bank robber, killed in a gun battle with law officers.

VITO GENOVESE (1897–February 14, 1969) St. John's Cemetery, Middle Village, Queens, New York
Mafia "Boss of all Bosses," died in the penitentiary.

HENRY JUDD GRAY (1893–January 12, 1928) Rosedale Cemetery, Montclair, New Jersey
Corset salesman Gray and his mistress, Ruth Brown Snyder, were convicted of murdering her husband in a sensational trial of the 1920s.

CHARLES JULIUS GUITEAU (1844–June 30, 1882) **D.C.
Jail and Asylum, Washington, D.C.** Authorities refused to turn
the body of President Garfield's (see Presidents) assassin over to
his family and instead buried it beneath the northeast corridor of
the old Washington, D.C., jail. Prison officials were none too
fond of Guiteau's sister, whom they accused of having brought a
poison-filled bouquet to the jail so that the deranged murderer
could die of arsenic and cheat the hangman's noose. The assassin's execution produced an outpouring of Guiteau-mania. Souvenir shops in Washington sold pieces of the hanging rope,
facsimiles of the murder bullets, and photographs of him.

JOHN H. "DOC" HOLLIDAY (1852–1887) Glenwood Cemetery, Glenwood Springs, Colorado

The gunslinger, Wyatt Earp's (see Explorers and Settlers) ally at the famous gunfight at the OK Corral, died of consumption in the Glenwood Springs sanitarium. On the table near his bed were his nickel-plated six-gun, a shotgun, and a bowie knife he had worn around his neck for ten years. Tossing down a final shot of whiskey, Holliday noted with horror that his feet were bare. "Dammit," he screamed at the nurses, "put 'em back on." But it was too late; one of the West's most dangerous killers died with his boots off. No actual grave site for Holliday is known, but a marker was erected for him in the old cemetery showing guns and a poker hand on it.

TOM HORN (1861–November 20, 1903) Columbia Cemetery, Boulder, Colorado

Horn, a well-known gunslinger, was found guilty of murder in 1902, largely through the efforts of a crusading prosecutor who had vowed to end "gun rule" in Wyoming. Plenty of folks thought that Tom had received a bad deal. As he looked out the window of his Cheyenne prison he saw written in the snow "keep your nerve." He followed that advice. Two days before the execution, he was visited by a Catholic priest and then an Episcopal minister, accompanied by a singing choir. As the minister was shepherding his singers down the stairs, Tom banged on the bars and called for his supper: "Hurry up, you sons of bitches. I'm hungry." He faced the hangman cheerfully after bidding good-bye to friends who sang a final hymn, "Life Is Like a Mountain Railroad."

JESSE JAMES (1847–April 3, 1882) Mount Olivet Cemetery, Kearney, Missouri/FRANK JAMES (1843–February 18, 1915) Hill Park, Independence, Missouri

Jesse James, the most daring bank and train robber of the American West, was killed by one of his own gang for the ten-thousand-dollar reward. The state militia was ordered to stand twenty-four-hour watch at the funeral parlor to prevent theft of the body by sympathizers. Jesse was first buried in an elegant galvanized iron casket at the foot of a coffee bean tree in the yard of the family farm; his one-armed mother offered twenty-five-cent tours of the house and sold pebbles from the grave. The gravestone noted that James was "Murdered by a traitor and coward whose name is not worthy to appear here." As the coffin was being moved to Mount Olivet in 1902 it fell apart and Jesse's skull rolled back into the grave twice and was recovered. The bullet hole could be seen behind his left ear. His brother and fellow outlaw, Frank, watching the proceedings, expressed a desire to be cremated.

THOMAS "THREE-FINGER BROWN" LUCHESE
(1903–July 13, 1967) Calvary Cemetery, Woodside, Queens, New York   Mafia chieftain.

CHARLES "LUCKY" LUCIANO (1897–January 26, 1962)
St. John's Cemetery, Middle Village, Queens, New York   Gangland leader; his simple Greek vault stands on consecrated ground, a privilege denied by the Church to many mobsters.

GEORGE "BUGS" MORAN (1893–February 26, 1957)
Cemetery of Leavenworth Penitentiary, Leavenworth, Kansas   Gang leader of the Prohibition era, he died in prison of lung cancer.

CHARLES DION "DEANIE" O'BANNION (1892–November 10, 1924) Mount Carmel Cemetery, Hillside, Illinois
Powerful Chicago bootlegger; his funeral was an underworld classic: 1,500 mourners, 1,000 autos, 26 truckloads of flowers, and burial in a $10,000 coffin.

LEE HARVEY OSWALD (1939–November 24, 1963) Rose Hill Memorial Park, Fort Worth, Texas   Rose Hill was not happy to have John F. Kennedy's (see Presidents) accused assassin among its permanent residents but under Texas law could not refuse burial, since Oswald's mother had purchased the four-grave plot some time before. A local minister who had driven out to the cemetery on his own performed the funeral service when the family's clergyman did not appear. So few people were in attendance that reporters had to carry the body from the chapel to the grave. In October 1981 Oswald's coffin was exhumed to verify charges that his was not the body inside. These suspicions turned out to be incorrect.

ETHEL ROSENBERG (1915–June 19, 1953) **JULIUS RO-SENBERG** (1918–June 19, 1953) **Wellwood Cemetery, Pinelawn, Long Island, New York**   Convicted of turning atomic secrets over to the Russians, they were the first in U.S. history to be executed by the government for espionage.

ARNOLD ROTHSTEIN (1882–November 4, 1928) **Union Field Cemetery, Ridgewood, Queens, New York**   Noted gambler; shot in a poker game, he refused to reveal his killer's name.

JACK RUBY (1911–January 3, 1967) **Westlawn Cemetery, Chicago, Illinois**   Slayer of Lee Harvey Oswald, died in prison while awaiting retrial.

DUTCH SCHULTZ (Arthur Flegenheimer) (1902–October 23, 1935) **Gate of Heaven Cemetery, Hawthorne, New York**   Mortally wounded in a Newark restaurant, the erratic gangster raved and babbled incoherently for days before expiring. His body lay unclaimed in a New York funeral home while a dispute over his burial raged between his mother, an orthodox Jew, and his wife, a Catholic. A priest was able to prove that he had baptized Schultz into the Catholic faith a few hours before his death and arrangements were made at last for a secret funeral and burial near the graves of many distinguished Catholics.

BENJAMIN "BUGSY" SIEGEL (1906–June 20, 1947) **Hollywood Memorial Park Cemetery, Los Angeles, California**   Gangland leader and well-known Hollywood figure.

JEFFERSON "SOAPY" SMITH (1860–July, 1898) **Skagway Town Cemetery, Skagway, Alaska**   Outlaw, gambler, and onetime dictator of Skagway; his reign was ended by an enraged vigilante committee. Smith was buried with local honors: a pea and three shells were thrown into his grave.

RUTH BROWN SNYDER (1894–January 12, 1928) **Woodlawn Cemetery, Bronx, New York**   Executed with her lover, Henry Judd Gray, for the murder of her husband. A reporter smuggled a camera into the death chamber, strapped to his leg, and photographed her execution for the front pages.

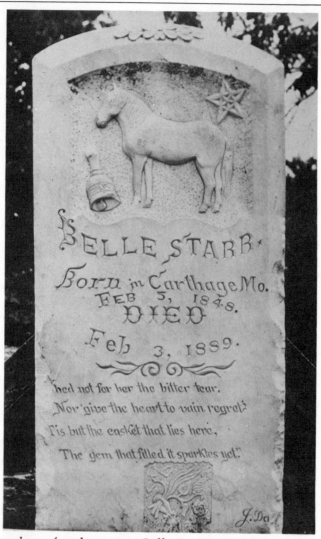

BELLE STARR
Born in Carthage Mo.
FEB 5, 1848.
DIED
Feb 3, 1889.

Shed not for her the bitter tear,
Nor give the heart to vain regret;
Tis but the casket that lies here,
The gem that filled it sparkles yet.

The daughter of outlaw queen Belle Starr commissioned this poetic gravestone for her mother. It has long since disappeared. (Oklahoma Historical Society)

BELLE STARR (1848–February 3, 1889) **Belle Starr Cabin, Porum, Oklahoma** The "bandit queen," popular with her Indian-territory neighbors, was shot in the back by an unknown assailant. Indian and white women dressed her for burial in her favorite black dress and jewelry and placed her prized possession, a six-shooter given to her by her lover Cole Younger, in her hands. Six heavily armed Indians served as pallbearers and, according to Cherokee custom, dropped small pieces of corn bread into the coffin, food for the departed's journey to the next world. One of the mourners was arrested for her murder (he was acquitted). The jewelry and six-shooter were later stolen by grave robbers.

ROBERT FRANKLIN STROUD, THE "BIRDMAN OF ALCATRAZ" (1887–November 21, 1963) Masonic Cemetery, Metropolis, Illinois   Became a respected ornithologist while serving fifty-four years in prison.

MARY E. SURRATT (1820–July 17, 1865) Mount Olivet Cemetery, Washington, D.C.   The first woman in U.S. history to die on the gallows, she was convicted of involvement in John Wilkes Booth's plot to kill Lincoln (see Presidents), although there was much doubt about her guilt. Her daughter made a hurried visit to the White House on the morning of the execution, but President Andrew Johnson refused to see her. Still, even the general in charge of the prisoner expected a reprieve to arrive and ordered relays of swift horses stationed between the White House and the execution site so that he could receive the message quickly. It never came.

WILLIE SUTTON (1901–November 2, 1980) Holy Cross Cemetery, Brooklyn, New York   Bank robber Sutton, called "Willie the Actor" for his many disguises, escaped from prison three times.

BEN THOMPSON (1843–March 11, 1884) Oakwood Cemetery, Austin, Texas   The most fearless and dangerous of Texas gunfighters, he became City Marshal of Austin at the end of his career and was so tough that there was no serious crime within city limits during his term. On March 11, 1884, Thompson was lured into an ambush staged by an old enemy in a San Antonio variety theater. His murder outraged Austin residents who bore his body to the cemetery in a cortege of sixty-two vehicles. Ironically, the gunman's substantial property now belongs to a Bible college.

COLE YOUNGER (1844–March 21, 1916) **Lee's Summit Cemetery, Lee's Summit, Missouri**   Noted western outlaw, cousin of Jesse James and a member of his gang.

JOSEPH ZANGARA (1902–March 21, 1933) **Cemetery of Union Correctional Institution, Raiford, Florida**   Attempted to assassinate President-elect Franklin D. Roosevelt in 1933 (see Presidents), but his bullet killed Mayor Anton J. Cermak of Chicago instead.

SUPREME COURT JUSTICES

HUGO L. BLACK (1886–September 25, 1971) **Arlington National Cemetery, Arlington, Virginia**   Stressed the inviolability of the Bill of Rights; buried in a coffin made of knotty pine from his Alabama hills, a copy of the U.S. Constitution inside his coat pocket.

LOUIS D. BRANDEIS (1856–October 5, 1941) **School of Law, University of Louisville, Belknap Campus, Louisville, Kentucky**   First Justice to use sociological evidence in preparing decisions; his ashes were buried beneath the porch of the Law School.

BENJAMIN N. CARDOZO (1870–July 9, 1938) **Shearith Israel Cemetery, Glendale, Queens, New York**   A spokesman for the idea that the law can be a means for social change; he decided in favor of much of the legislation associated with the New Deal.

SALMON P. CHASE (1808–May 7, 1873) **Spring Grove Cemetery, Cincinnati, Ohio**   Chief Justice (1864–73) during Reconstruction, Chase took a moderate position; presided over impeachment trial of Andrew Johnson (see Presidents). Established national bank system as Lincoln's Secretary of the Treasury.

WILLIAM O. DOUGLAS (1898–January 19, 1980) **Arlington National Cemetery, Arlington, Virginia**   Longest term on Court (1939–75); a cowboy friend he had asked to "wash your jeans and polish your boots and come East" to sing "The Lord's Prayer" at his funeral died before the hearty Justice, so a member of the U.S. Army Chorus sang the prayer.

FELIX FRANKFURTER (1882–February 22, 1965) **Mount Auburn Cemetery, Cambridge, Massachusetts**   Leader of the advocates of "judicial restraint."

JOHN MARSHALL HARLAN (1833–October 14, 1911) **Rock Creek Cemetery, Washington, D.C.**   Noted for his strict judicial construction of the Constitution.

JOHN MARSHALL HARLAN (1899–December 29, 1971) **Cemetery of Emmanuel Church, Weston, Connecticut**   Conservative voice of dissent on the Warren Court; grandson of the other Justice Harlan.

OLIVER WENDELL HOLMES, JR. (1841–March 6, 1935) **Arlington National Cemetery, Arlington, Virginia**   His eloquent defenses of social legislation earned him the title the "Great Dissenter"; developed the "clear and present danger" test to protect free speech. "Why should I fear death?" he said a few weeks before he died at ninety-three, "I have seen him often. When he comes he will seem like an old friend."

CHARLES EVANS HUGHES (1862–August 27, 1948) **Woodlawn Cemetery, Bronx, New York**   As Chief Justice, he resisted attempts to "pack" the Court with additional Justices favorable to President Franklin Delano Roosevelt.

JOHN MARSHALL (1755–July 6, 1835) **Shockoe Cemetery, Richmond, Virginia**   Chief Justice (1801–35), established power of the Supreme Court; while tolling for his funeral in Philadelphia, the Liberty Bell cracked.

HARLAN FISKE STONE (1872–April 22, 1946) **Rock Creek Cemetery, Washington, D.C.**   Known as the "great dissenter," joined with Brandeis and Cardozo in many liberal opinions.

ROGER B. TANEY (1777–October 12, 1864) **St. John's Cemetery, Frederick, Maryland**   Argued in the Dred Scott decision (1857) that slaves did not possess rights of citizenship.

FRED M. VINSON (1890–September 9, 1953) **Pine Hill Cemetery, Louisa, Kentucky**   As Chief Justice, frequently upheld the powers of the federal government in relation to the rights of the individual.

EARL WARREN (1891–July 9, 1974) Arlington National Cemetery, Arlington, Virginia   The Warren Court (1953–68) surprised those who thought him a "safe" conservative with its championing of individual rights. The first deceased member to lie in state in the Court's Grand Foyer, the Chief Justice's body rested on part of the black velvet-covered catafalque used for Lincoln, a special congressional resolution permitting its use for the first time for a nonpresident.

ADDRESS
UNKNOWN

JIM AVERILL (?–July 21, 1889) ELLA "CATTLE KATE" WATSON (1861–July 21, 1889) (Criminals) Watson, one of the few women rustlers of the Old West, and her partner/lover Averill received swift justice from a Wyoming lynch mob. Water seeped into their shallow grave, which soon disappeared; coyotes scattered the bones.

JIM BOWIE (1795–March 6, 1836) DAVID "DAVY" CROCKETT (1786–March 6, 1836) (Explorers and Settlers) Frontiersmen Bowie and Crockett died at the Alamo. The bodies of the Texan defenders were destroyed by the Mexicans in a huge funeral pyre as a calculated insult. Some time later, Sam Houston (see Government Leaders) sent out a detail to collect the bones and bury them. They may have been buried in a mass grave near the Alamo or near the altar railing of San Antonio's San Fernando Cathedral (a box of charred remains was discovered there in 1936)—or they may not have been buried at all.

213

ROBERTO CLEMENTE (1934–December 31, 1972) (Sports Figures)   Batting champion Clemente was killed in the crash on takeoff of a plane he had chartered to carry relief supplies from San Juan to the victims of an earthquake in Nicaragua. Day after day divers searched for his body, but it was never found.

ALBERT EINSTEIN (1879–April 18, 1955) (Scientists and Inventors)   Einstein requested that there be no funeral service, grave, or monument because he wanted no place to become his shrine. As he wished, the disposal of his ashes was kept secret; a friend drove to a river near Trenton, New Jersey, and dropped them in without ceremony.

JOE HILL (1879–November 19, 1915) (Social Reformers)   A union organizer and hero of the radical labor movement, Hill was executed by a firing squad for killing a prominent Salt Lake City businessman. His ashes were scattered in every state of the union, except Utah.

HENRY HUDSON (?–1611) (Explorers and Settlers)   Discoverer of the Hudson River and Hudson's Bay, the explorer was set adrift without provisions after his men mutinied. He was never seen again.

JUMBO (1865–September 15, 1885) (Entertainers)   The twelve-foot, six-and-a-half-ton elephant had grossed millions of dollars for showman P. T. Barnum (see Entertainers) before a locomotive plunged into him, killing him instantly. Jumbo's hide, weighing 1,538 pounds, was put on a frame and exhibited with the circus. It was later displayed at Tufts University until it was destroyed in a fire.

DUKE KAHANAMOKU (1890–January 22, 1968) (Sports Figures)   The Olympic swimming champion, who introduced the freestyle stroke, had a "beach boy" funeral with more than fifteen thousand people lining Waikiki Beach. Beach boys in thirty canoes escorted an outrigger carrying his ashes, which were scattered over the Pacific.

NATHAN LEOPOLD (1906–August 30, 1971) (Criminals)
Paroled thirty-five years after he was sentenced to life imprisonment for the sensational Leopold-Loeb murder (1924), he died in San Juan, Puerto Rico, where he had been working with a church medical mission for ten dollars a month. He donated his eyes to two blind people and the rest of his body to a medical school for research.

THOMAS PAINE (1737–June 5, 1809) (Colonists and Patriots)
Ten years after his death, the coffin of the ardent revolutionary was stolen from his New Rochelle, New York, farm and taken to England, where the remains were exhibited in an attempt to rally the masses against the British government. No one responded, and eventually the bones vanished, as illustrated in the English schoolboys' chant: "Poor Tom Paine/Here he lies/Nobody laughs and nobody cries/Where he's gone and how he fares/Nobody knows and nobody cares."

E. W. SCRIPPS (1854–March 12, 1926) (Journalists) Organizer of the Scripps-Howard newspaper chain, Scripps died in Liberia after roaming the world for four years on his yacht and gaining the title "hermit of the seas." He seldom went ashore, and spent his time in the yacht's thousand-volume library. He was buried at sea.

NAT TURNER (1800–November 11, 1831) (Social Reformers) The leader of the slave uprising (1831) that terrified the white South, Turner was captured, convicted of insurrection, and hanged. His body was dissected by surgeons, and legend has it that souvenir purses were made of his skin.

BILL WILLIAMS (1787–March 14, 1849) (Explorers and Settlers) One of the most skilled trappers and guides of the West, Williams was killed by a band of Ute Indians who were actually his friends. They mistook him and his companion for members

216

of a company of soldiers that had recently massacred a Ute village. When the error was discovered, the Indians gave Williams a chief's burial on the spot where he died on the Upper Rio Grande River in southern Colorado. The grave site is unmarked.

SARAH WINNEMUCCA (c. 1844–October 16, 1891) (Social Reformers) A Paiute Indian, she became a lecturer and agitator against the injustices being done to her people. At her request, she was buried on a mound overlooking Henry's Lake in northern Idaho—a crossroads for early Indian travel where she had first served as an interpreter for the U.S. Army. In 1960 a development of summer houses was built on the lake, probably covering her unmarked grave.

Cremated and ashes scattered according to their own wishes

ARCTIC OCEAN *Explorers and Settlers* Louise Arner Boyd (1887–September 14, 1972). **ATLANTIC OCEAN** *Musicians* Eddy Duchin (1909–February 9, 1951); Woody Guthrie (1912–October 3, 1967); Frank Loesser (1910–July 28, 1969). *Social Reformers* Victoria Claflin Woodhull (1838–June 9, 1927). **CALIFORNIA** *Entertainers* Steve McQueen (1930–November 7, 1980) Santa Paula Valley. **CARIBBEAN SEA** *Entertainers* Veronica Lake (1919–July 7, 1973). *Scientists and Inventors* J. Robert Oppenheimer (1904–February 18, 1967). **ILLINOIS** *Social Reformers* Clarence Darrow (1857–March 13, 1938) Jackson Park, Chicago. **INDIA** *Religious Leaders* Annie Wood Besant (1847–September 20, 1933) River Adyar. **MAINE** *Artists* Marsden Hartley (1877–September 2, 1943) Androscoggin River; William Zorach (1887–November 5, 1966) Goose Rock Passage, mouth of Robinhood Cove. **MASSACHU-SETTS** *Entertainers* Ted Shawn (1891–January 9, 1972) Jacob's Pillow Festival, Lee. **MICHIGAN** *Social Reformers* Walter Reuther (1907–May 9, 1970) Black Lake, near Onway. **NEW YORK** *Government Leaders* Norman M. Thomas (1884–December 19, 1968) Long Island Sound. *Journalists* Edward R. Murrow (1908–April 27, 1965) Pawling. *Musicians* Fats Waller (1904–December 15, 1943) Harlem, New York City. *Writers* Carl Van Vechten (1880–December 21, 1964) Shakespeare Gardens, Central Park, New York City. **PACIFIC OCEAN** *Artists* Edward Weston (1886–January 1, 1958). *Criminals* Caryl Chessman (1921–May 2, 1960). *Entertainers* Bud Abbott (1895–April 24, 1974); Van Heflin (1910–

July 23, 1971); William Holden (1918–c. November 16, 1981); Darryl F. Zanuck (1902–December 22, 1979). **Government Leaders** Jeannette Rankin (1880–May 18, 1973). **Military** Joseph W. Stilwell (1883–October 12, 1946). **Musicians** Janis Joplin (1943–October 4, 1970); André Kostelanetz (1901–January 13, 1980). **Social Scientists and Educators** Thorstein B. Veblen (1857–August 3, 1929). **PENNSYLVANIA** *Artists* John Sloan (1871–September 7, 1951) Lock Haven.

Ashes retained by family

Artists Alexander Calder (1898–November 11, 1976). **Entertainers** Fredric March (1897–April 14, 1975); Robert Montgomery (1904–September 27, 1981). **Journalists** Drew Pearson (1897–September 1, 1969). **Religious Leaders** Robert Ingersoll (1833–July 21, 1899). **Writers** Jacqueline Susann (1921–September 21, 1974).

Lost—in air or at sea

Colonists and Patriots Peter Minuit (1580–June, 1638). **Entertainers** Leslie Howard (1890–June 2, 1943). **Explorers and Settlers** Amelia Earhart (1898–July 2, 1937).

Lost—grave site no longer known or unburied

MASSACHUSETTS *Colonists and Patriots* William Brewster (1567–April 10, 1644) Plymouth; John Carver (c. 1576–April 5, 1621) Plymouth; John Endicott (c. 1589–March 16, 1665). **MISSISSIPPI RIVER** *Explorers and Settlers* Hernando De Soto (1500–May 21, 1542). **NEBRASKA** *Military Leaders* Crazy Horse (c. 1842/44–September 6, 1877) in the panhandle. **NEW YORK** *Colonists and Patriots* Nathan Hale (1755–September 22, 1776) Long Island; Anne Hutchinson (1591–1643) Bronx, New York City. **NORTH CAROLINA** *Colonists and Patriots* Virginia Dare (1587–c. 1587) Roanoke Island? **TEXAS** *Explorers and Settlers* Robert Cavelier Sieur de la Salle (1643–March 19, 1687) Brazos River. **VIRGINIA** *Colonists and Patriots* Nathaniel Bacon (1647–October 1676) Gloucester County; John Rolfe (1585–1622).

Body donated to medicine

Musicians Bobby Darin (1936–December 20, 1973).

BURIED ABROAD

GRACE KELLY (Princess Grace of Monaco) (1929–September 14, 1982) (Entertainers) Cathedral of Monaco, Monte Carlo, Monaco. The movie star who became a princess died in a controversial motor accident on the coast of France. First reports covered up the extent of her injuries, and statements after her death blamed failed brakes on her automobile. The exact cause of death was finally reported to be a stroke that led the princess to lose control of her car.

GEORGE S. PATTON, JR. (1885–December 21, 1945) (Military) Luxembourg American Cemetery, near Hamm, Luxembourg "Old Blood and Guts," commander of the Third Army in World War II, was killed in a car accident. Mrs. Patton gave up plans to ship her husband home when she learned that the bodies of other U.S. soldiers were not being returned while the war continued. "I know George would want to lie beside the men of his Army who have fallen," she said, choosing the cemetery with the largest number of Third Army casualties.

JAMES ALBERT PIKE (1913–September 1969) (Religious Leaders) St. Peter's Protestant Cemetery, Jaffa, Israel The respected Episcopal clergyman turned to spiritualism after the death of his son. On a trip to the Middle East, Pike became lost in the Judean wilderness west of the Dead Sea and was dead by the time search parties found him. As Bishop Pike was buried in the small cemetery, his young wife placed a "peace cross" in the coffin.

ARCTIC *Explorers and Settlers* Charles Francis Hall (1821–November 8, 1871) Thank God Harbor, or Hall's Rest. **AUSTRIA** *Musicians* Arnold Schoenberg (1874–July 13, 1951) Central Cemetery, Vienna. **BOLIVIA** *Criminals* Butch Cassidy (Robert Leroy Parker) (1866–?), Sundance Kid (Harry Longbaugh) (1865–?) San Vincente. **BRAZIL** *Musicians* Carmen Miranda (1913–August 5, 1955) Rio de Janeiro. **CANADA** *Business and Finance* Cyrus Stephen Eaton (1883–May 9, 1979) Upper Blandford, Nova Scotia. *Explorers and Settlers* Robert "Bob" Bartlett (1875–April 28, 1946) Methodist Churchyard, Brigus, Newfoundland; Samuel de Champlain (c. 1567–December 25, 1635) Quebec; Louis Joliet (1645–May 1700) Mignan Island. *Scientists and Inventors* Alexander Graham Bell (1847–August 2, 1922) Beinn Breagh Mountain, Nova Scotia; Jacob Schick (1877–July 3, 1937) Mount Royal Cemetery, Montreal. **DENMARK** *Musicians* Lauritz Melchior (1890–March 18, 1973) Copenhagen. **ECUADOR** *Artists* Thomas Nast (1840–December 7, 1902) Guayaquil. **ENGLAND** *Artists* John Singleton Copley (1737–September 9, 1815) Highgate Cemetery, London; Jacob Epstein (1880–August 19, 1959) Putney Vale Cemetery, near London; Benjamin West (1738–March 11, 1820) St. Paul's Church, London. *Colonists and Patriots* George Calvert, Lord Baltimore (c. 1580–April 15, 1632); James Edward Oglethorpe (1696–June 30, 1785); William Penn (1644–July 30, 1718); Pocahontas (c. 1595–March, 1617) St. George's Churchyard, Gravesend; John Smith (1579–June 21, 1631). *Entertainers* Alfred Hitchcock (1899–April 29, 1980); Boris Karloff (1887–February 3, 1969) London area; Anna Pavlova (1881–January 23, 1931) London; George Sanders (1906–April 25, 1972). *Military* Benedict Arnold (1741–June 14, 1801) Crypt of St. Mary's Church, Battersea. *Musicians* John Lennon (1940–December 8, 1980); Leopold Stokowski (1882–

September 13, 1977) St. Marylebone Cemetery, London. **FRANCE** *Artists* Mary Cassatt (1845–June 24, 1926) Department of Oise, Mesnil-Théribus; Jo Davidson (1884–January 2, 1952) estate at Azay-le-Rideau, near Tours. *Entertainers* Maurice Chevalier (1888–January 1, 1972) Marnes-la-Coquette, Paris suburb; Isadora Duncan (1878–September 14, 1927) Père Lachaise Cemetery, Paris; Maria Montez (1919–September 7, 1951) Montparnasse Cemetery, Paris; Vaslav Nijinsky (1890–April 8, 1950) Montmartre Cemetery, Paris; Jean Seberg (1938–September 8, 1979) Paris; Pearl White (1889–August 4, 1938) Passy Cemetery, Passy. *Government Leaders* Judah P. Benjamin (1811–May 8, 1884) Père Lachaise Cemetery, Paris. *Journalists* James Gordon Bennett, Jr. (1841–May 14, 1918) Paris. *Musicians* Sidney Bechet (1897–May 14, 1959) Paris; Maria Callas (1923–September 16, 1977) Père Lachaise Cemetery, Paris; Jim Morrison (1943–July 3, 1971) Père Lachaise Cemetery, Paris. Lili Pons (1904–February 13, 1976) Cannes. *Writers* Gertrude Stein (1874–July 27, 1946) Père Lachaise Cemetery, Paris; Edith Wharton (1862–August 11, 1937) Versailles; Richard Wright (1908–November 28, 1960) Père Lachaise Cemetery, Paris. **GERMANY** *Artists* George Grosz (1893–July 6, 1959) Berlin. **GHANA** *Social Reformers* W. E. B. DuBois (1868–August 27, 1963) outside Government House, Accra. **IRELAND** *Entertainers* Barry Fitzgerald (1888–January 4, 1961) Graveyard of St. Patrick's Protestant Church, Dublin. **ISRAEL** *Artists* Jacques Lipchitz (1891–May 26, 1973) Jerusalem. *Writers* Meyer Levin (1905–July 9, 1981) Jerusalem. **ITALY** *Criminals* Nicola Sacco (1891–August 23, 1927), Bartolomeo Vanzetti (1888–August 23, 1927) Turin. *Musicians* Arturo Toscanini (1867–January 16, 1957) Milan. **JAMAICA** *Social Reformers* Marcus Garvey (1887–June 10, 1940) King George VI Memorial Park, Kingston. **MEXICO** *Explorers and Settlers* Francisco Vásquez de Coronado (c. 1510–September 22, 1554). **MONACO** *Entertainers* Josephine Baker (1906–April 10, 1975). **POLAND** *Colonists and Patriots* Thaddeus Kosciuszko (1746–October 15, 1817) Wawel Castle, Cracow. *Entertainers* Helena Modjeska (1845–April 8, 1909) Cracow. **SPAIN** *Musicians* Lucrezia Bori (1888–May 14, 1960) Valencia; Pablo Casals (1876–October 22, 1973) Vendrell. **SWEDEN** *Entertainers* Ingrid Bergman (1915–August 29, 1982) Stockholm.

SWITZERLAND *Entertainers* Charles Chaplin (1889–December 25, 1977) Corsier Cemetery, Corsier. *Musicians* Paul Hindemith (1895–December 23, 1963) Blonay by Vevy. **TRINIDAD** *Scientists and Inventors* Charles W. Beebe (1877–June 4, 1962) Mucurapo Cemetery, Mucurapo. **USSR** *Journalists* John Reed (1887–October 19, 1920) Kremlin wall, Moscow.

The Moscow funeral of journalist John Reed prior to his burial in the Kremlin. (Houghton Library, Harvard University)

GEOGRAPHICAL GUIDE TO CEMETERIES

The geographical portion of *Permanent Addresses* is intended to be as specific as possible in helping you locate a particular cemetery and the individual in it. Information about the cemeteries is organized alphabetically by state and by town. We have tried to pinpoint town locations, the hours the cemetery and/or office are open, and sometimes the lot locations of the famous people buried there.

Many large cemeteries provide maps and materials for visitors, and these are noted. It is best to phone ahead before visiting any cemetery, because the times that they are open may vary. Generally speaking, however, you can expect to find cemetery gates open during daylight hours, with offices open during regular business hours plus a half or full day on Saturdays; they may be closed during the lunch hour. Small-town cemeteries are less likely to have an office, although they usually have a caretaker on the premises. If this person is not available when you arrive, check at the local town hall for information, or, if it is a churchyard, in the church itself. Even though small country cemeteries may be listed as open at all times, it is unwise to plan to visit them during the winter months or in inclement weather.

This geographical breakdown also notes other sites of interest in the locality related to the famous people buried there that you might enjoy visiting, such as restored homes, historic sites, museums, or festivals.

ALABAMA

MONTGOMERY Oakwood Annex, 1305 Upper Wetumpka Rd. ½ mi. E of city police station. Always open. *Musicians* Hank Williams, bear R at top of hill, monument visible on L, grave covered with artificial turf.
TUSKEGEE INSTITUTE (35 mi. E of Montgomery) Tuskegee Institute. The Institute maintains a small cemetery on campus. *Scientists and Inventors* George Washington Carver. *Social Scientists and Educators* Booker T. Washington.

ALASKA

SITKA (near Juneau) U.S. Government Cemetery. *Sports Figures* Charles William Paddock.
SKAGWAY (N of Juneau) Skagway Town Cemetery. *Criminals* Jefferson "Soapy" Smith.

ARIZONA

PHOENIX Greenwood Memorial Park, 2300 W. Van Buren Ave. *Journalists* Walter Winchell.
TOMBSTONE (40 mi. E of Tucson, off I-10) Boot Hill Graveyard. Originally called the Tombstone Cemetery; became known as "Boothill" because of the violent deaths many buried there had met. Victims of outlaws, hangings, lynchings, and suicides are buried alongside the perpetrators and innocent bystanders. Open 8–6 M–Su. *Explorers and Settlers* John Swain Slaughter. Also: the Clantons and McLaurys, killed in a gunfight with Wyatt Earp.

CALIFORNIA

CARMEL (near Monterey, on Rte. 1) Basilica, Mision de San Carlos Borromeo del Puerto de Monterey. Open 9:30–4:30 M–Sa,

10:30–4:30 Su; closed Easter, Christmas, Thanksgiving. *Religious Leaders* Junipero Serra.

COLMA (just S of San Francisco, on Rte. 82) Cypress Lawn Memorial Park, El Camino Real. Open dawn to dusk; office: 8–4 M–F. *Journalists* William Randolph Hearst, lots 1 and 2, sect. H, private mausoleum. *Social Reformers* Tom Mooney.

Hills of Eternity Cemetery, El Camino Real. Open 8–5 M–F, 10–3 Sa. *Explorers and Settlers* Wyatt Earp.

COMPTON (Los Angeles suburb) Woodlawn Memorial Park, 1715 W. Greenleaf Blvd. *Entertainers* Irene Ryan. Also: Francis E. Townsend (1867–1960) social reformer.

GLENDALE (Los Angeles suburb) Forest Lawn Memorial Park, 1712 Glendale Ave., Glendale; 6300 Forest Lawn Dr., Los Angeles. Open 9–5:30. *Business and Finance* King Camp Gillette, private mausoleum in begonia corridor; William Wrigley, Jr., Great Mausoleum. *Entertainers* Gracie Allen; Warner Baxter; Wallace Beery; Humphrey Bogart; Clara Bow; Joe E. Brown; Francis X. Bushman; Godfrey Cambridge; Jack Carson; Lon Chaney; Dorothy Dandridge; Walt Disney; Marie Dressler; William Farnum; W. C. Fields; Errol Flynn; Clark Gable, Great Mausoleum; Samuel Goldwyn; Sydney Greenstreet; Jean Harlow; Gabby Hayes; Buster Keaton; Ernie Kovacs; Alan Ladd; Carole Landis; Charles Laughton; Stan Laurel; Harold Lloyd; Carole Lombard, Great Mausoleum; Marjorie Main; Chico Marx; Harpo Marx; Victor McLaglen; Tom Mix; Alla Nazimova; Jack Oakie; Mary Pickford; Dick Powell; Freddie Prinze; George Raft; Wallace Reid; Will Rogers; Ruth St. Denis; David O. Selznick; Robert Taylor; Irving Thalberg; Spencer Tracy; Ben Turpin; Ed Wynn; Florenz Ziegfeld. *Musicians* Nat "King" Cole; Rudolph Friml; Red Nichols, Hollywood Hills Section. *Religious Leaders* Aimee Semple McPherson. *Sports Figures* Casey Stengel; Jess Willard. *Writers* Theodore Dreiser, lot 1132, Whispering Pines section; Clifford Odets, Columbarium of Honor. Also: Gutzon Borglum, sculptor; Russ Columbo, bandleader; John Gilbert, actor; Jean Hersholt, actor; Gus Kahn, composer; Ernst Lubitsch, director; Tod Sloan (1874–1933) jockey; Jack Teagarden, musician; Lawrence Tibbett, singer; Grant Withers, actor.

INGLEWOOD (Los Angeles suburb) Inglewood Park Cemetery, 720 E. Florence Ave. *Entertainers* Edgar Bergen; Louise Fazenda; Hoot Gibson; Betty Grable; Gypsy Rose Lee. *Sports Figures* James

Jeffries. Also: "The Flying Cordonas," circus aerialist family;
Ferde Grofé (1892–1972) composer.
LOS ANGELES Calvary Cemetery, 4201 Whittier Blvd. Open 7–
6 M–Su. *Entertainers* Ethel Barrymore; John Barrymore; Lionel
Barrymore; Lou Costello, mausoleum; Ramon Novarro.

Hillside Memorial Park, 6001 Centinela Ave. *Entertainers*
Jack Benny; Ben Blue; Eddie Cantor; Jeff Chandler; George Jessel;
Al Jolson.

Hollywood Memorial Park Cemetery, 6000 Santa Monica
Blvd., entrance between Van Ness Ave. and Gower St. Open 7:30–
4:30 M–Su; mausoleums: 8:30–4:15 M–Su, Beth Olam mauso-
leums closed Sa. Map available. *Criminals* Bugsy Siegel, Beth
Olam Mausoleum. *Entertainers* Louis Calhern; Marion Davies;
sect. 8; Cecil B. De Mille, sect. 8; Douglas Fairbanks, Sr., sect. 11,
Sunken Garden; Peter Finch, sect. 11, Hollywood Cathedral Mau-
soleum; Peter Lorre, sect. 11, Hollywood Cathedral Mausoleum;
Adolphe Menjou, sect. 8; Paul Muni, sect. 14, Beth Olam; Tyrone
Power, sect. 8; Norma Talmadge, Abbey of the Psalms; Clifton
Webb, Abbey of the Psalms; Rudolph Valentino, sect. 11, Hol-
lywood Cathedral Mausoleum. *Musicians* Nelson Eddy, sect. 8;
Cass Elliott. Also: Harry Cohn, movie producer; Bebe Daniels
(1901–71) near Chapel of Psalms, silent movie comedian.

Holy Cross Cemetery, 5835 West Slauson Ave. Open 7–6 M–
Su; mausoleum: 8–5 M–Sa, 11–5 Su and hol.; office: 8:30–5 M–
Sa. Map available. *Entertainers* Richard Arlen, grave 130, tier 57,
sect. T; Charles Boyer, grave 5, tier 186, sect. "Grotto," St. Anne
Garden; Bing Crosby, grave 1, tier 119, sect. "Grotto"; Jimmy
Durante, grave 6, tier 96, sect. F (St. Joseph); John Ford, grave 5,
lot 304, sect. M; Jack Haley, 2, 100, sect. "Grotto"; Frank Lovejoy,
grave 5, lot 306, sect. P; Bela Lugosi, grave 1, tier 120, sect.
"Grotto"; William Lundigan, grave 3, lot 269, sect. D; Rosalind
Russell, grave 2, lot 536, sect. M; Mack Sennett, grave 1, lot 490,
sect. N; Sharon Tate, grave 6, tier 152, sect. "Grotto," St. Anne's.
Journalists Louella Parsons, grave 8, lot 235, sect. D, Sacred
Heart. *Musicians* José Iturbi, crypt E-1, block 16, mausoleum;
Spike Jones, crypt A-7, block 70, mausoleum; Mario Lanza, crypt
D-2, block 46, mausoleum. *Sports Figures* Ralph De Palma; Bar-
ney Oldfield, grave 11, lot 290, sect. D, Sacred Heart. Also: Keefe
Brasselle (d. 1981) actor, 168, 29, sect. R; Joan Davis (1907–61)
actress, crypt D-1, block 46, mausoleum.

Home of Peace Cemetery, 4334 Whittier Blvd. Open 9–5 M–F, Su, closed Sa. Map available. *Entertainers* Fanny Brice; Louis B. Mayer.

Rosedale Memorial Park, 1831 W. Washington Blvd. *Entertainers* Anna May Wong.

Westwood Memorial Park, 1218 Glendon Ave. at Wilshire. *Entertainers* Sebastian Cabot, urn garden, grave 6, lot 200, row 1, East; Richard Conte, grave 2, lot 62, sect. D; Marilyn Monroe, crypt 24, sect A, Corridor of Memories; Natalie Wood. *Musicians* Oscar Levant, 26-A, Sanctuary of Love; Gregor Piatigorsky, grave 6, lot 154, sect. D; Helen Traubel, inurned in niche C-11, Sanctuary of Remembrance. Also: John Boles (1895–1969), silent movie star, crypt C-62, Sanctuary of Serenity; Anita Louise (1917–1970), actress, crypt B-12, Sanctuary of Devotion.

MARTINEZ (about 25 mi. NE of San Francisco) John Muir National Historic Site, intersection of John Muir Parkway and Ponoma St. Open daily except major holidays. Movie and self-guiding tours available. *Scientists and Inventors* John Muir, in family cemetery once part of Muir/Strenzel Ranch. Home and grounds may be visited.

MISSION HILLS (N of Los Angeles) Eden Memorial Park, 11500 Sepulveda Blvd. *Entertainers* Lenny Bruce; Groucho Marx.

San Fernando Mission Cemetery, 11160 Stranwood Ave., off Sepulveda Blvd. Open 8–6 M–Su; office: 8:30–5 M–Sa. Six buildings have been restored to show how they were when mission was established in 1797. *Entertainers* William Bendix, grave 10, lot 247, sect. D, across from Mausoleum, 14 graves up from 241; William Frawley, grave 4, lot 66, sect. C, 64 curb, 6 graves up. *Scientists and Inventors* Lee De Forest, grave 2, lot 416, sect. C, 406 curb, 22 graves up.

NEWPORT BEACH (S of Los Angeles, on Rte. 1) Pacific View Memorial Park, 3500 Pacific View Dr. *Entertainers* John Wayne.

NORTH HOLLYWOOD (Los Angeles area) Valhalla Memorial Park, 10621 Victory Blvd. Office: 8–5 M–F, 9–4 Sa, Su. Map available. *Entertainers* Oliver Hardy, Lot 48, Row D, Garden of Hope; Mae Murray, Lot 6, sect. 6328, Block G. Also: Bea Benaderet (1906–1968) character actress, Mausoleum of Hope, Garden of

Love; Gorgeous George, wrestler, Graceland; Gail Russell (1924–1961), actress, Evergreen.

OAKLAND (E of San Francisco) Mountain View Cemetery, 5000 Piedmont Ave. *Business and Finance* Charles Crocker; Henry J. Kaiser, crypt in Main Mausoleum. *Writers* Frank Norris.

PALO ALTO (near San Francisco) Stanford Family Mausoleum, Stanford University. *Business and Finance* A. Leland Stanford.

SACRAMENTO Sacramento City Cemetery, 10th St. and Broadway. *Business and Finance* Mark Hopkins (his tomb is the largest in the cemetery).

St. Mary's Cemetery and Mausoleum, 6700 21st Ave. *Sports Figures* Max Baer.

SAN BRUNO (outside San Francisco) Golden Gate National Cemetery, 1300 Sneath Lane, corner Junipero Serra Blvd., eastern border, El Camino Real. Open 8–5 M–Su, 8–7 Memorial Day; office: 8–4:30 M–F. Map available. *Military* Chester Nimitz, grave 1, sect. C-1. *Sports Figures* Tom Sharkey.

SAN DIEGO Cypress View Mausoleum, 3953 Imperial Ave. at 40th St., just W of Freeway 805. Open 8:30–4:45 M–Su. The Great Hall contains an art museum. *Musicians* Amelita Galli-Curci, Great Hall.

Greenwood Memorial Park, I-805 and Imperial Ave. *Musicians* Ernestine Schumann-Heink.

Mount Hope Cemetery, 3751 Market St. Map available. *Writers* Raymond Chandler, sect. 3. Also: early settlers and local leaders.

SANTA BARBARA (60 mi. N of Los Angeles, on Rte. 101) Santa Barbara Cemetery, E. Cabrillo Blvd., overlooking Pacific Ocean. *Entertainers* Ronald Colman, Ridge sect., lot 663. *Social Scientists and Educators* Robert Maynard Hutchins, Summit sect., S. G. 501, Addition M.

SANTA ROSA (50 mi. N of San Francisco) Burbank Home, Tupper St. and Santa Rosa Ave. *Scientists and Inventors* Luther Burbank.

STOCKTON (50 mi. E of San Francisco, on I-5) Parkview Cemetery, French Camp Rd. and Highway 99. Open 8–5 M–F; office and mausoleum: 8–5 M–F. Map available. *Sports Figures* Amos Alonzo Stagg, mausoleum, niche bank.

VICTORVILLE (60 mi. NE of Los Angeles) Roy Rogers–Dale Evans Museum, 15650 Seneca Rd. *Entertainers* Trigger.

COLORADO

BOULDER Columbia Cemetery, 9th St. and College Ave. Also called Pioneer Cemetery. *Criminals* Tom Horn, in the southwest section.

DENVER Buffalo Bill Memorial Museum and Grave, Lookout Mountain Rd., 5 mi. W of Golden, take I-70 W to Exit 256, Lookout Mt., 15 mi. from downtown Denver. Always open. Museum open 9–4 Oct. 1–Apr. 30; 9–5 May 1–Sept. 30. *Explorers and Settlers* Buffalo Bill.

GLENWOOD SPRINGS (100 mi. W of Denver, on I-70) Glenwood Cemetery, also called Old Hill. *Criminals* Kid Curry; John H. "Doc" Holliday.

CONNECTICUT

BRIDGEPORT Mountain Grove Cemetery, 2675 North Ave. Open sunup–sunset every day; office: 8:30–4 M–F. *Entertainers* P. T. Barnum, sect. 9; Tom Thumb, sect. 8.

CORNWALL (15 mi. W of Torrington, on Rte. 4) Cornwall Hollow Cemetery, Rte. 43, 5 mi. N of the intersections of Rtes. 4, 128, and 43, on R of 43 going N opposite Civil War monument to Major General John Sedgwick. *Writers* Mark Van Doren.

DANBURY (60 mi. N of New York City) Wooster Cemetery, 20 Ellsworth Ave., accessible from I-84, which runs through the city. Open until 4 M–F, until 12 Sa; office: 8:30–12:30 M–F. Map available. *Musicians* Charles Edward Ives, sect. M. Also: David Wooster, Revolutionary War general.

FARMINGTON (on Rte. 202, outside Hartford) Riverside Cemetery, Garden St. *Entertainers* William Gillette.

GREENWICH Putnam Cemetery, Parsonage Rd. *Musicians* Ezio Pinza.

HAMDEN (outside New Haven) Mount Carmel Cemetery, 3801 Whitney Ave., beyond Sleeping Giant Park, on R. *Writers* Thornton Wilder.

HARTFORD Cedar Hill Cemetery, 453 Fairfield Ave. Open 7–sunset; office: 9–4 M–F. Map available. *Artists* William Glackens, lot 104, sect. 1. *Business and Finance* J. Pierpont Morgan. *Scientists and Inventors* Samuel Colt. *Writers* Wallace Stevens.

Center Congregational Churchyard, Main St. *Colonists and Patriots* Thomas Hooker.

NEW CANAAN (N of Stamford) Lakeview Cemetery, Main St. and Millport Ave., about 6 blocks from town center. Open at all times. *Writers* Maxwell Perkins, sect. K, east half of lot 23, grave 2.

NEW HAVEN Evergreen Cemetery, 92 Winthrop Ave. Always open; office: 9–3:30. *Sports Figures* Walter Camp; George Weiss.

Grove Street Cemetery, 227 Grove St. between Prospect and Ashmun Sts. Map available with tour of cemetery notes the graves of 80 "eminent men"; also brochure with history of the cemetery. Dating from 1796, the cemetery is one of the earliest to be laid out with a grid pattern of streets. *Colonists and Patriots* Roger Sherman, Maple Ave. *Scientists and Inventors* Charles Goodyear, Sycamore Ave.; Eli Whitney, Cedar Ave. *Social Scientists and Educators* Ezra Stiles, Maple Ave. *Writers* Noah Webster, Cedar Ave. Also: Lyman Beecher (1775–1863) religious leader, Cedar Ave.; David Humphreys, Revolutionary War soldier; Benjamin Silliman, Sr. (1779–1864) educator, corner Hawthorne and Cedar; Benjamin Silliman, Jr. (1816–85) educator, Maple Ave.

Yale University Art Gallery, corner High and Chapel Sts. Open 9–5 Tu–F during school year. *Artists* John Trumbull (a black marble tablet marking the location of his vault can be found in the area between the History of Art office and the Sculpture Hall in the old Art Gallery).

NEW LONDON Gardner Cemetery, Ocean and Pequot Aves. *Entertainers* Richard Mansfield.

RIDGEFIELD (20 mi. N of Norwalk, on Rtes. 7 and 35) Fairlawn Cemetery, Rte. 116 and Maple Shade Rd., short distance from center of town, off Main St. *Artists* Cass Gilbert.

SHERMAN (10 mi. N of Danbury) North Cemetery, on Church Rd., off Rte. 39, next door to Sherman Congregational Church. *Artists* Arshile Gorky, plot 83.

WESTON (3 mi. N of Westport) Cemetery of Emmanuel Church, Lyons Place Rd. *Supreme Court Justices* John Marshall Harlan (d. 1971).

WETHERSFIELD (near Hartford) Emanuel Cemetery, Berlin Turnpike. *Entertainers* Sophie Tucker.

WINDSOR LOCKS (10 mi. N of Hartford) St. Mary's Cemetery, Spring St. *Government Leaders* Ella T. Grasso.

DELAWARE

GREENVILLE (near Wilmington) Du Pont Family Cemetery, Buck Rd., near intersection of Rtes. 100 and 141. *Business and Finance.* Éleuthère Irénée Du Pont.

DISTRICT OF COLUMBIA

Congressional Cemetery, 18th and E St. SE, 1½ mi. SE of Capitol on Anacostia River. From 1807 until 1876, when Arlington National Cemetery became the principal burial ground, nearly every congressman who died in office was buried here. A cenotaph or empty tomb was built in memory of each congressman who had died in office, even those who were buried elsewhere. By 1876 nearly a hundred senators and representatives, two vice-presidents, several Supreme Court Justices, and the first five mayors of the District of Columbia had been buried there. Three presidents, John Adams, Harrison, and Taylor, lay in a public vault before being transported to their home states, as did Dolley Madison, John C. Calhoun, and Henry Clay. *Artists* Mathew B. Brady. *Government Leaders* Elbridge Gerry; J. Edgar Hoover; Edwin M. Stanton. *Musicians* John Philip Sousa. Also: Choctaw chief Push-Ma-Ta-Ha and several Revolutionary War generals.

D.C. Jail and Asylum (Old Washington Jail), 19th and Independence Ave., SE. *Criminals* Charles Julius Guiteau.

Mount Olivet Cemetery, 1300 Bladensburg Rd. NE. Open 8–5 M–Su; office: 8:30–4 M–F. Map available. *Criminals* Mary E. Surratt, sect. 12-F, lot 31.

Oak Hill Cemetery, 3001 R St. NW. Open 9–5 M–F. *Government Leaders* Dean Acheson. Also: Edward D. White (1845–1921) Supreme Court Justice.

Rock Creek Cemetery, Rock Creek Church Rd. and Webster St. NW. Established in 1719, and the oldest cemetery in the District, it contains St. Paul's Church, the oldest church in the District. *Scientists and Inventors* Cleveland Abbe. *Supreme Court Justices* John Marshall Harlan (d. 1911); Harlan Fiske Stone. *Writers* Henry Adams. Also: Terence Vincent Powderly (1842–1924) labor leader; Sumner Welles (1892–1961) government leader.

Smithsonian Institution. *Military* Kidron, Museum of Natural History, Research Collection, Mammals. *Sports Figures*

Lexington, Museum of Natural History, Osteology Hall; Old Henry Clay, Museum of Natural History, Attic.

Washington Cathedral, Wisconsin Ave. and Woodley Rd. Also called National Cathedral and, formally, Cathedral Church of Saint Peter and Saint Paul. Open 10–4:30. Tours, maps, shops available. *Government Leaders* Cordell Hull. *Military* George Dewey. *Presidents* Woodrow Wilson, Wilson Bay. *Social Reformers* Helen Keller. *Social Scientists and Educators* Anne Sullivan Macy.

FLORIDA

DAYTONA BEACH (60 mi. S of Jacksonville, on I-95) Adjacent to Bethune-Cookman College Campus. *Social Scientists and Educators* Mary McLeod Bethune.

FORT LAUDERDALE Lauderdale Memorial Gardens and Mausoleum, 400 N.W. 27th Ave. *Sports Figures* Rocky Marciano, mausoleum, unit 2, lower level (Prayer level).

MIAMI Our Lady of Mercy Cemetery, 11411 N.W. 25th St. *Sports Figures* Benny "Kid" Paret.

RAIFORD (20 mi. NE of Gainesville, on Rte. 121) Cemetery of Union Correctional Institution. Open to public. *Criminals* Joseph Zangara.

GEORGIA

ATLANTA Oakland Cemetery, 248 Oakland Ave. SE. Visitor center: 8–4:30 M–Sa, 1–4:30 Su. Maps and brochures available. *Sports Figures* Bobby Jones, near Memorial D. *Writers* Margaret Mitchell.

South View Cemetery, 1990 Jonesboro Rd. SE. *Social Reformers* Martin Luther King, Jr.

CARROLLTON (20 mi. SW of Atlanta, on Rte. 166) Our Lady's Memory Garden, Cemetery of Our Lady of Perpetual Help Church, on Center Point Rd. off Highway 113, N of Carrollton. *Entertainers* Susan Hayward (tombstone reads "Mrs. F. E. Chalkley," sign nearby notes actress's grave).

CRAWFORDVILLE (80 mi. E of Atlanta, off I-20) Liberty Hall, Alexander H. Stephens Memorial State Park, 2 blocks N of intersection of US 278 and Rte. 22. *Government Leaders* Alexander H. Stephens, on lawn of home.

GAINESVILLE Alta Vista Cemetery, Broad St. *Military* James Longstreet, lot 36, block 3.
MILLEDGEVILLE (30 mi. NE of Macon, on Rte. 49) Memory Hill Cemetery, West Franklin St., S on Wayne St., R for 2 blocks on Franklin, cemetery on L. Open daylight hours. *Writers* Flannery O'Connor.
ROYSTON (30 mi. NE of Athens, off Rte. 29) Rose Hill Cemetery, off Hwy. 17S near city limits. Always open. *Sports Figures* Ty Cobb.
SAVANNAH Johnson Square, N end of Bull St. *Military* Nathanael Greene, in center of square.

HAWAII

HONOLULU National Memorial Cemetery of the Pacific, 2177 Puowaina Dr. *Journalists* Ernie Pyle.
KIPAHULU, MAUI Kipahulu Hawaiian Churchyard. *Explorers and Settlers* Charles A. Lindbergh.

IDAHO

BOISE Morris Hill Cemetery, 317 No. Latah St., within 1 mile of the heart of the city. *Government Leaders* William E. Borah, block 1, grave 1, in large triangular plot across from mausoleum.

ILLINOIS

ALSIP (Chicago suburb) Burr Oak Cemetery, 127th and 44th Ave. Cemetery and office open 8:30–4:30 M–Su. *Musicians* Dinah Washington, lot 155, grave 4, Elmgrove sect.
BLOOMINGTON (30 mi. SE of Peoria, on I-74) Evergreen Memorial Cemetery, 302 E. Miller St. Always open; office: 8–4:30 M–F. *Government Leaders* Adlai E. Stevenson. Also: Adlai E. Stevenson (1835–1914) vice-president 1893–97.
CEDARVILLE (6 mi. N of Freeport) Cedarville Cemetery, off the railroad. *Social Reformers* Jane Addams.
CHICAGO Douglas Monument Park, E end of 35th St. *Government Leaders* Stephen A. Douglas, 96-foot-tall tomb surmounted by 46-foot column supporting 9-foot-9-inch bronze statue.
     Graceland Cemetery, 4001 North Clark St. Map available. *Artists* Louis Henry Sullivan, Lakeside sect. *Business and*

Finance Philip D. Armour, Ridgeland sect.; Vincent Bendix, Lakeside sect., lot 81; Marshall Field, Ridgeland sect.; Potter Palmer, Willomere sect.; Allan Pinkerton, Chapel sect. *Journalists* Joseph Medill, Ridgeland sect.; Eleanor "Cissy" Medill Patterson. *Scientists and Inventors* Cyrus H. McCormick, Ridgeland sect.; George Mortimer Pullman, Fairlawn sect. *Sports Figures* Bob Fitzsimmons, sect. 12; William A. Hulbert, sect. E and F; Jack Johnson, Bellevue sect. Also: John P. Altgeld (1847–1902) Illinois governor, Lakeside sect.

Lincoln Cemetery, 123rd and Kedzie. *Musicians* Lil Hardin.

Mount Hope Cemetery, 11500 S. Fairfield. *Business and Finance* Gustavus Franklin Swift.

Oak Woods Cemetery, 1035 E. 67th St. *Scientists and Inventors* Enrico Fermi, sect. V, Lot 145, Plot 12. *Sports Figures* Kenesaw Mountain Landis.

Rosehill Cemetery, 5800 N. Ravenswood. *Business and Finance* Oscar Ferdinand Mayer; Richard Warren Sears, compartment H, Community Mausoleum; Montgomery Ward, Community Mausoleum. *Government Leaders* Charles G. Dawes. Also: Julius Rosenwald (1862–1932) merchant.

Rosemont Park Cemetery, 6758 W. Addison St., CTA Addison St. Bus to 6800 West. Office open 9:30–4:30 M–F, Su. Map available. *Sports Figures* Barney Ross, sect. N, lot 19.

Westlawn Cemetery, 7801 W. Montrose Ave. *Criminals* Jack Ruby, next to his parents, Fannie and Joseph Rubenstein.

EVANSTON Memorial Park Cemetery, 2500 Ridge. *Business and Finance* James L. Kraft.

EVERGREEN PARK (Chicago suburb) St. Mary's Cemetery, W. 87th and South Hamlin Ave. *Sports Figures* Brian Piccolo.

FOREST PARK (Chicago suburb) Waldheim/Forest Home Cemetery, 863 S. Des Plaines Ave., main entrance on Des Plaines Ave. Gates open 8:30–5. Area originally used as Pottawatomie Indian burying ground. Notable for burying those executed for inciting the Haymarket riot when no other cemetery would accept their remains. Now one section of the cemetery is known as Dissenters' Row because of the numerous rebels buried there. A large monument recalling the Haymarket incident is across from the chapel. *Entertainers* Mike Todd. *Religious Leaders* Billy Sunday, sect. 32. *Social Reformers* Emma Goldman, to the left of the Haymarket graves; Bill Haywood.

GALESBURG Hope Cemetery, W of Academy St., Main St., near downtown. *Journalists* S. S. McClure, S 6 feet of the W half of lot 634. *Social Scientists and Educators* George Washington Gale, lot 112, 1 block inside cemetery, a four-sided limestone marker topped by a pyramid.

Linwood Cemetery, Rte. 34, W. Main St. Open year round. *Military* Mary Ann "Mother" Bickerdyke, block 61, lot 1 in SE part of cemetery. Statue of Bickerdyke in County Court Yard, downtown.

Carl Sandburg Birthplace, 331 E. Third St. *Writers* Carl Sandburg, Remembrance Rock, in backyard. Birthplace open 9–12, 1–5 Tu–Sa, 1–5 Su, closed M, Thanksgiving, Christmas, New Year's Day.

HILLSIDE (Chicago suburb) Mount Carmel Cemetery, Roosevelt and Wolf Rds. *Criminals* Al Capone; Charles Dion "Deanie" O'Bannion.

METROPOLIS (10 mi. NW of Paducah, Ky., off I-24) Masonic Cemetery. *Criminals* Robert Franklin Stroud.

MOLINE Riverside Cemetery, 2712 6th Ave. *Sports Figures* Warren Giles.

MOUNT OLIVE (50 mi. S of Springfield) Union Miners' Cemetery. *Social Reformers* Mother Jones.

NAUVOO (60 mi. SW of Galesburg, on Rte. 96) Joseph Smith Homesite, between Mississippi River and log cabin, the oldest structure in town, built 1803. *Religious Leaders* Joseph Smith, also wife Emma and brother Hyrum.

PEKIN (10 mi. S of Peoria) Glendale Memorial Gardens, Rte. 9, 3 mi. E of town. *Government Leaders* Everett McKinley Dirksen.

PETERSBURG (20 mi. NW of Springfield) Petersburg Oakland Cemetery. *Writers* Edgar Lee Masters, on main drive. Also: Ann Rutledge, Lincoln's friend, inscription by Masters.

SPRINGFIELD Oak Ridge Cemetery, 1441 Monument Ave., end of street. Map and tour available. *Presidents* Abraham Lincoln. Inside tomb in niches are 4-foot statuettes of Lincoln commemorating periods of his life. A 117-foot spire with four heroic bronze groups about the base and a 10-foot statue S of the shaft. Mary Lincoln and three of their four children are buried here. *Writers* Vachel Lindsay, block 13. Also: John L. Lewis (1880–1969) labor leader, block 22, lot 135, grave 3.

WHEATON Cantigny Estate, 1 S 151 Winfield Rd., 30 mi. W of

Chicago Loop via Eisenhower Expwy. and East-West Tollway. Exit N at Naperville Rd. to Butterfield Rd. Go W to Winfield Rd., then N to estate. Open daily until dusk. Museum, concerts, movies available. This is the 500-acre country estate of Robert McCormick and formerly that of his grandfather, Joseph Medill. Originally a farm called Red Oaks; McCormick renamed it after a French village, site of the American army's first offensive in Europe during the First World War. *Journalists* Robert R. McCormick, buried in the center of a large horseshoe-shaped bench of white granite designed by himself. A statue of a German police dog lies at the head of the grave.

WORTH (Chicago suburb) Holy Sepulchre Cemetery, 6001 W. 111th St. Open 9–7, May–Aug., 9–5 Sept.–Apr.; office: 9–4 M–F, 9–1 Sa. Map available. *Government Leaders* Richard Daley, grave 6, lot AA, block 1, sect. 19. *Musicians* Helen Morgan, grave 2, lot 10, block 2, sect. 14.

INDIANA

ANDERSON (25 mi. NE of Indianapolis) Anderson Memorial Park, State Rd. 9S, 2 blocks N of Interchange of I-69 and State Rd. 9S. Map available. *Sports Figures* Ray Harroun, grave 3, sect. 223, block B.

BLOOMINGTON (45 mi. S of Indianapolis, on Rte. 37) Rose Hill Cemetery, W. 4th St. Map available. *Scientists and Inventors* Alfred C. Kinsey, sect. H. Also: Ross Lockridge, writer.

FAIRMOUNT (60 mi. NE of Indianapolis, off I-69) Park Cemetery, 150 East (Main St.), State Rd. 26, N at Main St. (flashing light), ½ mi. *Entertainers* James Dean. Museum Days in late September include Dean events.

INDIANAPOLIS Crown Hill Cemetery, 700 W. 38th St., 3 mi. NW of downtown, main entrance on 34th St. Open 8–5 Oct. 1–Mar. 30, 8–6 Apr. 1–Sep. 30; office: 8:30–5 M–F. Transportation within cemetery's 50 mi. of paved roads available at nominal fee. Maps and brochures available with locations of some famous burial places. Opened in 1864, the cemetery is listed on the National Register of Historic Places. The Waiting Station, a restoration of the building first used as a gathering place for mourners, designed in the Romanesque Revival style. *Criminals* John Dillinger, sect. 44. *Presidents* Benjamin Harrison, sect. 13. *Writers* James Whitcomb Riley, special tomb at the crown of Crown Hill, near sect. 61; Booth Tarkington, mausoleum in sect. 13. Also: Charles Warren Fairbanks (1852–1918) vice-president 1905–09; Richard Jordan Gatling (1818–1903) inventor; Thomas Andrews Hendricks (1819–85) vice-president (1884); Eli Lilly (1839–98) scientist; Thomas Riley Marshall (1854–1925) vice-president (1913–21); and other statesmen, writers, and notables.

LAFAYETTE (50 mi. NW of Indianapolis) Rest Haven Memorial Park Cemetery, 1200 Sagamore Pkwy. N., US 52, between Greenbush and Union Sts. Office 8–12, 1–4 M–F, 8:30–10:30 Sa. *Entertainers* Emmett Kelley, Sunset Terrace sect. between entrance and exit drives, W of an apple tree.

NEW HARMONY (15 mi. NW of Evansville, on US 460) Paul Tillich Park, intersection of Main and North Sts., just behind the Red Geranium Restaurant. *Religious Leaders* Paul Tillich. Rocks in the park are carved with verses from his writings; bust of Tillich by Rosatti cast in bronze.

PERU (50 mi. W of Fort Wayne) Mount Hope Cemetery, from Rte. 24 going W, turn L on Business 31 and R on 12th after the high school. The cemetery is before the hospital. *Musicians* Cole Porter.

RUSHVILLE (30 mi. SE of Indianapolis) East Hill Cemetery, ½ mi. E on Ind. 44. *Government Leaders* Wendell L. Wilkie.

SOUTH BEND Highland Cemetery, 2257 Portage Ave., 2½ mi. from the stadium, entrance corner Lathrop St. Map and brochure available. Cemetery contains Council Oak, site of meeting between Indian chieftains and La Salle in 1679. *Sports Figures* Knute Rockne.

Riverview Cemetery, 2300 Portage Ave. *Business and Finance* Clement Studebaker.

TERRE HAUTE Highland Lawn Cemetery, 4520 Wabash Ave. *Social Reformers* Eugene V. Debs.

IOWA

ANAMOSA (20 mi. E of Cedar Rapids) Riverside Cemetery, in SW part of city on N side of Wapsipinicon River. Open sunup–sundown. *Artists* Grant Wood, ⅗ of the way around cement drive, on N side. Annual Grant Wood Art Festival, 2nd week in June, other related points of interest nearby.

DAVENPORT Oakdale Cemetery, 25th and Eastern. Office: 9–4:30 M–F, 9–noon Sa, caretaker on premises. *Musicians* Bix Beiderbecke. Annual "Bix Fest" held the last weekend in July at LeClaire Park on the levee.

DES MOINES Glendale Cemetery, University Ave. *Government Leaders* Henry A. Wallace.

DUBUQUE Julien DuBuque Monument Preserve, S of Dubuque, beyond the end of Rowan St. *Explorers and Settlers* Julien DuBuque. Also: Dubuque's wife, Petosa, and his father-in-law, Chief Peosta.

NEWTON (20 mi. E of Des Moines) Newton Union Cemetery, 1600 W. 4th St. N. *Business and Finance* Elmer Henry Maytag; Frederick Louis Maytag.

WEST BRANCH (outside Iowa City) Herbert Hoover National Historic Site, Birthplace, and Grave, off I-80. Open 8–sunset 365 days a year. *Presidents* Herbert Hoover, buried just behind the museum and library.

KANSAS

ABILENE (about 80 mi. W of Topeka) Eisenhower Center, Place of Meditation, SE 4th St., E of Kansas Hwy. 15, 2 mi. S of Abilene exit from I-70. Open 9–5 every day except Thanksgiving, Christmas, and New Year's Day. No fee, except for museum exhibits. Center also includes Eisenhower home and library. *Presidents* Dwight David Eisenhower.

COFFEYVILLE (15 mi. S of Independence, on US 166) Elmwood Cemetery, 16th and Maple. *Criminals* Bob Dalton; Grat Dalton, buried in common grave with Bill Powers (on tombstone: Power). Also: Frank Dalton, a brother on the side of the law, buried several blocks away with an elaborate, tall, inscribed monument. Dalton Defenders Museum in downtown, and other points of interest.

EMPORIA (midway between Topeka and Wichita) Maplewood/Memorial Lawn Cemeteries, 2000 block of N. Prairie. *Journalists* William Allen White.

INDEPENDENCE Old Mount Hope Cemetery, N. Penn Ave. and Oak St., N. Hwy. 75. *Writers* William Inge, lot 100-E.

LAWRENCE (between Topeka and Kansas City) Dyche Hall, University of Kansas Museum of Natural History. *Military* Comanche.

Lawrence Memorial Park Cemetery, 1517 E. 15th St. *Sports Figures* James Naismith, at far end of central drive in the S end of the cemetery. A Masonic shaft with a group of graves circling it, and in the inner circle a red granite stone marks grave.

Oak Hill Cemetery, 1605 Oak Hill. *Sports Figures* Forrest C. Allen.

LEAVENWORTH (outside Kansas City) Cemetery of Leavenworth Penitentiary. Cemetery not open to the public. *Criminals* George "Bugs" Moran.

KENTUCKY

FRANKFORT (20 mi. NW of Lexington) Frankfort Cemetery, E. Main St. *Explorers and Settlers* Daniel Boone.

HOPKINSVILLE (60 mi. W of Bowling Green, on Rte. 68) Riverside Cemetery, 530 N. Main St. *Religious Leaders* Edgar Cayce, buried near entrance to Riverside Chapel in the cemetery. A marker near entrance notes burial.

LEXINGTON Kentucky Horse Park, Iron Works Pike, Rte. 6. Open 9–7 M–Su Memorial Day–Labor Day; hours, days vary rest of year. Entrance free; movies, tours, camping, riding available with admission charge. Maps, brochures available. State-operated theme park showing shops where riding equipment is made; Horse Museum, exhibiting the history of the horse in America. *Sports Figures* Man O' War.

Lexington Cemetery, 833 W. Main St. Open 8–7:30 M–Su Easter Sunday–Mother's Day, 8–5 rest of year. Map available. Sunken gardens, lily pools, 3-acre flower garden. *Government Leaders* Henry Clay, sect. M. Also: John C. Breckinridge (1821–75), vice-president (1857–61), sect. G; John Hunt Morgan (1825–64) Confederate general, sect. C; the Todds (Mrs. Abraham Lincoln's family) and other historic persons. Plus 500 Confederate and 1,300 Union veterans in specially designed plots.

University of Kentucky, Thomas Hunt Morgan Building, corner Washington and Rose Sts. Open 8 A.M.– end of classes. *Sports Figures* Hanover, room 200, 2nd fl.

LOUISA (20 mi. S of Ashland) Pine Hill Cemetery, just W of town. *Supreme Court Justices* Fred M. Vinson.

LOUISVILLE Cave Hill Cemetery, 701 Baxter Ave., E end of Broadway. Open 8–5 M–Su. Tours may be arranged. Rare trees, shrubs, and plants, all labeled; also swans, geese, and wildlife on

300 acres. *Business and Finance* Harland Sanders, lot 57, sect. 33. *Colonists and Patriots* George Rogers Clark. Clark home, Locust Grove, in Louisville may be visited.

Springfield, 5608 Apache Rd., 7 mi. E on Brownsboro Rd., US 42. *Presidents* Zachary Taylor, monument at site of his home as an infant. The surrounding area is a national military cemetery; home not open to public.

University of Louisville, School of Law, Belknap Campus. *Supreme Court Justices* Louis D. Brandeis, under the porch.

TRAPPIST (near Bardstown, 20 mi. S of Louisville) Community Cemetery, Abbey of Gethsemani. *Religious Leaders* Thomas Merton. Since the cemetery is within the monastic enclosure and not open to women, the grave may be seen only by men who are there on retreat, not the general public.

LOUISIANA

BATON ROUGE State House, N. 3rd St. and Boyd Ave. *Government Leaders* Huey Long, in sunken gardens in front.

METAIRIE (New Orleans suburb) Providence Memorial Park, 8200 Airline Hwy. *Musicians* Mahalia Jackson.

NEW ORLEANS Metairie Cemetery, 5100 Pontchartrain Blvd. Map available. Originally a racetrack at which Lexington (see Sports Figures) raced Lecomte in 1854; landscaping has retained the racetrack configuration. Heritage Trail traces burials of historical interest. *Military* John Bell Hood. Also: P. G. T. Beauregard (1818–93) Confederate general, the Army of Tennessee Memorial and tomb; Richard Taylor, son of President Zachary Taylor.

St. Louis Cemetery #1, 400 Basin St., contact caretaker at 3421 Esplanade Ave. *Sports Figures* Paul Morphy, tomb 11, alley No. 2, left facing Basin St.

MAINE

AUGUSTA Blaine Memorial Park, Blaine Ave., adjacent to Forest Grove Cemetery, overlooking city and State Capitol. *Government Leaders* James G. Blaine.

GARDINER (5 mi. S of Augusta) Gardiner Cemetery, at the end of Danforth St. Take Lincoln Ave. E from main square to Danforth, turn R at foot of block. *Writers* Edwin Arlington Robinson, family plot located between the fourth and fifth maple trees on L of road in second line of plots from the road. Robinson birthplace at 67 Lincoln Avenue, corner Danforth.

MARYLAND

ANNAPOLIS Chapel, U.S. Naval Academy, off King George St. and Maryland Ave. Open 9–5 M–Sa, 12–5 Su. Museum; map and tours available. *Military* John Paul Jones.

BALTIMORE Green Mount Cemetery, Greenmount Ave. and Oliver St. Map and brochure available. *Business and Finance* Johns Hopkins, lot 8–9, Summit. *Criminals* John Wilkes Booth, lot 9–11, Dogwood. Also: Allen Dulles (1893–1969) director CIA, lot 51, McDonogh; Sidney Lanier (1842–81) poet, lot 25, Sycamore.

Loudon Park Cemetery, 3801 Frederick Ave. Map available. *Scientists and Inventors* Ottmar Mergenthaler, sect. O, lot 184. *Writers* H. L. Mencken, sect. W, lot 224S½, in family plot.

New Cathedral Cemetery, 4300 Old Frederick Rd. Open 8:30–5 M–Su; office: 8:30–4:30 M–F, 8:30–Noon Sa. Map available. *Sports Figures* John J. McGraw, sect. L, private mausoleum.

Westminster Presbyterian Churchyard, SE corner Fayette and Greene Sts. *Writers* Edgar Allan Poe, between mother-in-law, Maria Clemm, and wife, Virginia, under a monument. Six small square markers each with a "p" define boundaries of family plot. Also: David Poe, Sr., his grandfather.

CHESTERTOWN (about 30 mi. S of Wilmington, Del., on Rte. 213) Saint Paul's Churchyard, 7 mi. W on Rte. 20, turn L at sign at Sandy Bottom Rd. and continue 1 mi. *Entertainers* Tallulah Bankhead, nearest the lake and nearest the trees, NE corner of cemetery.

EMMITSBURG (40 mi. NW of Baltimore, on Rte. 32) Seton Shrine Chapel, St. Joseph's Provincial House, Daughters of Charity. Open 10–5 M–Sa. Tours available. *Religious Leaders* Elizabeth Seton.

FREDERICK Mount Olivet Cemetery, S end of Market St. *Colonists and Patriots* Barbara Fritchie. *Writers* Francis Scott Key.

St. John's Cemetery, East St. between 3rd and 4th Sts. Open M–Su. *Supreme Court Justices* Roger B. Taney.

FROSTBURG (11 mi. W of Cumberland, on Rte. 40) Frostburg Memorial Park. Open 8–4 M–Su. *Sports Figures* Lefty Grove, sect. 9, lot 94.

OELLA (just W of Baltimore, between Rtes. 40 and 144) West-chester Grade School grounds, intersection of Oella Rd. and West-chester Ave. *Scientists and Inventors* Benjamin Banneker.

PIKESVILLE (NW of Baltimore, on Rte. 140) Druid Ridge Ceme-tery, Park Heights Ave. and Old Court Rd. *Musicians* Rosa Pon-selle.

ROCKVILLE (NW of Washington, on I-70S) Saint Mary's Ceme-tery, 600 Veirsmill Rd. (Rte. 28W), corner Rockville Pike (Rte. 355) down street from new County Court House. Always open. *Writers* F. Scott Fitzgerald, near his wife, Zelda.

SILVER SPRING Gate of Heaven Cemetery, 13705 Georgia Ave. *Social Reformers* George Meany.

MASSACHUSETTS

AMESBURY (38 mi. N of Boston, on I-95) Union Cemetery, Rte. 110 (the Haverhill Rd.), follow signs. *Writers* John Greenleaf Whittier, Friends' sect., follow signs. Whittier's home, a national historic landmark, in vicinity, also other points of historical in-terest.

AMHERST (5 mi. from Northampton, on Rte. 9) West Cemetery, Triangle St. *Writers* Emily Dickinson.

ANDOVER (SE of Lawrence) Andover Chapel Cemetery, Phillips Academy, behind main classroom building. *Writers* Harriet Beecher Stowe.

BARRE (20 mi. NW of Worcester, on Rte. 122) Riverside Ceme-tery, take Rte. 62E from town center, turn R on dirt road after 2¼ mi., turn L opposite old house after 1 mi. *Social Reformers* Jacob A. Riis, marker notes his grave, by an unmarked boulder. Riis farm site on Rte 62 beyond turn for cemetery.

BOSTON Central Burying Ground, Boston Common, SW corner, near Boylston St. *Artists* Gilbert Stuart.

Copp's Hill Burying Ground, Hull and Snow Hill Sts. *Religious Leaders* Cotton Mather.

Forest Hills Cemetery, 95 Forest Hills Ave., Jamaica Plain. *Social Reformers* William Lloyd Garrison; Lucy Stone. *Social Scientists and Educators* Frederick Lewis Allen. *Writers* E. E. Cummings; Edward Everett Hale; Eugene O'Neill.

Granary Burying Ground, Tremont St. at the head of Brom-field St., N of Beacon Hill. *Colonists and Patriots* Crispus At-tucks; Paul Revere. *Government Leaders* Samuel Adams; John

Hancock. *Social Reformers* Wendell Phillips. Also: James Otis (1725–83) colonial political leader; Robert Treat Paine (1731–1814) Revolutionary leader.

King's Chapel Burying Ground, Tremont and School Sts. *Colonists and Patriots* John Winthrop.

Old Calvary Cemetery, Forest Hills, entrances on Harvard St. and Cummings Highway. *Sports Figures* John L. Sullivan.

St. Joseph Cemetery. 990 LaGrange St., West Roxbury. *Government Leaders* John W. McCormack. *Musicians* Arthur Fiedler. Also: mayors of Boston and governors of Massachusetts.

BROOKLINE (Boston suburb) Holyhood Cemetery, Walnut Ave. and Amarillo Rd. *Business and Finance* Joseph P. Kennedy.

Walnut Hills Cemetery, 96 Grove St., Chestnut Hill. *Artists* Henry Hobson Richardson.

CAMBRIDGE (Boston suburb) City of Cambridge Cemetery, 76 Coolidge Ave. *Social Scientists and Educators* William James. *Writers* Henry James, near his family, including his parents, sister, Alice, and brother, William. Also: William Dean Howells (1837–1919) writer.

Mount Auburn Cemetery, 580 Mount Auburn St. Open 8–7 May 1–Oct. 1, otherwise 8–5. Map available. The oldest garden cemetery in the country, opened in 1831. *Artists* Charles Dana Gibson, Halcyon Ave., lot 3629; Horatio Greenough, Cedar Ave.; Walter Gropius; Winslow Homer, Lily Path; Harriet Hosmer, Hemlock Path. *Entertainers* Edwin Booth, Anemone Path; Charlotte Cushman, Palm Ave. *Government Leaders* Henry Cabot Lodge, Oxalis Path, in large family plot; Charles Sumner, Arethusa Path. *Religious Leaders* Mary Baker Eddy, Halcyon Ave. (her monument is a Greek temple copied from the choragic monument of Lysicrates in Athens); G. Bromley Oxnam. *Scientists and Inventors* Louis Agassiz, Bellwort Path. *Social Reformers* Dorothea Dix, Columbine Path. *Social Scientists and Educators* Charles William Eliot, Thistle Path; Abbott L. Lowell, Bellwort Path; Francis Parkman; William Graham Sumner. *Supreme Court Justices* Felix Frankfurter. *Writers* Oliver Wendell Holmes, Sr., Lime Ave.; Henry Wadsworth Longfellow, Indian Ridge Path; Amy Lowell, Bellwort Path. Also: John Bartlett, Cypress Ave.; William Ellery Channing (1780–1842) Unitarian minister, Greenbrier Path; Edward Everett (1794–1865) orator and statesman, Magnolia Ave.; Julia Ward Howe (1819–1910) writer and social reformer; James Russell Lowell (1819–1891) writer, Bellwort Path; Josiah Royce (1855–1916) philosopher.

CHARLTON (10 mi. SW of Worcester, on Rte. 31) Bay Path Cemetery, Main St. Cemetery contains three photograph stones, headstones with glass-covered niches for daguerreotypes of the deceased. *Explorers and Settlers* Grizzly Adams.

CHILMARK (Martha's Vineyard) Abel's Hill Cemetery, South Rd. Always open. *Entertainers* John Belushi.

CONCORD (10 mi. NW of Boston, near Rte. 2) Sleepy Hollow Cemetery, Court Lane, N of town square, reached from Bedford St. *Artists* Daniel Chester French. *Writers* Louisa May Alcott, near two of her sisters (a stone commemorates a third, Abba May, buried in France); Ralph Waldo Emerson; Nathaniel Hawthorne, "Authors' Ridge," near crest in secluded spot; Henry David Thoreau.

DANVERS (10 mi. N of Boston, on Rte. 128) 149 Pine St., take Exit 24 from Rte. 128, N on Endicott St., R on Sylvan St., bear L on Pine St. *Colonists and Patriots* Rebecca Nurse, in backyard. Homestead is open to public.

EASTHAM (Cape Cod, on Rte. 6, 20 mi. S of Provincetown) Evergreen Cemetery, Rte. 6, 2 mi. toward Provincetown on L. *Sports Figures* Freeman Hatch, close to front on L side.

FAIRHAVEN (immediately W of New Bedford) Riverside Cemetery, 274 N. Main St. *Business and Finance* Henry Huttleston Rogers.

FALL RIVER Oak Grove Cemetery, 765 Prospect St. Office: 9–12, 1–4 M–F, 9–1 Sa. *Criminals* Lizzie Borden.

HANOVER (10 mi. E of Brockton, on Rte 3) Portiuncula Chapel, Cardinal Cushing School and Training Center. Open 9–5 M–F, 10–6 Sa, Su. *Religious Leaders* Richard James Cushing, under the front of the altar in the chapel, which is a replica of one in Assisi, Italy, and is made of stones and frescoes imported from Italy.

LYNN (8 mi. N of Boston, on Rte. 1A) Pine Grove Cemetery, 145 Boston St. Map available. *Business and Finance* George Swinnerton Parker, lot 147, Fuchsia Path, grave 3; Lydia E. Pinkham, lot 1343, Hackmatack Ave., grave 8.

MARSHFIELD (about 25 mi. SE of Boston, off Rte. 3) Governor Winslow Cemetery, Cemetery Rd., off Webster St. Always open. *Colonists and Patriots* Peregrine White. *Government Leaders* Daniel Webster, on a knoll about 200 yards from the road.

NANTUCKET (Nantucket Island) Prospect Hill Cemetery, between Milk St. and Hummock Pond Rd. *Scientists and Inventors* Maria Mitchell. *Writers* Robert Benchley, lots 1146 and 1147.

NEWBURYPORT (30 mi. N of Boston, on Rte. 1) Sawyer's Hill Burying Ground, Curzon's Mill. *Writers* John P. Marquand.

NORTH ANDOVER (just E of Lawrence) First Burial Ground, near N end of Academy Rd., off Massachusetts Ave., Old Center Village. *Writers* Anne Bradstreet, under some pines, not marked with a stone.

OXFORD (S of Worcester, on Rte. 12) North Cemetery. Main St., on Rte. 12, next to high school. *Social Reformers* Clara Barton: entering cemetery on Central Ave., to the R of flagpole, take first R, East Ave., grave on R marked by tall gray granite marker topped by red granite cross.

PEABODY (10 mi. N of Boston, on Rte. 128) Harmony Grove Cemetery, 30 Grove St., on Salem/Peabody line on Tremont St. Always open. *Business and Finance* George Peabody. Peabody Museum in Salem has items relating to Peabody and his funeral.

PLYMOUTH (30 mi. SE of Boston, off Rte. 3) Burial Hill, W of town square. *Colonists and Patriots* William Bradford.

QUINCY (just S of Boston, on Rte. 3) First Unitarian Church, Church of the Presidents, 1306 Hancock St. Built of Quincy granite and designed in the Greek Revival style by Alexander Parris. *Colonists and Patriots* Abigail Adams. *Presidents* John Adams; John Quincy Adams, crypt open upon application to the sexton.

SHARON (18 mi. SW of Boston, on I-95) Rockridge Cemetery, East St. Always open. *Military* Deborah Sampson Gannett, to rear of grave site is a small boulder bearing a plaque by the Deborah Sampson Chapter of the DAR. Deborah Sampson Gannett House, 300 East St.

SOUTH DUXBURY (20 mi. S of Boston, off Rte. 3) Old Burying Ground, Chestnut St. The second burying ground in the Plymouth Colony. *Colonists and Patriots* John Alden; Priscilla Mullens; Miles Standish.

SOUTH NATICK (15 mi. W of Boston) Glenwood Cemetery, Glenwood St. *Writers* Horatio Alger, Jr.

STOCKBRIDGE (10 mi. S. of Pittsfield, on Rte. 7) Stockbridge Cemetery, corner Main St. and Church St. across from Town Hall and Congregational Church. Always open. *Artists* Norman

Rockwell. *Business and Finance* Cyrus West Field. *Religious Leaders* Reinhold Niebuhr.

SUDBURY (W of Boston, off Rte. 20) Chapel near St. Elizabeth's Episcopal Church, 451 Concord Rd., opposite Plympton Rd. *Artists* Ralph Cram, grave site is 40 ft. N of chapel, accessible from path through woods beginning at parking lot. Chapel, originally part of Cram's estate, Whitehall, was given to St. Elizabeth's Church.

TISBURY (Martha's Vineyard) Village Cemetery, Franklin St. behind Town Hall. *Entertainers* Katharine Cornell, bench near grave.

TRURO (Cape Cod, 10 mi. S. of Provincetown on Rte. 6) Snow Cemetery, near Truro Town Hall. Always open. *Artists* Hans Hofmann, plot dominated by huge granite block, largest monument in cemetery.

WELLESLEY (W of Boston, on Rte. 135) Chapel, Wellesley College. *Social Scientists and Educators* Alice Freeman Palmer, George Herbert Palmer, buried next to each other.

WELLFLEET (Cape Cod, 12 mi. S of Provincetown on Rte. 6) Pleasant Hill Cemetery. *Writers* Edmund Wilson.

WORCESTER Hope Cemetery, overlooking Hadwen Park. *Scientists and Inventors* Robert Goddard.

MICHIGAN

BATTLE CREEK Oak Hill Cemetery, 255 South Ave. *Business and Finance* John Harvey Kellogg; Will Keith Kellogg; Charles William Post. *Social Reformers* Sojourner Truth.

DETROIT The Ford Cemetery, St. Martha's Episcopal Church, 15801 Joy Rd. Cemetery open by appointment only, see rector. *Business and Finance* Henry Ford.

Woodlawn Cemetery, 19975 Woodward, between 7 and 8 Mile Rds. Open 8–4:30 M–Su; office: 8:30–4:30, Su–F, Sa until 3. Map available. *Business and Finance* Horace Elgin Dodge, John Francis Dodge; both in family mausoleum; Edsel Ford. *Writers* Edgar A. Guest. Also: J. L. Hudson, department store magnate, after whom the Hudson Motor Car was named.

Woodmere Cemetery, 9400 W. Fort St. *Business and Finance* David Dunbar Buick, sect. Allendale, lot 631; Henry Martyn Leland, sect. G, lot 119.

GRAND RAPIDS Oakhill Cemetery, 647 Hall S. E. *Government Leaders* Arthur H. Vandenberg, lot 45, block 2, grave 8.

LANSING Mt. Hope Cemetery, 1709 E. Mount Hope Rd. Map available. *Business and Finance* Ransom Eli Olds, Olds Mausoleum, lot 157, sect. F, in center crypt.

MIDLAND (100 mi. NW of Detroit, on I-75) Midland Cemetery, 3017 Orchard Drive. *Business and Finance* Herbert Henry Dow.

PONTIAC (10 mi. NW of Detroit) Mount Hope Cemetery, 727 Orchard Lake Rd. *Sports Figures* Terry Sawchuk.

SAGINAW (70 mi. NW of Detroit on I-75) Oakwood Cemetery, 6100 Gratiot. *Writers* Theodore Roethke.

ST. IGNACE (N shore of the Straits of Mackinac, on I-75) Fr. Marquette Monument, downtown St. Ignace. *Explorers and Settlers* Jacques Marquette, grave adjacent to monument. Fr. Marquette National Memorial and Museum.

SOUTHFIELD (Detroit suburb) Holy Sepulchre Cemetery, 25800 W. Ten Mile Rd. Mausoleum open 9–4 M–Su; office: 9–4:30 M–F, 9–2:30 Sa, closed Su, hols., holy days. Maps available. *Sports Figures* Walter C. Hagen, mausoleum, Chapel Floor, sect. 101-W, crypt A-3.

TROY (N of Detroit, on I-75) White Chapel Memorial Cemetery, 621 W. Long Lake Rd. *Artists* Albert Kahn.

MINNESOTA

AUSTIN (80 mi. S of St. Paul) Oakwood Cemetery, 1800 NW 4th St. *Business and Finance* George Albert Hormel.

MINNEAPOLIS Lakewood Cemetery, 3600 Hennepin Ave. *Government Leaders* Hubert H. Humphrey.

ROCHESTER (60 mi. S of St. Paul) Oakwood Cemetery. *Scientists and Inventors* Charles Horace Mayo; William J. Mayo.

ST. PAUL Resurrection Cemetery, 2101 Lexington Ave. S. *Writers* John Berryman.

SAUK CENTRE (80 mi. NW of Minneapolis, off I-95) Greenwood Cemetery. *Writers* Sinclair Lewis, in family burial plot.

MISSISSIPPI

BOND (60 mi. NE of New Orleans, on Rte. 49, near Wiggins) Bond Cemetery. *Sports Figures* Dizzy Dean.

MERIDIAN (100 mi. E of Jackson, on I-20) Oak Grove Cemetery, next to Oak Grove Baptist Church, 1002 Oak Grove Dr., reached from Hwy. 19 S Exit off I-20-59. *Musicians* Jimmie Rodgers, near street about midway in the second row of graves. Week-long Jimmie Rodgers Festival, end of May.

OXFORD (50 mi. SE of Memphis, Tenn., on Rte. 6) St. Peter's Cemetery, Jefferson and N. 16th St., 3 blocks from the Holiday Inn. Visitors always welcome. *Writers* William Faulkner. Faulkner's home, Rowan Oak, open to visitors.

MISSOURI

BELTON (17 mi. S of Kansas City, off Rte. 71) Belton Cemetery, on Cambridge W of Scott Ave., across from elementary school. *Social Reformers* Carry Nation, SE corner. Also: Dale Carnegie (1888–1955), N of tool house, stones and chain around grave site.

INDEPENDENCE (outside Kansas City) Courtyard, Harry S. Truman Library and Museum, off US 24. Open 9–7 summer, 9–5 winter, closed Thanksgiving, Christmas, and New Year's Day. No fee for courtyard. *Presidents* Harry S. Truman. Truman boyhood home, summer White House, "walking statue," and other points of interest nearby.

Hill Park, 23rd St. between Sterling and Maywood. *Criminals* Frank James, stone fence surrounds plot.

Mount Washington Cemetery, 614 Brookside Dr., off Truman Rd. and I-435. Open 8–5 M–Su; office: 8–5 M–F, Sa. Map available in roadside park. *Explorers and Settlers* Jim Bridger.

KANSAS CITY Calvary Cemetery, 6901 Troost. *Government Leaders* Thomas Pendergast.

KEARNEY (outside Kansas City, on I-35) Mount Olivet Cemetery, on M-92. *Criminals* Jesse James. Annual Jesse James Day Parade and Festival. James Farm, 3 mi. NE of Kearney, first gravesite fenced in.

LEE'S SUMMIT (outside Kansas City, on Rte. 50) Lee's Summit Cemetery, 3rd and Independence (M-291). *Criminals* Cole Younger, near corner of Langsford Rd. (2nd St.) and M-291. Younger home on M-291, not open to public.

ST. CHARLES (NW of St. Louis, on I-70) Memorial Shrine of Blessed Philippine Duchesne, grounds of the Academy of the Sa-

cred Heart, 619 N. 2nd St. Open 8–5 M–Su. Tours available, except Tu. *Religious Leaders* Rose Philippine Duchesne.
ST. LOUIS Bellefontaine Cemetery, 4947 W. Florissant Ave. Open 8–5 M–Su; office: 8–4:30 M–F, 8–12 Sa. Guided tour and map available. *Business and Finance* Adolphus Busch, Woodbine Ave., elaborate mausoleum. *Explorers and Settlers* William Clark, Meadow Ave. *Government Leaders* Thomas Hart Benton, Laurel Ave., in Brant lot. *Writers* Sara Teasdale. Also: other local notables.

Calvary Cemetery, 5279 W. Florissant Ave. *Military* William Tecumseh Sherman. *Scientists and Inventors* Thomas A. Dooley.

MONTANA

BOZEMAN Sunset Hills Cemetery, E end of Main St. *Explorers and Settlers* Henry T. P. Comstock. *Journalists* Chet Huntley, lot 219, block 61, in new addition.

NEBRASKA

McCOOK (S of North Platte, on Rte. 83) Memorial Park, West M St. *Government Leaders* George W. Norris, in family plot.

NEVADA

LAS VEGAS Paradise Memorial Gardens, 6200 S. Eastern Ave. *Sports Figures* Sonny Liston.

NEW HAMPSHIRE

CONCORD (on Rte. 93) Old North Cemetery. *Presidents* Franklin Pierce, Minot enclosure. Franklin Pierce homestead, N end of Main St.
CORNISH (40 mi. NW of Concord, near Vt. border) Saint-Gaudens Memorial, on State 12A, 2 mi. N of the Windsor, Vt., covered bridge. Originally a country tavern built around 1800, then Saint-Gaudens's home. *Artists* Augustus Saint-Gaudens. Two studios open to public contain some of his work and a picture gallery.

GILMANTON (20 mi. SE of Laconia, on Rte. 140) Smith Meeting House Cemetery. *Writers* Grace Metalious.

JAFFREY CENTER (10 mi. E of Keene, on Rte. 124) Old Burying Ground, located behind the original Meeting House. *Writers* Willa Cather. Also: Amos Fortune, early patriot and ex-slave.

MOULTONBOROUGH (20 mi. NE of Laconia on Rte. 113) Red Hill Cemetery, Bean Road. Take Bean Road from Rte. 25 at the Center Harbor–Moultonborough town line for 1½ mi. to second cemetery on right. *Entertainers* Claude Rains, headstone is black marble.

NORTH HAMPTON (10 mi. S of Portsmouth, on Rte. 286) Little River Cemetery, corner Woodland Rd. and Atlantic Ave. *Writers* Ogden Nash.

PETERBOROUGH (21 mi. E of Keene, on Rte. 101) MacDowell Colony, less than 1 mi. from center of town on R of High St., a short distance beyond Monadnock Country Club. Colony is host to artists and writers and composers. *Musicians* Edward Mac-Dowell.

STRATFORD (about 20 mi. S of Canadian border, on Rte. 3) Stratford Center Cemetery, Rte. 3, 8 mi. N. of Groveton across from Stratford Grange Hall. *Writers* Paul Goodman, at back, near hills.

NEW JERSEY

BASKING RIDGE (20 mi. S of Paterson, on I-287) Cemetery of the Basking Ridge Presbyterian Church, Oak St. and North Finley Ave., large white church in center of town. *Business and Finance* Samuel Shannon Childs, in family plot.

BORDENTOWN (outside Trenton) Bordentown Cemetery, 210 Crosswicks Rd. *Journalists* Jeannette Leonard Gilder; Richard Watson Gilder, lot B, sect. 6.

CAMDEN Harleigh Cemetery, Haddon Ave. *Social Reformers* Ella Reeve Bloor. *Writers* Walt Whitman.

FAIRVIEW (about 5 mi. S of George Washington Bridge) Fairview Cemetery, 500 Fairview Ave. *Artists* John Marin.

HILLSIDE (SW of Newark on Rte. 22) Evergreen Cemetery, 1137 N. Broad St. *Writers* Stephen Crane.

LYNDHURST (3 mi. N of Newark, on Rte. 21) Hillside Cemetery, corner Rutherford Ave. and Orient Way, on Rte. 17S. Open 9–4:30 *Writers* William Carlos Williams, sect. D, lot 187.

MIDDLETOWN (30 mi. S. of Elizabeth, on Rte. 35) Mount Olivet Cemetery, Chapel Hill Rd., ¼ mi. E of Rte. 35. *Sports Figures* Vince Lombardi, sect. 30.

MONTCLAIR (4 mi. NE of Newark, on Rte. 506) Rosedale Cemetery, 408 Orange Rd., Exit 148 on Garden State Parkway. Map available. *Criminals* Henry Judd Gray.

PARAMUS (10 mi. W of George Washington Bridge, junction Rtes. 4 and 17) Cedar Park Cemetery, Forest Ave. off Rte 4. *Entertainers* Joe E. Lewis. *Writers* Delmore Schwartz.

PATERSON Cedar Lawn Cemetery, McLean Blvd. and Crooks Ave. *Social Scientists and Educators* Nicholas Murray Butler.

PRINCETON (10 mi. N of Trenton, on Rte. 206) Princeton Cemetery, Witherspoon and Wiggins Sts. Brochure available. *Government Leaders* Aaron Burr. *Presidents* Grover Cleveland. *Religious Leaders* Jonathan Edwards. *Writers* John O'Hara. Also: Sylvia Beach (1887–1962) first publisher of Joyce's *Ulysses.*

ROOSEVELT (10 mi. E of Trenton, off I-195) Roosevelt Cemetery. Open until 8 M–F, stop at Municipal Building for directions. *Artists* Ben Shahn.

SADDLE BROOK (5 mi. W of Fort Lee, on Rte. 80) Riverside Cemetery, off Market St. Open 8–5 M–F, Su; office: 8:30–4 (closed 12–1) M–F, 8:30–1 Su, closed Sa and some Jewish holidays. Map available. *Journalists* Meyer Berger, family sect. 3, plot 103, grave 4, block A, sect. 2, take Roosevelt Drive to first R, Hillside Rd.

TRENTON Cemetery of the First Presbyterian Church of Ewing, 100 Scotch Rd. Office: 9–4:30 M–F, 8–12 Sa. *Musicians* Paul Whiteman, private mausoleum.

Riverview Cemetery, off Lalor St. on 800 block of Centre St., which runs into cemetery. Office: 9–12, 12:30–4:30 M–F. *Military* George Brinton McClellan. Also: John A. Roebling, designer and builder of Brooklyn Bridge, and other notables.

St. Mary's Cemetery, Cedar Lane. *Artists* Edward Boehm.

WEST ORANGE (5 mi. W of Newark, on I-280) Glenmont, Llewellyn Park, closed M, Tu, and legal holidays. Request permit to enter grounds from Edison Laboratory, the Edison National Historic Site at Main and Lakeside Aves., near I-280. Open 9–5. *Scientists and Inventors* Thomas A. Edison, on grounds of estate. Tours of home available, tours of laboratory available 9:30–3.

NEW MEXICO

FORT SUMNER (65 mi. SE of Las Vegas, on US 60) Old Fort Sumner Military Cemetery, 2 mi. E of town on US 60. *Criminals* Billy the Kid. Also: Lucien A. Maxwell, proprietor of the Maxwell Land Grant.

SANTA FE National Cemetery, Espanola Highway. Brochure available. *Writers* Oliver La Farge, grave 300, sect. O. Also: Charles Bent, first territorial governor of New Mexico.

TAOS (50 mi. NE of Santa Fe, on US 64) Kit Carson Cemetery, Kit Carson State Memorial Park, end of Dragoon Lane. *Explorers and Settlers* Kit Carson. Kit Carson Home and Museum.

NEW YORK

ALBANY Albany Rural Cemetery. Albany-Troy Rd., Menands. Office: 8:30–4:30 M–F, 8:30–12:00 Sa. Maps, brochure available. Scenically beautiful cemetery founded in 1841; 32 mi. of winding roads. *Presidents* Chester A. Arthur: a winged angel guards his tomb. Also: Peter Gansevoort (1749–1812) Revolutionary War hero; Philip Schuyler (1733–1804) Revolutionary figure, grave marked by a 36-foot-high Doric column; Thurlow Weed (1797–1882) powerful political figure.

AMAWALK (Westchester County) Amawalk Friends Cemetery, Quaker Church Rd., 1 mi. E of center of Yorktown Heights. Take L off Rtes. 35–202, Quaker Meeting House and Cemetery are on L ⅙ mi. down the road. *Artists* Robert Capa, grave to R of Meeting House.

ARDEN (Westchester County) Cemetery of St. John's Episcopal Church. *Business and Finance* Edward Henry Harriman, in private plot not open to the public.

AUBURN Fort Hill Cemetery, 19 Fort St., in south central sect. of city. Always open, office: 9–12, 1–4. *Criminals* Leon Czolgosz. *Government Leaders* William H. Seward. *Military* Emory Upton.

AU SABLE FORKS Kent Estate, office of Rockwell Kent Legacies, about 8 mi. from Burlington, Vt., off Rte. 9N–44. Private estate; grave site is open to the public, but grounds are patrolled by guard dogs; phone ahead. *Artists* Rockwell Kent.

AUSTERLITZ (20 mi. SE of Albany, near end of Taconic Pkwy.)

Steepletop. Open by appointment, call ahead (518) 392-3003. Former estate of Edna St. Vincent Millay, now the Millay Colony for the Arts. *Writers* Edna St. Vincent Millay, grave about 1 mi. down a wooded path, not suitable for winter access.

BRONX (New York City) St. Anne's Episcopal Churchyard, E. 140th St. and St. Anne's Ave. *Government Leaders* Gouverneur Morris. Also: other prominent members of the Morris family.

St. Raymond's Cemetery, E. 177th St. and Lafayette Ave. *Musicians* Billie Holiday. Also: Vincent "Mad Dog" Coll (1909–32) gangster.

Woodlawn Cemetery, 233rd St. and Webster Ave., adjacent to Van Cortland Park. Map, brochure available; concerts, tours. Features an extraordinary diversity of cemetery art and sculpture set amid a rolling landscape of 3,500 trees. Many of the rich and famous are buried here. *Artists* Joseph Stella. *Business and Finance* Arde Bulova; Joseph Bulova; Jay Gould; Collis P. Huntington; Samuel Henry Kress; James Cash Penney; Rudolph Jay Schaefer; J. Walter Thompson; Frank Winfield Woolworth. *Criminals* Ruth Brown Snyder. *Entertainers* Nora Bayes; Irene Castle; Vernon Castle; Lotta Crabtree; Marilyn Miller, in a tiny white mausoleum in the style of a Greek temple; Florence Mills; Laurette Taylor. *Explorers and Settlers* Matthew A. Henson; Bat Masterson. *Government Leaders* Ralph Bunche; Fiorello H. La Guardia; Adam Clayton Powell, Jr. *Journalists* Nellie Bly; Joseph Pulitzer; Grantland Rice. *Military* David G. Farragut. *Musicians* George M. Cohan; Duke Ellington; W. C. Handy; Victor Herbert; Fritz Kreisler. *Scientists and Inventors* Edwin Howard Armstrong. *Social Reformers* Carrie Chapman Catt; Elizabeth Cady Stanton. *Sports Figures* Frankie Frisch; Vincent Richards. *Supreme Court Justices* Charles Evans Hughes. *Writers* Clarence Day; Herman Melville. Also: Rudolph Fisher (1897–1934) mystery writer; Chauncey Olcott (1858–1932) popular singer; Joseph "King" Oliver (1885–1938) jazz musician; George Browne Post (1837–1913) architect; Michael I. Pupin (1858–1937) inventor; Theodore Reik, (1888–1969) psychologist; Julian Alden Weir (1852–1919) impressionist artist; Harry Payne Whitney (1872–1930) millionaire sportsman.

BROOKLYN (New York City) Cypress Hills Cemetery, 833 Jamaica Ave., Jamaica and Cypress Aves. *Entertainers* Mae West. *Sports Figures* Jim Corbett; Jackie Robinson.

Evergreen Cemetery, Bushwick and Conway Aves. *Entertainers* Bill "Bojangles" Robinson.

Friends Cemetery, in Prospect Park, 8th traffic light past Grand Army Plaza. Caretaker on premises, phone ahead for appointment, (212) 768-8298, or write Religious Society of Friends, 15 Rutherford Place, N.Y., N.Y. 10003. *Entertainers* Montgomery Clift.

Green-Wood Cemetery, 5 Ave. and 25 St. Open every day 8–5. List of celebrities available. Built in 1835, this rural cemetery was once a prime tourist attraction; called the "Garden City of the Dead" because of its beautiful settings—drives, lakes, ponds, and rolling hills. *Artists* George Catlin, lot 717/20, sect. 60; Nathaniel Currier, lot 8325, sect. 108; Asher Brown Durand, lot 1053, sect. 60. *Business and Finance* "Diamond Jim" Brady; Peter Cooper, lot 3932, sect. 97/101; Charles Lewis Tiffany; John Thomas Underwood. *Criminals* Albert Anastasia, number 182, lot 38325. *Entertainers* William S. Hart; Lola Montez, lot 12730, sect. 8; Gus Williams, lot 22246, sect. 47/48. *Government Leaders* William M. Tweed, lot 6447, sect. 55; DeWitt Clinton, Clinton Dell. *Journalists* Horace Greeley, lot 2344, sect. 35; James Gordon Bennett, Sr., lot 865, sect. 107. *Musicians* Louis Moreau Gottschalk, lot 19581, sect. M/N. *Religious Leaders* Henry Ward Beecher, lot 25911, sect. 140. *Scientists and Inventors* Elias Howe; Samuel F. B. Morse, lot 5761/9, sect. 25/32; Elmer A. Sperry. *Social Reformers* Henry George, lot 29673, sect. P. Also: George Wesley Bellows (1882–1925) lot 478/479, sect. 24, artist; Marcus Daly (1841–1900) copper tycoon; Joey Gallo, lot 40314, gangster; Duncan Phyfe (1768–1854) cabinetmaker; Samuel Chester Reid (1783–1861) designer of the flag, flagpole near his grave; William Steinway (1836–96) sect. 46/47, founder of piano firm.

Holy Cross Cemetery, Tilden Ave. *Criminals* Willie Sutton. *Sports Figures* Jim Fitzsimmons; Gil Hodges. *Writers* Quentin Reynolds. Also: W. R. Grace (1832–1904), steamship magnate.

Salem Fields Cemetery, 775 Jamaica Ave. *Business and Finance* Daniel Guggenheim; Harry Guggenheim; Meyer Guggenheim; Simon Guggenheim; Solomon Guggenheim; Felix M. Warburg. Also: Adolph Lewisohn (1849–1938), banker.

BUFFALO Forest Lawn Cemetery, 1411 Delaware Ave. *Business and Finance* William George Fargo. *Presidents* Millard Fillmore.

CANTON Evergreen Cemetery, about 12 mi. from Ogdensberg on US 11. *Artists* Frederic Remington. Frederic Remington Museum, 303 Washington St., Ogdensberg.

CASTILE Letchworth State Park, about 3 mi. S of Castile on Rte. 245. Brochure available. *Colonists and Patriots* Mary Jemison, grave and statue are on a bluff above the Pioneer and Indian Museum and the Glen Iris Mansion.

CLINTON (10 mi. SW of Utica, on Rte. 12B) Hamilton College Cemetery, on College Hill between Campus and Griffin Rds., adjacent to the campus. Always open. *Government Leaders* Elihu Root. *Writers* Alexander Woollcott. Also: Samuel Kirkland, founder of Hamilton; Chief Skenandoah, Kirkland's Indian friend.

COLD SPRING HARBOR (on Long Island, 3 mi. N of Huntington Station) Memorial Cemetery of St. John's Church, Rte. 25A, top of hill at Cove Rd. *Business and Finance* Alfred P. Sloan. *Government Leaders* Henry L. Stimson. Also: Otto Herman Kahn (1867–1934) financier.

COLONIE (outskirts of Albany) Shaker Cemetery, on Rte. 155 (Watervliet-Shaker Rd.), near Albany County Airport. Cemetery is in what was one of the earliest Shaker settlements. *Religious Leaders* Ann Lee: her gravestone is slightly larger than the others in the cemetery, all of which are uniform in size. Twenty-five Shaker buildings remain in the area.

CONESUS (about 20 mi. S of Rochester, on US 15) Union Cemetery, West Lake Rd., Rte. 256S, between Lakeville and Dansville. *Colonists and Patriots* Daniel Shays.

COOPERSTOWN (20 mi. N of Oneonta, on Rte. 28) Christ Churchyard, 69 Fair St. *Writers* James Fenimore Cooper. Fenimore House, 1 mi. N of town on Rte. 80.

CROTON-ON-HUDSON (Westchester County) Beth El Cemetery, Old Post Rd. S, R turn at first traffic light in Croton-on-Hudson. Assistance available at Swanson Florist, near cemetery. *Writers* Lorraine Hansberry.

EAST HAMPTON (S fork of Long Island, on Rte. 27) Cedar Lawn Cemetery, Cooper Lane. Open 8–4 M–F. *Artists* Childe Hassam, lot 32, sect. C.

Green River Cemetery, Accabonac Highway, take Rte. 27 to light past the pond, make L, turn L at 2nd light, go straight ahead. *Artists* Stuart Davis; Jackson Pollock.

EAST MARION (tip of North Fork of Long Island, on Rte. 25)
East Marion Cemetery. *Artists* Mark Rothko, grave is straight
down the road toward lake, on the R.

ELMIRA Woodlawn Cemetery, 1200 Walnut St., N end of street.
Writers Mark Twain. Mark Twain Study, Park Pl., near Washington Ave.

FARMINGDALE (on Long Island, near Levittown) Mount Ararat
Cemetery, Southern State Pkwy. *Artists* Max Weber.

Pinelawn Memorial Park and Cemetery, Pinelawn Rd.
Musicians John Coltrane; Guy Lombardo. *Social Reformers* Roy
Wilkins.

FLEISCHMANNS (3 mi. N of Belleayre Mountain Ski Ctr., in
Catskill resort area) Clovesville Cemetery, on old Rte. 28 just
outside of Village of Fleischmanns. *Entertainers* Gertrude Berg,
in Jewish sect. of cemetery.

FRANKLIN (12 mi. SW of Oneonta, on Rte. 357) Ouleout Cemetery, on Rte. 357, northeastern end of upper Main St.
Artists Lewis W. Hine.

GARRISON (S of West Point, on Rte. 9D) Cemetery of St. Philips
Church in the Highlands. *Government Leaders* Hamilton Fish,
in Fish family plot.

HARTSDALE (Westchester County) Ferncliff Cemetery, Secor
Rd. Brochure, celebrity list available. Seventy-acre parklike cem-
etery with a noted mausoleum designed by James Baird, builder
of the Lincoln Memorial. *Business and Finance* Charles Revson.
Entertainers Joan Crawford; Michel Fokine, Shrine of Memories
Mausoleum; Judy Garland; "Moms" Mabley; Basil Rathbone,
Shrine of Memories Mausoleum; Diana Sands. *Journalists* Ed
Sullivan. *Musicians* Béla Bartók; Connee Boswell; Jerome Kern;
Thelonious Monk; Paul Robeson; Richard Rodgers; Sigmund
Romberg. *Scientists and Inventors* Karen Horney; Otto Rank. *So-
cial Scientists and Educators* Charles A. Beard, plot 309, grave 1;
Mary R. Beard, plot 309, grave 2. *Social Reformers* Malcolm X;
Whitney M. Young, Jr. *Writers* Maxwell Anderson; Moss Hart.
Also: Bugs Baer, boxer; "Peaches" Browning, 1920s nymphet;
Hattie Carnegie, dress designer; Mady Christians (1900–51) ac-
tress; Emanuel Feuermann (1920–42) cellist; Lew Fields (1867–
1941) vaudevillian; John Gunther, Jr., (John Gunther wrote *Death
Be Not Proud* about his early death); Elsa Maxwell, society leader;
"Toots" Shor, restaurateur; Conrad Veidt (1893–1943) character

actor; Frank Dan Waterman (1869–1938) founder of the pen company.

HASTINGS-ON-HUDSON (Westchester County) Temple Israel Cemetery (Mount Hope), Jackson Ave. and Saw Mill River Rd. *Entertainers* Sol Hurok. *Musicians* George Gershwin.

Westchester Hills Cemetery, 400 Saw Mill River Rd. *Entertainers* John Garfield; Judy Holliday; Max Reinhardt; Billy Rose; Lee Strasberg. *Religious Leaders* Stephen S. Wise. *Social Reformers* Sidney Hillman.

HAVERSTRAW (Rockland County) Mount Repose Cemetery, on Rte. 92. *Musicians* Kurt Weill.

HAWTHORNE (Westchester County) Gate of Heaven Cemetery, Stevens and Bradhurst Aves. Walking-tour map available. Located on 250 acres of wooded hills. *Business and Finance* Charles Michael Schwab. *Criminals* Dutch Schultz. *Entertainers* Fred Allen, plot 1, sect. 47; Anna Held, plot 295, sect. 42; Sal Mineo, sect. 2. *Journalists* Bob Considine, crypt; Dorothy Kilgallen, sect. 23; Westbrook Pegler, plot 859, sect. 40. *Sports Figures* Babe Ruth, sect. 25. Also: Tim Mara (d. 1959) owner of the football Giants; Mike Quill, labor leader; James J. Walker (1881–1946) sect. 41, N.Y.C. mayor.

Mount Pleasant Memorial Park, 80 Commerce Ave. *Government Leaders* Henry Morgenthau, Jr. *Musicians* Lillian Roth. *Religious Leaders* Felix Adler.

HOOSICK FALLS (about 10 mi. W of Bennington, Vt., on Rte. 22) Maple Grove Cemetery, off Main St. *Artists* Grandma Moses.

HYDE PARK (about 5 mi. N of Poughkeepsie, on US 9) Franklin D. Roosevelt National Historic Site, 1 mile S of town center on US 9. Open 9–4:30. Brochure available. *Government Leaders* Eleanor Roosevelt, in Rose Garden. *Presidents* Franklin D. Roosevelt, in Rose Garden. Roosevelt Home and Library.

ITHACA Sage Chapel, Cornell University, on Tower Rd., near McGraw Tower. Campus is on E side of town overlooking Cayuga Lake. *Business and Finance* Ezra Cornell, in a crypt.

JAMESTOWN Lake View Cemetery, 907 Lakeview Ave. *Business and Finance* Benjamin Franklin Goodrich.

JOHNSTOWN North Market St., next to St. John's Episcopal Church, which adjoins Sir William Johnson Park. *Colonists and Patriots* William Johnson. Johnson Hall, Hall Avenue, restored home.

KINDERHOOK (25 mi. S of Albany, on US 9) Kinderhook Cemetery. *Presidents* Martin Van Buren.

KINGSTON Old Dutch Churchyard, Main St. between Wall and Fair Sts., within the original stockade area of the city. Always open. Earliest gravestone here dates from 1710. *Colonists and Patriots* George Clinton, grave marked by large monument with a torch on top.

LAKE RONKONKOMA (on Long Island, 5 mi. from Central Islip) Cenacle Convent, Cenacle Rd., take County Rd. 19 (Exit 61 of Long Island Expressway), follow road to end, make R turn, turn L at second light. Open to visitors at any time, check at Retreat Office. *Entertainers* Maude Adams, in a small cemetery on convent grounds.

LIBERTY (in Catskill resort area, on Rte. 17) Ahavath Israel Cemetery. *Business and Finance* Jennie Grossinger.

NEW LEBANON (10 mi. W of Pittsfield, Mass., on US 20) Presbyterian Church Cemetery. *Government Leaders* Samuel Tilden.

NEW ROCHELLE (Westchester County) Holy Sepulchre Cemetery, 66 Highland Ave. *Entertainers* Eddie Foy.

NEW YORK CITY (Manhattan) General Grant National Memorial, Riverside Dr. at W 122nd St. Open 9–5 W–Su, closed Christmas and New Year's Day. *Presidents* Ulysses S. Grant.

Saint Cabrini Chapel, Missionary Sisters of the Sacred Heart, 701 Fort Washington Ave. *Religious Leaders* Saint Frances Xavier Cabrini, beneath altar in the main chapel. Photo exhibit. Gift Shop.

St. Mark's Church-in-the-Bowery, 10th St. at 2nd Ave. Built in 1795–99, it is one of the city's rare eighteenth-century buildings. *Colonists and Patriots* Peter Stuyvesant, Stuyvesant vault, permanently sealed since 1953, is located under the church on the E side of the building. Also: Nicholas Fish, Revolutionary War hero; Daniel Tompkins, vice-president under James Monroe.

St. Patrick's Cathedral, the crypt, 5th Ave. and 50th St. Cathedral open 6–9:30 every day. *Religious Leaders* Fulton J. Sheen; Francis Joseph Spellman (his crypt is last on the top row, extreme right). Crypt below the main altar holds the remains of six archbishops of New York. It is visible from behind the altar, with plaques identifying occupants. Crypt is not open to the public except on special occasions such as All Souls' Day, Nov.2.

St. Thomas Church, 1 West 53 St. *Business and Finance* John Jacob Astor.

Trinity Cemetery, 155th St. and Riverside Dr. Cemetery, on both sides of Broadway, belongs to Trinity Church (see below). Opened in 1842, it stands on land that was once part of the Audubon farm. *Artists* John James Audubon. *Writers* Clement Clarke Moore. Also: Madame Eliza B. Jumel, chatelaine of the Jumel Mansion. Monument to Audubon near Broadway and 155th St.

Trinity Churchyard, 74 Trinity Pl. Standing at the head of Wall St., the cemetery has been in existence for almost 300 years. No longer in use for burials, it serves today as a pocket park in the crowded financial district. *Government Leaders* Albert Gallatin; Alexander Hamilton, obelisk with his portrait marks the grave. *Journalists* John Peter Zenger. *Military* James Lawrence. *Scientists and Inventors* Robert Fulton. Also: Francis Lewis (1713–1803) only signer of the Declaration of Independence buried in Manhattan.

NORTH ELBA (near Lake Placid) John Brown Farm, off Rte. 73 about 2 mi. S of Lake Placid, opposite Lake Placid Horse Show grounds. Open 9–5 W–Su, early May to late Dec.; also open Memorial Day, July 4, and Labor Day. *Social Reformers* John Brown, large boulder marks grave site.

NORTH TARRYTOWN Rockefeller Family Cemetery, Pocantico Hills Estate, on Rte. 9, outside the village of North Tarrytown. Three-acre cemetery, not open to the public, abuts Sleepy Hollow Cemetery (see below). *Business and Finance* John D. Rockefeller, Jr. *Government Leaders* Nelson A. Rockefeller. Also: Abby Aldrich Rockefeller; John D. Rockefeller III.

Sleepy Hollow Cemetery, on Rte. 9 outside the village of North Tarrytown, take Exit 9 off the New York State Thruway. Open 8–4:30 every day; office: 8:30–4:30 M–F, 9–12 Sa. Map available. Cemetery surrounds the Old Dutch Church, oldest church on the Hudson River (1685). *Business and Finance* Andrew Carnegie, Hebron sect., off Dingle Rd.; Walter Percy Chrysler, mausoleum, Altona sect.; William Rockefeller, mausoleum; Thomas John Watson. *Entertainers* Major Edward Bowes, Gideon sect., off Vernon Ave. *Government Leaders* Carl Schurz, Horeb sect., off Fairmont Ave. *Journalists* Whitelaw Reid; Henry Villard; Oswald G. Villard. *Social Reformers* Samuel Gompers. *Writers* Washington Irving. Also: Mark Hellinger, producer.

NYACK (Rockland County) Oak Hill Cemetery, 140 N. Hilland Ave., N of Rte. 9W. *Artists* Edward Hopper. *Writers* Carson McCullers. Also: Joseph Cornell, painter. Edward Hopper House, 82 N. Broadway, may be seen.

OYSTER BAY (on Long Island, 5 mi. E of Glen Cove, on Rte. 106N) Young's Cemetery, Cove Rd. Open 9–5 every day. *Presidents* Theodore Roosevelt. Sagamore Hill National Historic site, Cove Neck Rd., Roosevelt's home.

PAWLING (20 mi. SE of Poughkeepsie, on Rte. 22) Pawling Cemetery, W side of Rte. 22 in the Village of Pawling. Open during daylight hours. *Government leaders* Thomas E. Dewey, in mausoleum. Also: Rear Admiral John L. Worden, commander of the USS *Monitor* in her battle with the *Merrimac.*

PINELAWN (Long Island) Wellwood Cemetery, Wellwood Ave. *Criminals* Ethel Rosenberg, Julius Rosenberg.

QUEENS (New York City) Belmont Park Race Track, Hempstead Tnpk. and Plainfield Ave., Elmont. *Sports Figures* Ruffian, beneath the flagpole.

Beth El Cemetery, Cypress Hills, Glendale. *Entertainers* Edward G. Robinson, in Goldenberg family plot.

Calvary Cemetery, 49-02 Laurel Hill Blvd., Woodside. Open 8–4:30. *Criminals* Thomas "Three-Finger Brown" Luchese, sect. 69, plot 164, grave 13. *Entertainers* Nita Naldi. *Government Leaders* Alfred E. Smith, stone reads "Smith/ Glynn." *Writers* Claude McKay.

Flushing Cemetery, 163-06 46 Ave., Flushing. *Government Leaders* Bernard M. Baruch. *Musicians* Louis "Satchmo" Armstrong.

Linden Hills Cemetery, 52-22 Metropolitan Ave., Maspeth. *Business and Finance* Joseph Bernard Bloomingdale. *Entertainers* David Belasco.

Machpelah Cemetery, 82-30 Cypress Hills, Glendale. *Entertainers* Harry Houdini.

Montefiore Cemetery, 121-83 Springfield Blvd., St. Albans. *Artists* Barnett Newman.

Mount Carmel Cemetery, Cypress Hills Rd., Glendale. *Entertainers* Jacob Adler. *Journalists* Abraham Cahan. *Social Reformers* Meyer London. *Sports Figures* Benny Leonard. Also: Joseph Barondess (1867–1928) union leader.

Mount Hebron Cemetery, Rodman Ave., and Long Island

Expwy., Flushing. *Entertainers* Maurice Schwartz. *Religious Leaders* Solomon Schechter.

Mount Lebanon Cemetery, 78-00 Myrtle Ave., Glendale. *Musicians* Richard Tucker.

Mount Neboh Cemetery, 82-07 Cypress Hills, Glendale. *Writers* Sholem Aleichem.

Mount Olivet Cemetery, 65-50 Grand Ave., Maspeth. *Criminals* Jack "Legs" Diamond.

Mount Zion Cemetery, 59-63 54 Ave., Maspeth. *Musicians* Lorenz Hart. Also: Nathanael West.

St. John's Cemetery, 80-01 Metropolitan Ave., Middle Village. Open 7:30–5. Map available. *Criminals* Vito Genovese, sect. 11, range E, plot 9; "Lucky" Luciano, sect 3, range E.

St. Michael's Cemetery, 72-02 Astoria Blvd., Astoria. Open 8–4:30, 11–3 Sa, Su, hols. *Criminals* Frank Costello, vault to L of main entrance. *Musicians* Scott Joplin.

Shearith Israel Cemetery, 2 Cypress Hills, Glendale. *Sports Figures* Emanuel Lasker. *Supreme Court Justices* Benjamin N. Cardozo.

Union Field Cemetery, Cypress Ave., Ridgewood. *Criminals* Arnold Rothstein. *Entertainers* Bert Lahr.

REMSEN (20 mi. N of Utica, on Rte. 12) Steuben Memorial, Starr Hill Rd., 2½ mi. W of Rtes. 12 and 28. Brochure available. Open 9–5 M–Sa, 1–5 Su, Apr. 15–Oct. 15. Closed Easter and Oct. 16–Apr. 14. *Military* Friedrich Wilhelm von Steuben. Steuben's cabin.

ROCHESTER Mt. Hope Cemetery, 1133 Mt. Hope Ave., between Elmwood and Highland Aves. Open every day until 6; office: 8:30–3:30 M–Sa. Brochure, map available. *Social Reformers* Susan B. Anthony, sect. C, off Linden, Ave.; Frederick Douglass, sect. T, off East Ave. Also: Jacob H. Meyer, inventor of the voting machine; Lewis Henry Morgan, sect. F, anthropologist; Colonel Rochester, who gave his name to the city.

ROSLYN (on Long Island) Roslyn Cemetery, N side of Northern Blvd., immediately W of Glen Cove Rd. Map available. *Writers* William Cullen Bryant, at rear of cemetery; Christopher Morley, on L of road leading from entrance.

ROXBURY (10 mi. N of Belleayre Mountain Ski Ctr., in Catskill resort area, on Rte. 30) Burroughs Memorial Field, Burroughs Memorial Rd., just N of Roxbury. Always open. *Scientists and*

Inventors John Burroughs. Woodchuck Lodge, Burrough's home.
RYE (Westchester County) John Jay Cemetery, E side of Boston
Post Rd., about 300 ft. S of Rye Golf Club. *Government
Leaders* John Jay, sect. 121A. John Jay Homestead, Jay St., Ka-
tonah.
SACKETS HARBOR (8 mi. W of Watertown, on Rte. 3) Military
Cemetery, across the road from village cemetery. *Explorers and
Settlers* Zebulon Pike.
SAG HARBOR (on S fork of Long Island, off Rte. 114) Oakland
Cemetery, Jermain Ave. *Writers* Nelson Algren.
ST. JAMES (on Long Island, about 8 mi. SW of Port Jefferson, off
Rte. 25A) St. James Episcopal Church Graveyard, 490 N. Country
Rd. *Artists* Stanford White.
SARATOGA SPRINGS Greenridge Cemetery, 17 Greenridge Pl.,
1 block E of Rte. 95, in SW sect. of the city. Office: 9–2 M–F,
closed Sa, Su, and hols. *Entertainers* Monty Woolley, inscription
reads "Edgar M. 'Monty.' "
SOUTHAMPTON (on S fork of Long Island, on Rte. 27A) Sacred
Heart Cemetery, North Hwy. *Entertainers* Gary Cooper, grave
marked by rose-colored, three-ton boulder.
SPARKILL (Rockland County) Rockland Cemetery. Kings Hwy.
Open 10–4 every day. *Explorers and Settlers* John C. Fremont,
sect. H on the upper plateau. Signs indicate direction to grave
site. Large monument overlooks Hudson River.
STATEN ISLAND (New York City) Moravian Cemetery, Todt
Hill Rd., N of Richmond Rd. *Business and Finance* Cornelius
Vanderbilt; William Henry Vanderbilt; William Kissam Vander-
bilt. Vanderbilt mausoleum, in rear of cemetery, is carved out of
"living rock" and has an ornate entrance. Mausoleum area not
open to the public.
　　　Silver Mount Cemetery, 918 Victory Blvd. *Writers* Wallace
Thurman.
TIVOLI (about 20 mi. N of Poughkeepsie, off Rte. 402) St. Paul's
Episcopal Church. *Government Leaders* Robert R. Livingston,
buried directly beneath church structure, not possible to view
grave. Clermont, Livingston's estate, in Clermont State Historic
Park, R.D. 1, Germantown.
TROY Oakwood Cemetery, Oakwood Ave., in NW sect. of Troy.
Open 9–4:30 every day. Map available. *Business and
Finance* Russell Sage. *Social Scientists and Educators* Emma

Willard. Also: Sam Wilson, meatpacker, who created the term "Uncle Sam," which became symbol of the U.S. A flag is raised and lowered by his grave every day.

TUXEDO PARK (near Sterling Forest Gardens, off Rte. 17) St. Mary's Cemetery, off Rte. 17, just inside Tuxedo Park gate. *Writers* Emily Post.

VALHALLA (Westchester County) Kensico Cemetery, Virginia Rd., water tower marks entrance, take Exit 4 (Rte. 100–A Hartsdale) off Westchester Expwy. Office: 9–5 M–F, 9–4 Sa, Su. Brochure available. Beautifully landscaped rural cemetery. *Business and Finance* Jacob Ruppert. *Musicians* Tommy Dorsey; Sergei Rachmaninoff. *Religious Leaders* Evangeline Cory Booth, Salvation Army plot. *Social Scientists and Educators* Allan Nevins, lot 124. *Sports Figures* Lou Gehrig; William A. Muldoon. *Writers* Ayn Rand.

WEST POINT West Point Cemetery, U.S. Military Academy, near the Old Cadet Chapel. Always open. Map of campus available. More than 4,000 men and women are buried here, representing every war in which the U.S. has taken part. *Military* Lucius D. Clay; Margaret Corbin; George Armstrong Custer; Winfield Scott. *Scientists and Inventors* George Washington Goethals, in NW corner of cemetery. Also: Sylvanus Thayer (1785–1872) father of the military academy; Edward H. White (1930–67) astronaut, first man to walk in space.

NORTH CAROLINA

ASHEVILLE Riverside Cemetery, Birch St. off Pearson Dr. *Writers* O. Henry; Thomas Wolfe.

DURHAM Maplewood Cemetery, Duke University Rd. Open every day 7:30–5:00 Sep. 1–Mar. 1, 7:30–7:00 Mar. 1–Sep. 1. *Business and Finance* James Buchanan Duke, Benjamin Newton Duke, both in family mausoleum in old part, annex A.

FLETCHER (10 mi. S of Asheville, on US 25) Calvary Churchyard. Always open, supt. on duty 8–4 M–F. *Journalists* Bill Nye, in old sect., lot 105.

GREENSBORO New Garden Friends Cemetery, 801 New Garden Rd. Open 7:30–5:00, caretaker on grounds 8–5 M–F. *Writers* Randall Jarrell.

OHIO

CANTON McKinley Memorial, 7th St. NW and Monument Rd. Open 9–5 every day. *Presidents* William McKinley, domed white granite tomb with statue of McKinley in front, McKinley Museum of History, Science and Industry, adjacent.
CINCINNATI Indian Hill Episcopal-Presbyterian Churchyard, 6000 Drake Rd. *Government Leaders* Robert A. Taft.

Spring Grove Cemetery, 4521 Spring Grove Ave., North Gate on Gray Rd. Open 7:30–5 M–F, 8–5 Sa, Su; office: 7:30–4 daily. Brochure, map available. Founded in 1845, it is the largest nonprofit cemetery in the U.S.—733 acres with 426 different species of trees and shrubs. *Business and Finance* William Cooper Proctor. *Social Reformers* Levi Coffin, Friends Soc. sect. 101. *Supreme Court Justices* Salmon P. Chase, monument is a granite shaft.
CLEVELAND Lake View Cemetery, 12316 Euclid Ave., Euclid and 123 St. Brochure, map available; floral car-tour routes laid out in spring, summer, and autumn. The 285-acre cemetery is a garden spot and wildlife center. *Business and Finance* John D. Rockefeller, Sr., between Chapel and Glen Rds. (his is largest obelisk monument in cemetery). *Government Leaders* John Hay, off Detour Rd. *Presidents* James A. Garfield, off Garfield Rd. (his monument is an 18-foot circular tower; frieze on exterior of building depicts his life). Garfield Monument is open every day, Apr. 1–Nov. 15. Also: Newton D. Baker, off Cross and Circle Rds., Secy. of War under Woodrow Wilson; Charles W. Chesnutt (1858–1932) novelist; Mark Hanna (1837–1904) "President-maker."
COLUMBIANA (10 mi. S of Youngstown, off Rte. 14) Columbiana Cemetery, East Park St. Open 9–dark; office closes at 4:30. *Business and Finance* Harvey Samuel Firestone.
COLUMBUS Greenlawn Cemetery, 1000 Greenlawn Ave. *Military* Eddie Rickenbacker. *Writers* James Thurber.
COSHOCTON South Lawn Cemetery, 1401 Cemetery Dr. Office: 8–4 M–F, 8–12 Sa. Map available. *Social Reformers* William Green.
DAYTON Woodland Cemetery, 118 Woodland Ave., near Brown and Wyoming Sts. Open 7:30–sunset every day; office: 8–4:30 M–F, 8–12 Sa. Brochure, map available. Cemetery is also an arboretum. *Government Leaders* James M. Cox, sect. 121. *Scientists and Inventors* Orville Wright, Wilbur Wright, both in sect.

101. *Writers* Paul Laurence Dunbar, sect. 101. Also: Johnny Morehouse, a child; his memorial statue *Dog and the Boy*, a sleeping boy and his dog, is the most famous in the cemetery.

EVANSTON (a few mi. NE of Cincinnati) Walnut Hills Cemetery, 3400 Montgomery Rd. Open 7:30–4 every day. *Religious Leaders* Isaac Mayer Wise.

FREMONT Rutherford B. Hayes State Memorial, 1337 Hayes Ave. at Buckland Ave., 2 mi. E of intersection of Rtes. 6 and 53. Open 9–5 Tu–Sa. 1:30–5 Su, M, and hols. Brochure available. A 25-acre estate. *Presidents* Rutherford B. Hayes. Rutherford B. Hayes Library and Museum.

GREENVILLE (30 mi. NW of Dayton, on US 127) Brock Cemetery, on the Beamsville–St. Mary's Rd., off Rte. 185, NE of Greenville. *Entertainers* Annie Oakley. Also: Frank Butler, her husband and fellow sharpshooter. Garst Museum, 205 N. Broadway, contains world's largest collection of Oakley memorabilia.

LUCAS (3 mi. SE of Mansfield, on Rte. 39) Malabar Farm State Park, on Pleasant Valley Rd., 3 mi. S of Lucas. Map, self-guided tour available, Bromfield's home; wagon tours of farm; hiking and bridle trails; cross-country skiing; picnicking; seasonal events. *Writers* Louis Bromfield, in cemetery below farm complex.

MARION Harding Memorial, US 23 and Vernon Heights Blvd., next to Marion Cemetery. *Presidents* Warren G. Harding.

NORTH BEND (25 mi. W of Cincinnati, on US 50) William Henry Harrison Memorial State Park, Loop Ave., S of Harrison Ave., near US 50 and Rte. 128. Fourteen acres overlooking the Ohio River. *Presidents* William Henry Harrison, tomb open during daylight hours, illuminated at night.

UPPER SANDUSKY (15 mi. N of Marion, off US 23) Old Mission Church Cemetery, Church St. at N. 4 St., between Sandusky Ave. and Mission Dr. Brochure available. *Explorers and Settlers* John Stewart. Also: many Indian graves.

WARREN Oakwood Cemetery, 860 Niles Rd. SE. *Business and Finance* James Ward Packard.

OKLAHOMA

AKINS (60 mi. SE of Tulsa, off I-40) Akins Cemetery, 8 mi. outside of Sallisaw on Rte. 101. Open every day during daylight hours. *Criminals* "Pretty Boy" Floyd, footstone has been badly chipped by souvenir hunters.

FORT SILL (3 mi. N of Lawton on US 277/281) Apache Cemetery, Elgin and Dodge Hill Rds., 2 mi. N of museum. Grave site open every day during daylight hours. Brochure available. *Military* Geronimo. Fort Sill Military Museum and original buildings.

GEARY Jesse Chisholm Gravesite, 8 mi. N of Geary on US 270/281, near Greenfield. *Explorers and Settlers* Jesse Chisholm, site belonged to Chisholm's friend, Chief Left Hand, and is still owned by his heirs.

OKLAHOMA CITY Fairlawn Cemetery, 2700 N. Shartel Ave. *Explorers and Settlers* Wiley Post.

PONCA CITY Near White Eagle Monument, S of 101 Ranch, off US 177. *Sports Figures* Bill Pickett.

PORUM (20 mi. S of Muskogee, on Rte. 2) Belle Starr Cabin, Rte. 2, "Belle Starr Canyon," near Lake Eufaula Dam. Area, in private hands, is difficult to see from the road because it is overgrown. Small admission charge. *Criminals* Belle Starr, grave is unmarked.

WELCH (60 mi. N of Muskogee, on US 59) Williams Cemetery, go 4 mi. E of Welch, 1 mi. N, turn back R at cross cattle guard. *Criminals* Kate "Ma" Barker. Also: Arthur, Fred, and Herman Barker, her sons and fellow gang members.

OREGON

EUGENE Rest Haven Memorial Park, 3986 Willamette St. Open 24 hrs Su–Th, dawn–sunset F–Sa; office: 8–5 M–F. *Government Leaders* Wayne Morse. The Morse Ranch Park, Crest Dr., former Morse estate.

PORTLAND Mount Calvary Cemetery, 333 SW Skyline Blvd. *Sports Figures* Jack Dempsey.

PENNSYLVANIA

ALTOONA Rose Hill Cemetery, 1207 12th Ave., Pleasant Valley Blvd., on Rte. 220. Always open. *Journalists* Hedda Hopper.

BALA-CYNWYD (adjoins Philadelphia on W) West Laurel Hill Cemetery, 215 Belmont Ave., above City Line Ave. *Artists* Alexander Stirling Calder, family plot marked by Celtic cross. Also: Alexander Milne Calder, his father, a sculptor; Anna Reeves Jarvis (1864–1948) founder of Mother's Day.

Westminster Cemetery, Belmont Ave. and Levering Mill Rd. *Business and Finance* Charles Elmer Hires, sect. Valleyview 41, grave 2.

BETHLEHEM Nisky Hill Cemetery, 254 E. Church St., Church and Center Sts., overlooking Lehigh River. Cemetery has a Civil War section with a mounted cannon in the center. *Writers* H.D.

BRYN MAWR (western suburb of Philadelphia, off US 30) Cloisters of M. Carey Thomas Library, Bryn Mawr College, Old Gulph Rd. Cloisters are a colonnaded area in the center of the library. *Social Scientists and Educators* M. Carey Thomas, small plaque in the floor of the walkway notes where she is interred.

CARLISLE (20 mi. W of Harrisburg, off I-76) Old Graveyard, South St., 4 blocks from center square of Carlisle. Founded by the Penns, this burial ground contains many Revolutionary soldiers. *Military* Molly Pitcher: her monument, towering above all others in the cemetery, is a statue of a woman holding a cannon plunger, with a cannon in front of it.

DUNMORE (adjoins Scranton on the E) Dunmore Cemetery, Church St. *Business and Finance* George Whitfield Scranton, block 6, lots 21 and 27, Scranton family plot.

ELKINS PARK (in NW part of state, about 30 mi. S of N.Y. border) St. Paul's Churchyard, York and Ashbourne Rds. *Business and Finance* Jay Cooke, Cooke was instrumental in founding this church in 1866.

FARMINGTON (11 mi. E of Uniontown, on US 40) Braddock's Grave, 1 mi. W. of Fort Necessity National Battlefield, Brochure available. *Military* Edward Braddock, in Braddock Park, a detached sect. of the national battlefield.

GETTYSBURG Evergreen Cemetery, 799 Baltimore St., on Rte. 97. Open dawn to dusk; office: 8–5, M–F, or by appointment. *Writers* Marianne Moore. Also: Jennie Wade, a member of Baseball's Hall of Fame.

GLADWYNE (5 mi. W of Philadelphia, on Rte. 23) The Shrine, Woodmont Palace Mission Estate, Woodmont Rd. off Spring Mill Rd. Open 9–5 every day, 1–5 Su. Seventy-three-acre estate belonging to the sect founded by Father Divine. *Religious Leaders* Father Divine.

HERSHEY (10 mi. E of Harrisburg, off Rte. 422) Hershey Cemetery, One Chocolate Ave. *Business and Finance* Milton Snavely Hershey.

JIM THORPE (15 mi. SE of Hazelton, on Rte. 903) Jim Thorpe Monument, Rte. 903. *Sports Figures* Jim Thorpe, entombed in a square structure.

KENNETT SQUARE (adjoins Wilmington, Del.) Union Hill Cemetery, on Rte. 82, just outside of Kennett Square. Always open; caretaker on premises 8–4, *Entertainers* Linda Darnell.

LANCASTER Lancaster Cemetery, 205 E. Lemon St. Open 8–4:30 every day. *Artists* Charles Demuth, in family plot.

Shreiner's Cemetery, SE corner of North Mulberry and West Chestnut Sts., near city center. Always open. *Government Leaders* Thaddeus Stevens.

Woodward Hill Cemetery, 538 E. Strawberry St. *Presidents* James Buchanan.

LASHASKA (20 mi. N of Trenton, N.J.) Buckingham Friends Cemetery, Rte. 202. *Social Scientists and Educators* Margaret Mead.

LITITZ (about 8 mi. N of Lancaster, on Rte. 501) Lititz Moravian Cemetery, E. Main St., several blocks E of Rte. 501. Cemetery located in rear of Moravian Church. Church office hours: 8:30–4:30 daily. *Explorers and Settlers* John Sutter.

PEN ARGYL (halfway between Easton and Stroudsberg, on US 22, in Pocono resort area) Fairview Cemetery. *Entertainers* Jayne Mansfield, grave is near entrance to cemetery.

PERKASIE (between Doylestown and Quakertown, on Rte. 313) Green Hills Farm, Dublin Rd., off Rte. 313W. Maintained by the Pearl S. Buck Foundation. *Writers* Pearl S. Buck. Pearl S. Buck Home, tours available.

PHILADELPHIA Christ Church Burial Ground, 5th and Arch Sts., a few blocks N of Independence Hall. Open 9–4:30 mid-Apr. through Oct. except in inclement weather. Guide on duty. Booklet available. Probably no other nonmilitary cemetery in the U.S. has so many colonial and Revolutionary leaders. It was opened in 1719, when it became evident that the churchyard (see below) needed expansion. *Artists* William Rush. *Colonists and Patriots* Benjamin Rush. *Government Leaders* Benjamin Franklin, a few feet from the sidewalk, grave site is visible through opening in the wall.

Churchyard of Christ Church, 2nd St., between Market and Arch Sts. Oldest tombstone here is dated 1714 and can be seen near the entrance to the Tower Room. *Colonists and Patriots* Robert Morris. Also: Charles Lee (1731–82) Revolutionary War general.

Churchyard of St. James the Less, 3227 West Clearfield St. Open 9–5 M–F, weekends by appointment. *Business and Finance* John Wanamaker, in "Wanamaker Tower" crypt. Crypt gates permanently closed.

Congregation Mikve Israel Burial Ground, Spruce St. between 8th and 9th Sts. One of the smallest burying grounds in the U.S.; enclosed by a high brick wall, it contains the bodies of all Jews who died in Philadelphia during the colonial period. *Colonists and Patriots* Haym Salomon, grave is unmarked but the fact of burial is recorded in a memorial on the east wall. Also: Rebecca Gratz, model for Rebecca in Sir Walter Scott's novel *Ivanhoe*.

Eden Cemetery, 5410 Haverford Ave. *Writers* T. Thomas Fortune.

Friends Fair Hill Burial Ground, 45 W. School House Lane. *Social Reformers* Lucretia Coffin Mott.

Girard College, Founder's Hall, Corinthian and Girard Aves. Hall open to the public Thursday afternoons; other times by appointment. *Business and Finance* Stephen Girard.

Holy Sepulchre Cemetery, Cheltenham Ave. *Sports Figures* Connie Mack.

Laurel Hill Cemetery, 3822 Ridge Ave., adjoining Fairmont Park. Office: 9–4:30 M–F, 9–12:30 Sa. Brochure available. The first architect-designed rural park cemetery in the country, it became a widely copied model. Winding paths pass monuments by many renowned Victorian architects and sculptors; nature sanctuary growing every kind of local tree. *Artists* Thomas Sully. Also: Sarah Josepha Hale (1788–1879) editor, responsible for the establishment of Thanksgiving Day; Commodore Issac Hull (1773–1843) hero of the War of 1812; Elisha K. Kane (1820–57) explorer; George Gordon Meade (1815–72) Union general; William H. Sylvis (1828–69) social reformer; Joseph Wharton (1826–1909) founder of the Wharton School of Finance and Political Economy.

Montefiore Cemetery, Church Rd. and Borbeck St. *Artists* Louis Kahn.

Mother Bethel African Methodist Episcopal Church, 419 S.

6th St. Tour guides on duty 10–3 Tu–Th. Brochure available. *Religious Leaders* Richard Allen, in a crypt. Museum of the history of the A.M.E. Church.

Mount Moriah Cemetery, 62nd St. and Kingsessing Ave. *Colonists and Patriots* Betsy Ross.

Mount Sinai Cemetery, Bridge and Cottage Sts. *Business and Finance* Bernard F. Gimbel; Charles Gimbel; Ellis Gimbel.

Saint Paul's Episcopal Churchyard, S. 3rd St. at Willings Alley. Erected in 1761, no longer in use as a church. *Entertainers* Edwin Forrest.

Saint Peter's Churchyard, 3rd and Pine Sts. One of three eighteenth-century churches in the U.S. that have not been altered structurally. *Artists* Charles Willson Peale. *Business and Finance* Nicholas Biddle. *Military* Stephen Decatur, his monument, a granite pillar topped by an eagle, is the tallest in the churchyard.

Woodlands Cemetery, 40th St. and Woodland Ave. Open 8–4 daily; office: 8–4 M–F. Office, a National Historic Landmark, is an eighteenth-century mansion. *Artists* Thomas Eakins, in an unmarked spot near other Eakins family graves. Also: Frank R. Stockton (1834–1902) author; members of Philadelphia's prominent families.

PITTSBURGH Allegheny Cemetery, 4734 Butler St. Open 7–7 daily during summer months, 7–5 during winter months; office: 8:30–5 M–Sa. Walking-tour brochure available. The great families of Pittsburgh are housed in this 300-acre cemetery in tombs of all architectural styles. *Entertainers* Lillian Russell, in mausoleum, sect. 40, lot 5. *Musicians* Stephen C. Foster, sect. 21, lot 30. Also: Joshua Barney (1759–1818) naval hero; Galbraith Perry Rodgers (1879–1912) sect. 19, lot 102, aviation pioneer; "Rosey" Rowswell, sportscaster, "voice of the Pittsburgh Pirates"; Harry K. Thaw (1871–1947) slayer of architect Stanford White (see Artists).

Homewood Cemetery, Dallas and Aylesboro Aves. Open 7–5 Oct.–Apr., 7–9 May–Sep. Gates open at 8 on Su; office: 8:30–5 M–F, 8:30–4 Sa. Founded in 1878, it has 200 landscaped acres. *Business and Finance* Henry Clay Frick; Henry John Heinz.

PLEASANT HILLS (immediately S of Pittsburgh, on Rte. 51) Jefferson Memorial Park, Curry Hollow Rd. *Sports Figures* Honus Wagner, Garden of the Cross sect., lot 372C, grave 1.

SHARON HILL (1 mi. W of SW Philadelphia) Mount Lawn Cemetery, 84th St. and Hook Rd., in Darby Township. *Musicians* Bessie Smith.

SHENANDOAH (about 40 mi. SW of Wilkes-Barre, on Rte. 54) Annunciation Cemetery, 218 West Cherry St., Shenandoah Heights, adjoining Annunciation Church. *Musicians* Jimmy Dorsey.

TITUSVILLE (about 50 mi. NE of New Castle, on Rte. 36) Woodlawn Cemetery, 892 W. Spring St., on hill above town. *Journalists* Ida M. Tarbell.

WAYNE (6 mi. W of Philadelphia on US 30) St. David's (Radnor) Churchyard, Valley Forge Rd. Open daily during daylight hrs. Brochure available. *Military* Anthony Wayne, large monument, grave just outside gate.

WILKES-BARRE Hollenbach Cemetery, 540 North River St. *Artists* Franz Kline.

PUERTO RICO

SAN JUAN Metropolitan Cathedral, Cristo St. *Explorers and Settlers* Juan Ponce de Leon.

RHODE ISLAND

NEWPORT Island Cemetery, 30 Warner St. Office: 9–4 M–F. *Business and Finance* August Belmont. *Military* Oliver Hazard Perry; Matthew Calbraith Perry.

PROVIDENCE North Burial Ground Cemetery, corner of Branch Ave. and North Main St. Office: 8:30–4:30 M–F, closed at 4 July and Aug. *Social Scientists and Educators* Horace Mann, grave marked with replica of the "obelisk of the Vatican." Also: General William Barton, Revolutionary War hero; Samuel W. Foss (d. 1911), poet who wrote "House by the Side of the Road"; and Stephen Hopkins (1707–July 13, 1785), signer of the Declaration of Independence.

Roger Williams Memorial, Congdon St., off Prospect St. *Colonists and Patriots* Roger Williams, memorial is a WPA-style monument on a pavilion overlooking Providence.

SOUTH CAROLINA

CHARLESTON St. Michael's Cemetery, Broad and Meeting Sts. Brochure available. St. Michael's Church is the oldest in Charleston. *Colonists and Patriots* John Rutledge.

St. Philip's Churchyard, Church and Queen Sts. *Government Leaders* John C. Calhoun. *Writers* DuBose Heyward. Also: Charles Pinckney (1757–1824) signer of the U.S. Constitution; Edward Rutledge (1749–1800) signer of the Declaration of Independence.

COLUMBIA Trinity Churchyard, 1100 Sumter St. *Military* Wade Hampton.

MONCKS CORNER (30 mi. N of Charleston) Luce Family Cemetery, Roman Catholic Abbey of Our Lady of Mepkin, River Rd., about 9 mi. outside of Moncks Corner. Visitors welcome 9–4:30, call Abbey for appointment. Mepkin, Indian for "serene and lovely," is the former estate of colonial statesman Henry Laurens; it was donated to the monks by Henry R. Luce. *Journalists* Henry R. Luce; family cemetery is one of three cemeteries on the property.

ST. STEPHEN (about 70 mi. SE of Columbia, on US 52) Gabriel's Plantation, Belle Isle. *Military* Francis Marion.

SOUTH DAKOTA

DEADWOOD (20 mi. NW of Rapid City, off I-90) Mount Moriah Cemetery, off Lincoln Ave. Brochure available. *Explorers and Settlers* Calamity Jane; Wild Bill Hickok. Also: "Potato Creek Johnny," picturesque prospector; Henry Weston Smith, pioneer minister.

MOBRIDGE (60 mi. S of Bismarck, on US 12) Sitting Bull Monument, overlooking Lake Oahe (W of Mobridge, a short distance S of US 12). *Military* Sitting Bull, huge monument is by sculptor Korczak Ziolkowski.

TENNESSEE

CHATTANOOGA Forest Hills Cemetery, 40th St. and Tennessee Ave., in St. Elmo sect. of city at the foot of Lookout Mountain. Open 8–7 every day spring and summer, 8–6 fall and winter. *Musicians* Grace Moore. Also: Tennessee governors, senators, and Civil War generals.

GREENEVILLE (about 50 mi. E of Knoxville, on US 411) Andrew Johnson Cemetery, Monument Hill, 1 block S of West St., off US 411. Open 9–5 every day except Christmas. Brochure available. *Presidents* Andrew Johnson. Andrew Johnson Homestead, Main St.; Johnson Tailor Shop, corner of Depot and College Sts. With the cemetery, these comprise the Andrew Johnson National Historic Site.

HENDERSONVILLE (about 20 mi. NE of Nashville, on Rte. 109) Woodlawn East Memorial Park, 353 Gallatin Rd., 6 mi. from Rivergate Shopping Center. *Musicians* Maybelle Carter, Garden of Matthew sect.

HOHENWALD Meriwether Lewis Park, Natchez Trace Pkwy, 7 mi. E of Hohenwald and 35 mi. SW of Columbia on Rte. 20. Brochure available. *Explorers and Settlers* Meriwether Lewis, grave just N of Grinders Stand site where Lewis died; grave marked by a broken column, symbol of his early death. Museum about Lewis, picnic area.

MEMPHIS Forrest Park, Union St., between Dunlap and Manassas. *Military* Nathan Bedford Forrest.

Graceland (Presley Estate), 3764 Elvis Presley Blvd. Grounds open 9–4 Tu–Su. *Musicians* Elvis Presley, near the meditation pool.

NASHVILLE The Hermitage, 12 mi. E of Nashville on Rte. 70-N. Open 9–5 every day, closed Christmas. Free admission on Jan. 8, anniversary of the Battle of New Orleans; Mar. 15, birthday of Andrew Jackson. *Presidents* Andrew Jackson, in garden adjacent to mansion. Mansion, Museum, Hermitage Grove, Tulip Grove, "Rachel's Church," smokehouse, slave cabins.

State Capitol Grounds, Capitol Hill. *Presidents* James Knox Polk.

PALL MALL (about 46 mi N of Crossville, on Rte. 127) Alvin York's Farm and Grist Mill, signs in Pall Mall indicate direction to Mill and grave site. Grave site open at all times. *Military* Alvin York. Farm and Grist Mill, home of Sgt. York; his 82-year-old son, Andrew Jackson York, is the Ranger on duty.

TEXAS

AUSTIN Oakwood Cemetery, 1601 Navasota. Open 7– dusk every day; office: 8–4:30 M–F. *Criminals* Ben Thompson, sect. 1, lot 71. Also: many Austin pioneers.

State Cemetery, 901 Navasota, in the eastern sect. of the city. Open 8–5 M–Sa, Su and hols. Founded in 1854, this state-run cemetery is divided into two parts. The smaller contains over 200 graves of prominent Texans, the larger the graves of 2,047 Confederate veterans and their wives. *Government Leaders* Stephen F. Austin (inscription on grave marker gives his birth year as 1703 instead of 1793, a typographical error); "Ma" Ferguson.

BEAUMONT Forest Lawn Memorial Park, 4955 Pine St., at intersection of Pine and E. Lucas. Cemetery and offices open 8–5 every day. *Sports Figures* Babe Didrikson Zaharias.

BONHAM (about 40 mi. NE of Dallas, on US 82) Willow Wild Cemetery, W. 7th St. Open 8:30–5:00 M–F. *Government Leaders* Sam Rayburn.

DALLAS Calvary Hills Cemetery, 3235 Lombardy Lane, in NW sect. of Dallas. Open 8–7 spring and summer, 8–sunset winter months. Established in the 1920s as the official burial ground of Catholics of the Diocese of Dallas. *Business and Finance* Conrad Nicholson Hilton. Also: Tom Braniff, founder of Braniff International Airlines.

Crown Hill Memorial Park, 9718 Webbs Chapel. *Criminals* Bonnie Parker.

Sparkman-Hillcrest Memorial Park, 7405 West Northwest Highway, between Hillcrest and Central Expressway. *Business and Finance* H. L. Hunt. *Sports Figures* Maureen Connolly.

Western Heights Cemetery, 1617 Fort Worth Ave. *Criminals* Clyde Barrow.

DE KALB (20 mi. W of Texarkana, on US 82) De Kalb Cemetery, Front St. (US 82), coming from Texarkana, turn R at 646 Front St. Always open. *Entertainers* Dan Blocker.

EL PASO Fort Bliss National Cemetery, 5210 Fred Wilson Highway, Fort Bliss. Open 8–5 every day, 8–7 Memorial Day; office: closed Sa, Su, and hols. Brochure available. *Sports Figures* Goose Tatum.

FORT WORTH Rose Hill Memorial Park, 7301 E. Lancaster. *Criminals* Lee Harvey Oswald.

HOUSTON Glenwood Cemetery, 2525 Washington St. *Business and Finance* Howard Hughes.

Rice University, Center Campus Quadrangle, 610 South Main St., 3 mi. S of downtown Houston. Booklet available on University. *Business and Finance* William Marsh Rice, at the base of his statue at focal point of the campus.

HUBBARD (25 mi. NE of Waco, on Rte. 31) Fairview Cemetery, *Sports Figures* Tris Speaker.

HUNTSVILLE Oakwood Cemetery, 9th St. and Ave. I. Cemetery is noted for the Rawley Rather Powell Monument, a copy of Thorwaldsen's statue of Christ in the Denmark Church, Copenhagen. *Government Leaders* Sam Houston. Sam Houston Memorial Park and Museum, Sam Houston Ave. and 19th St.

JOHNSON CITY (35 mi. W of Austin, on US 290) LBJ Ranch, Johnson Family Cemetery, a few mi. W of Johnson City off US 290, entrance on Ranch Rd. No. 1. Brochure available on all Johnson sites; map of cemetery available. Cemetery, adjacent to ranch house, has remains of 25 Johnson family members and friends. *Presidents* Lyndon Baines Johnson, on R side of cemetery near his mother, Rebekah Baines Johnson. Bus tours of LBJ Ranch. Johnson's Boyhood Home and Johnson settlement area, Johnson City. LBJ Library, University of Texas, Austin.

KINGSVILLE Chamberlain Cemetery, off Armstrong St. in SW sect. of town. *Business and Finance* Henrietta Chamberlain King, at entrance to cemetery. Also: Richard King, her husband and founder of the King Ranch. King Ranch, auto tour, W of Kingsville on Rte. 141.

LUBBOCK City of Lubbock Cemetery, 2011 E. 34th St. Always open. Office: 9–12, 1–5, M–F. *Musicians* Buddy Holly, grave site just N of office.

PORT NECHES (about 10 mi. SE of Beaumont, on Rte. 347) Oak Bluff Memorial Park, 101 Block St. *Musicians* Tex Ritter, a cowboy boot is to the L of his name, a cowboy hat on R.

UTAH

SALT LAKE CITY Mormon Pioneer Memorial, 140 1st Ave. Open every day during daylight hours. Brochure available at Visitors Center, Temple Square. *Religious Leaders* Brigham Young.

VERMONT

BELLOWS FALLS (15 mi. N of Brattleboro, on Rte. 35) Immanuel Cemetery, 14 Church St., at top of Church St., adjacent to Immanuel Episcopal Church. Always open. *Business and Finance* Hetty Green, in Green family lot.

BENNINGTON Old Bennington Cemetery, Rte. 9, 1 mi. W of town center. *Writers* Robert Frost.

BRATTLEBORO Meetinghouse Hill Cemetery, Orchard St. *Sports Figures* Ely Culbertson.

Prospect Hill Cemetery, South Main St. Open during daylight hours. *Business and Finance* Jim Fisk, largest monument in cemetery.

BURLINGTON Dewey Memorial, University of Vermont, S. Prospect St., eastern edge of city. *Social Scientists and Educators* John Dewey, a simple monument much like a tombstone, on the lawn N of Ira Allen Chapel.

Greenmount Cemetery, SE side of Colchester Ave., on crest of hill overlooking village of Winooski. Always open during summer months. Booklet available. *Colonists and Patriots* Ethan Allen, large monument.

Lakeview Cemetery, W of North Ave. Open 7:30–8. Booklet available. *Military* Oliver Otis Howard. Also: Warren R. Austin, U.N. Ambassador; Admiral Henry T. Mayo, WWI naval hero.

DORSET (about 25 mi. S of Rutland, on Rte. 30) Maple Hill Cemetery, in town on Rte. 30. Always open during summer months. *Artists* Reginald Marsh, in middle sect. of cemetery, directly N of Fisher monument.

PLYMOUTH (20 mi. SE of Rutland, on Rte. 100A) Plymouth Cemetery, on unnamed dirt road off Rte. 100A. Always open; no caretaker on duty during winter months. Brochure available at Calvin Coolidge Visitors Center. *Presidents* Calvin Coolidge. Plymouth Notch Historic District: President Coolidge Homestead, Rte. 100A; Calvin Coolidge Birthplace.

VIRGINIA

ARLINGTON (directly W of Wash. D.C.) Arlington National Cemetery. Open 8–5 Oct.–Mar., 8–7 Apr.–Sept. Brochure, map available. Located on 1,100-acre estate that once belonged to the Custis-Lee family, Arlington is the pantheon of America's war dead; here lie soldiers from every war in which the nation has participated. Noted monuments are the Arlington Memorial Amphitheater and the Tomb of the Unknown Soldier on its Plaza;

the Confederate Monument, erected to symbolize the reunion of North and South, sect. 16, I–23; the Mast of the Maine, honoring those who lost their lives in that disaster, sect. 24, N–23½. *Artists* Pierre L'Enfant, sect. 2, S–3, in front of Lee Mansion. *Entertainers* Constance Bennett. *Explorers and Settlers* Richard E. Byrd, sect. 2, 4969–1; Robert E. Peary, sect. 8, S–15. *Government Leaders* William Jennings Bryan, sect. 4, 3118; John Foster Dulles, sect. 21, S–31; James Forrestal, sect. 30, 674; Robert F. Kennedy, sect. 45, 5–45A. *Journalists* Marguerite Higgins, sect. 2, 4705–B; Joseph Medill Patterson. *Military* Creighton Abrams; Henry "Hap" Arnold, sect. 34, 44–A; Omar N. Bradley; Roger B. Chaffee, sect. 3, 2502–F; Claire Chennault, sect. 2, 873–4; Virgil I. Grissom, sect. 3, 2503–E; William F. "Bull" Halsey, sect. 2, 1184; George Catlett Marshall, sect. 7, 8198; Audie Murphy, sect. 46, 366–11; John J. Pershing, sect. 34, S–19; Philip Sheridan; Jonathan Wainwright, sect. 1, 358–B; Leonard Wood. *Musicians* Ignace Jan Paderewski, entombed at the Mast of the Maine monument. *Presidents* John Fitzgerald Kennedy, sect. 45, S–45, some 300 ft. down the terrace from the Custis-Lee Mansion; William Howard Taft, sect. 30, S–14. *Scientists and Inventors* Walter Reed, sect. 3, 1864. *Social Reformers* Medgar Evers, sect. 36, 1431. *Sports Figures* Dwight Davis; Abner Doubleday, sect. 1, 61; Joe Louis, just down the slope from the Tomb of the Unknown Soldier. *Supreme Court Justices* Hugo L. Black; William O. Douglas; Oliver Wendell Holmes, Jr., sect. 5, 7004–A; Earl Warren, sect. 21, S–32. *Writers* Dashiell Hammett; Mary Roberts Rinehart. Also: Bernt Balchen (1899–1973) sect. 2, 4969–2, Admiral Perry's pilot; William "Wild Bill" Donovan (1883–1959) CIA chief; Ira Hayes, sect. 34, 479–A, American Indian who raised the flag on Iwo Jima; Lew Jenkins (1916–81) lightweight boxing champion; George Westinghouse (1846–1914) inventor of the air brake; Orde Charles Wingate (1903–44) British general in Burma during WW II.

BROOKNEAL (35 mi. S of Lynchburg, on Rte. 501) Red Hill Shrine, 5 mi. W of Brookneal on Rte. 600. Open 9–5 Apr. 1–Oct. 31, 9–4 Nov. 1–Mar. 31, closed Christmas. Brochure available. *Government Leaders* Patrick Henry, grave in garden. Red Hill, restoration of Henry's plantation: main house, museum, kitchen, smokehouse, law office, stables.

CHARLOTTESVILLE Monticello, Rte. 53, 1½ mi. SW of Charlottesville. Open every day 8–5 Mar. 1–Oct. 31, 9–4:30 Nov.

1–Feb. 28, closed Christmas. Brochure available. *Presidents* Thomas Jefferson, in graveyard near lower parking lot. Home, plantation buildings, and gardens.

HANOVER COUNTY (N of Richmond) "Marlbourne Estate," E side of US 360 at Rte. 628. *Government Leaders* Edmund Ruffin, grave on private property but may be seen.

LANCASTER (80 mi. NE of Richmond, on Rte. 3) St. Mary's Whitechapel Trinity Episcopal Churchyard, intersection of Rtes. 201 and 354. Always open. *Entertainers* Margaret Sullavan, grave is just after curve in path.

LEXINGTON Lee Chapel Museum, Washington and Lee University, off I–64. Open 9–5 M–Sa (9–4 after mid-Oct.), 2–5 Su. Brochure available. *Military* Robert E. Lee, in family crypt; Traveller, in grave outside the chapel, marker is visible. Also: "Light-Horse Harry" Lee (1756–1818) Revolutionary War hero and father of Robert E. Lee.

　　Stonewall Jackson Memorial Cemetery, South Main St. Open dawn to dusk every day. *Military* Stonewall Jackson, cemetery has statue of Jackson by Richmond sculptor Edward V. Valentine. Stonewall Jackson House may be seen.

LORTON (20 mi. from Washington, D.C., via I–95) Gunston Hall Plantation. Open 9:30–5 every day, closed Christmas. Brochure available. *Colonists and Patriots* George Mason, in family cemetery. Home and plantation. Seasonal events.

MARION (about 20 mi. NE of Bristol, Tenn., off I–81) Roundhill Cemetery, off South Park St., go R after Exit 16 off I–81, left on Cherry St. (first traffic light) to top of hill, L at stop sign (S. Park St.) to Cemetery St. *Writers* Sherwood Anderson.

MONTPELIER STATION (20 mi. SW of Culpepper, on Rte. 20) Montpelier Estate, 5 mi. W of Orange on Rte. 20. One of the few presidential homes in private hands; public may visit only the grave sites. *Colonists and Patriots* Dolley Madison. *Presidents* James Madison.

MOUNT VERNON Mount Vernon Estate, 14 mi. S of Washington, D.C., on Mount Vernon Memorial Highway. *Presidents* George Washington. Home and plantation.

NORFOLK MacArthur Memorial, City Hall Ave. Coming from the E, Exit I–264 at City Hall Ave., proceed 3 blocks W. From W, cross Downtown Tunnel from Portsmouth, turn L on St. Paul's Blvd., go 1 block, turn R on City Hall Ave., proceed 2 blocks W.

Open 10–5 M–Sa, 11–5 Su, closed New Year's Day, Thanksgiving Day, Christmas. Brochure available. *Military* Douglas Mac-Arthur, in rotunda of what used to be Norfolk City Hall. Eleven separate galleries, arranged in two levels around it, depict his life and display mementos. Theater (showing newsreels about MacArthur), Gift Shop, Library, Archives.

RICHMOND Hollywood Cemetery, 412 South Cherry St., Cherry and Albemarle Sts. Open 8–6 Apr.–Sept., 8–5 Oct.–Mar. Map available. This Victorian cemetery contains leading southerners. *Government Leaders* Jefferson Davis, C 2, on Davis Circle, statue of him on grave site; John Randolph, D 2. *Military* James Ewell Brown (JEB) Stuart, N 9, on top of a high hill. *Presidents* James Monroe, G 7, on Presidents Circle, in Gothic cast-iron tomb resembling an openwork latticed chapel, sarcophagus is visible inside; John Tyler, G 7, on Presidents Circle, imposing monument. *Writers* Ellen Glasgow, stark, white stone. Also: James Branch Cabell (1879–1958) writer; George Edward Pickett (1825–75) U 7, Confederate general.

Shockoe Cemetery, Hospital and 2nd Sts. *Supreme Court Justices* John Marshall. Also: Elizabeth L. Van Lew (1818–1900) a spy for the Union during the Civil War, her tombstone is a boulder from Capitol Hill in Boston.

WESTMORELAND COUNTY (about 40 mi. SE of Fredericksburg, off Rte. 202) Yeocomico Church, Tucker Hill. *Writers* John Dos Passos.

WINCHESTER Shenandoah Memorial Park, Rte. 1. Office: 9–12, 1–5 M–F, 9–12 Sa. *Musicians* Patsy Cline.

WASHINGTON

RENTON (about 10 mi. S of Seattle, off Rte. 167) Greenwood Memorial Park, 3401 N. 4th St. *Musicians* Jimi Hendrix.

WALLA WALLA Whitman National Monument, off State Hwy. 12, 6 mi. W. of Walla Walla. *Explorers and Settlers* Marcus Whitman, Narcissa Whitman. Mission site, self-guiding trails, picnic area.

WISCONSIN

APPLETON Cemetery of St. Mary's Roman Catholic Church, 2019 West Prospect Ave. Open 9–7 daily, sexton on grounds.

Government Leaders Joseph R. McCarthy, grave overlooks Fox River.

MADISON Forest Hill Cemetery, One Speedway Rd. Office: 7:30–4 M–F, 9–11 Sa. Map available. Cemetery has Indian mounds (on southern edge) estimated to be over a thousand years old. *Government Leaders* Robert M. La Follette.

MILWAUKEE Forest Home Cemetery, 2405 West Forest Home Ave., directly in the center of the S side of Milwaukee, bounded on W by 27th St. Office: 9–5 M–F, 9–noon Sa. Walking-tour booklet with map available. Two hundred acres of greenery and history in the heart of the city; many people prominent in the development of Milwaukee and Wisconsin are buried here. Cemetery is constructing a Hall of History Museum/Mausoleum to honor them and is planning to offer historical and botanical tours. *Business and Finance* Fred Pabst, sect. 40, lot 16. *Entertainers* Alfred Lunt, sect. 33, lot 42. *Military* William "Billy" Mitchell, sect. 32. Also: Edward P. Allis (1824–89) sect. 36, lots 11 & 12, founder of Allis Chalmers; Mathilde Anneke (1817–84) sect. 15, lots 2 & 3, founder of the first women's suffrage newspaper; Victor Berger (1860–1929) sect. 25, lots 3–5, "father of the Socialist Party in America"; 7 Wisconsin governors and 27 mayors of Milwaukee.

RHINELANDER (100 mi. NW of Green Bay, off Rte. 8) Rhinelander Cemetery. *Sports Figures* John W. Heisman, Grave D, lot 11, block 3.

SPRING GREEN (20 mi. NW of Madison, off State Highway 14) Unity Chapel, on County Trunk T, approximately ¼ mi. E of junction with Rte. 23, about 3½ mi. S of Spring Green. *Artists* Frank Lloyd Wright.

WISCONSIN DELLS (30 mi. N of Madison, off I–90/94) Spring Grove Cemetery, Rte. 23, just E of Wisconsin Dells. *Military* Belle Boyd.

WYOMING

CHEYENNE Lakeview Cemetery, 25th St. and Seymour. *Government Leaders* Nellie Tayloe Ross, Space G, lot 1086.

INDEX

281